MARIA BALDWIN'S WORLDS

FIGURE 1. Maria Baldwin. Cambridge Historical Commission, Cambridge Public Library Collection.

MARIA BALDWIN'S WORLDS

A STORY OF BLACK NEW ENGLAND AND THE FIGHT FOR RACIAL JUSTICE

Kathleen Weiler

University of Massachusetts Press

Amherst & Boston

ISBN 978-1-62534-478-6 (paper); 477-9 (hardcover)

Designed by Jen Jackowitz
Set in Palatino Linotype and Avenir Next
Printed and bound by Maple Press, Inc.

Cover design by Milenda Nan Ok Lee
Cover photo: *Maria Baldwin*. Cambridge Historical Commission,
Cambridge Public Library Collection.

Library of Congress Cataloging-in-Publication Data
Names: Weiler, Kathleen, author.
Title: Maria Baldwin's worlds : a story of Black New England and the fight
for racial justice / Kathleen Weiler.
Other titles: Story of Black New England and the fight for racial justice
Description: Amherst, MA : University of Massachusetts Press, [2019] |
Includes bibliographical references and index. | Summary: "Maria Baldwin
(1856–1922) held a special place in the racially divided society of her
time, as a highly respected educator at a largely white New England
school and an activist who carried on the radical spirit of the Boston
area's internationally renowned abolitionists from a generation earlier.
African American sociologist Adelaide Cromwell called Baldwin "the lone
symbol of Negro progress in education in the greater Boston area" during
her lifetime. Baldwin used her respectable position to fight alongside
more radical activists like William Monroe Trotter for full citizenship
for fellow members of the black community. And, in her professional and
personal life, she negotiated and challenged dominant white ideas about
black womanhood. In Maria Baldwin's Worlds, Kathleen Weiler reveals both
Baldwin's victories and what fellow activist W. E. B. Du Bois called her
"quiet courage" in everyday life." —Provided by publisher.
Identifiers: LCCN 2019020708 (print) | LCCN 2019022357 (ebook) | ISBN
9781625344779 (hardcover) | ISBN 9781625344786 (pbk.)
Subjects: LCSH: Baldwin, Maria, 1856–1922. | African American
intellectuals—Massachusetts—Cambridge--Biography. | African American
women school principals—Massachusetts—Cambridge—Biography. |
Professor Agassiz' School (Cambridge, Mass.) —Biography. | African
American civil rights workers—Massachusetts—Cambridge—Biography. |
African Americans—Civil rights—Massachusetts--Boston
Region—History—19th century. | Single
women—Massachusetts—Cambridge—Biography. | Boston Region
(Mass.) —Race relations—History—19th century.
Classification: LCC E185.89.I56 W45 2019 (print) | LCC E185.89.I56
(ebook) | DDC 370.92 [B] —dc23
LC record available at https://lccn.loc.gov/2019020708
LC ebook record available at https://lccn.loc.gov/2019022357

British Library Cataloguing-in-Publication Data
A catalog record for this book is available from the British Library

CONTENTS

PREFACE

Maria Baldwin is a well-known figure in Cambridge, Massachusetts, but is not widely recognized in the broader context of African American history. I initiated this research with the goal of writing an article that would bring her achievement as an African American public school principal in a predominantly white, middle-class school to a wider audience. But once I began exploring her life in the context of the history of African Americans in New England in the late nineteenth and early twentieth centuries, I began to see the parallel world in which she moved and the community of black activists of which she was a part. While knowledge of her own inner life is limited by the lack of surviving personal writings, the availability of US census, municipal, and state records has made it possible to trace at least the outlines of the lives of her family and other figures in her life. At the same time, advances in technology have greatly expanded the nature of historical research. Many university archives are now beginning to digitalize and make available their research collections. The W. E. B. Du Bois Papers available through the University of Massachusetts Amherst are a rich source of African American history and proved invaluable in understanding the broader political world of which Maria Baldwin was a part. I made particular use of the full series of *The Woman's Era* digitalized by Emory University and the minutes of the League of Women for Community Service and papers of Charlotte Hawkins Brown digitalized by the Schlesinger Library at the Radcliffe Institute for Advanced Study at Harvard. The collection of

Cambridge newspapers from the nineteenth century to the present digitalized by the Cambridge Public Library was essential in tracing the public lives of Maria Baldwin and her brother Louis.

I was greatly helped in this research by librarians and archivists in a number of Cambridge and Boston archives. I thank particularly Diana Carey of the Schlesinger Library, Alyssa Pacy of the Cambridge Room at the Cambridge Public Library, and Kit Hawkins, assistant director of the Cambridge Historical Commission. Thanks as well to the helpful librarians and archivists at the Houghton Library at Harvard, the Schlesinger Library, the Boston Athenaeum, the Boston Public Library, the Guardian of Boston Collection at the Howard Gotlieb Archival Research Center at Boston University, the South End Historical Society, the Massachusetts Historical Society, and Tisch Library at Tufts University. Brian Halley and Rachael DeShano at the University of Massachusetts Press provided invaluable guidance and advice throughout the process of preparing the book for publication. Amanda Heller's work copy editing the manuscript was exceptional. Technical expertise from Stephen Sylvester, Anna Steinman, and Helen Steinman was a great help in putting together the final text. The manuscript was greatly improved by the suggestions and careful readings of Lorraine Roses, Michele Clark, Sam Clark, Sandy Zagarell, Marilyn Johnson, Kit Hawkins, and especially Peter Weiler, whose love and support sustained me throughout this project.

MARIA
BALDWIN'S
WORLDS

INTRODUCTION

In 2000, Nathaniel Vogel, an eighth-grade student at the Agassiz Elementary School in Cambridge, Massachusetts, began a campaign to change the name of his school to the Maria Baldwin School. The Agassiz School had been named for the nineteenth-century Harvard professor Louis Agassiz, an internationally known geologist and zoologist. But Agassiz was also a follower of the theory of polygenism, which claimed that race is a scientific reality and that different races have separate origins and inherently different abilities, a hierarchical theory that justifies white privilege and racism. When Nathaniel Vogel read Stephen Jay Gould's condemnation of Agassiz's racist views in *The Mismeasure of Man,* he became ashamed that his school bore Agassiz's name. He already knew something about Maria Baldwin, who had once been his school's principal. There was a plaque commemorating her at the entrance to the school, and an annual award to an outstanding student was still given in her name. After he read the brief entry on Baldwin in Darlene Clark Hine's *Black Women in America: An Historical Encyclopedia* and contrasted Baldwin's accomplishments with Agassiz's scientific racism, he mobilized a campaign to change the name of the school.[1] Cambridge and Boston newspapers and local television news programs publicized the story. After a number of open meetings, in 2002 the Cambridge School Committee voted to change the name of the school from the Agassiz to the Maria Baldwin School.

Maria Baldwin is now well known in Cambridge, and her name appears in numerous reference works on notable African

American women. But while she is recognized as an accomplished and pioneering educator, her accomplishments and role in the black freedom struggle have largely been forgotten. In fact, she was a central member of a group of African American activists in Boston and Cambridge who fought for full citizenship and civil rights in the late nineteenth and early twentieth centuries, a period commonly termed the nadir of black experience in the United States after the abolition of slavery.[2] Knowledge of the active resistance to racism of these northern African Americans brings to light the ways in which racist practices and beliefs were named and contested in the era of Jim Crow. The figure of Maria Baldwin herself shows how a single individual could negotiate and challenge dominant white ideas of black womanhood. Unlike a militant figure such as Ida B. Wells, Maria Baldwin did not publicly condemn and denounce the racist violence of these years, but through her achievements and what W. E. B. Du Bois called her "quiet courage," she both called into question racist cultural images and assumptions in the white community and supported resistance in the black world.

Born in Cambridge in 1856, Maria Baldwin attended local elementary schools and graduated from what was then Cambridge High School in 1874 and the Cambridge teacher training program a year later. In 1881 she began teaching at the Agassiz Elementary School, a well-regarded public school attended by the children of Cambridge's academic and professional elite. The staff and the overwhelming majority of the children were white. In 1889 Baldwin was named principal of the school, and in 1916 was given the position of master, one of only two women in the Cambridge school system to hold this title. She was a progressive New England schoolmarm. She loved Dickens and Tennyson, was welcome in the parlors of the old abolitionists, belonged to socially elite and progressive organizations, and was a supporter of women's suffrage. Acquaintances and former pupils spoke of her in glowing terms. The poet e. e. cummings, who had been her pupil at the Agassiz School, described her as "a lady if ever a lady existed . . . blessed with a delicious voice, charming manners, and a deep understanding of children. . . . From her I marvellingly learned that the truest power is gentleness."[3] Accounts of Maria Baldwin's charismatic presence and abilities as an educator are remarkably consistent. Her accomplishments were unique. The African American sociologist Adelaide Cromwell called her "the lone symbol of Negro progress in education in the greater Boston area" during her lifetime.[4] Her friend W. E. B. Du Bois claimed in 1917 that she had gained "without doubt . . . the most distinguished position achieved by a person of Negro descent in the teaching world of America, outside cities where there are segregated schools."[5] For whites, Baldwin was a model citizen praised for her devotion to service and duty. For the African American community, she was a living example of the capabilities of the race. Throughout her life, she moved in and between these different worlds.

Baldwin was born in Massachusetts before the Civil War and came to adulthood during Reconstruction, that brief period of racial optimism in the North and black citizenship in the South. A person of great presence and dignity, she saw herself as a black New Englander, embodying the moral values of plain living and high thinking and the integrity and courage of the abolitionists. She embraced not only the social activism of the abolitionists but also the value of literature and poetry, the life of the mind. Her contemporary, the novelist Pauline Hopkins, a descendant of a long line of black New England activists who referred to herself as a "daughter of the revolution," later wrote, "May my tongue cleave to the roof of my mouth and my right hand forget its cunning when I forget the benefits bestowed upon my persecuted race in noble-hearted New England."[6] Although Baldwin's own parents were not native to New England, she, like Hopkins, saw herself as the inheritor of the "noble" culture of abolitionist New England, where both whites and blacks fought for the freedom of black people. Boston and Cambridge had been centers of the abolitionist movement before the Civil War. As a teenager and young adult, Maria Baldwin would have been aware of the black and white reformers who had been active in the movement— well-known figures who continued to support progressive causes.[7] She grew to womanhood in Cambridge at a time when the sacrifice of war and the prize of freedom seemed to promise a new world where both black and white Americans could share the privileges and obligations of citizenship.

The hopes of the abolitionists and the promise of the early years after the war were threatened in 1877, when Baldwin was twenty-one. In a political compromise with white southern leaders, the federal government ended its military presence in the South and its enforcement of the rights of black southerners. Over the next twenty years, white southerners created an apartheid society in which African Americans lost the right to vote, many were tied to a system of debt peonage, and all were forced into a segregated world maintained by state laws and lawless white violence. Lynching was only the best-known form of this violent oppression. More than 2,500 black people were lynched between 1884 and 1900.[8] The rise of Jim Crow in the South was paralleled by the intensification of racist practices in the North, even in comparatively progressive Massachusetts. African Americans in New England, who retained the right to vote and escaped legal segregation, nonetheless witnessed the growth of racist beliefs and a growing pattern of segregation in housing, employment, and social institutions throughout civil society. The ascendancy of eugenics and an entrenched belief in white racial superiority marked the scholarly as well as the cultural world. Maria Baldwin's maturity spanned these years of the nadir, in which she, like other African Americans, struggled to create a better life for herself and for her race. Over the years her dual identity as both black and a New Englander did not always coexist easily in the perception of others. In a famous passage from his classic work *The Souls of Black Folk,* W. E. B. Du Bois described the experience of being black in a racist society as one of "double-consciousness, the sense of always looking at one's self through the eyes of others, of measuring one's soul through the tape of a world that looks on in amused contempt and pity. One always feels his two-ness, an American, a Negro; two souls, two thoughts, two unreconciled strivings; two warring ideals in one dark body, whose dogged strength alone keeps it from being torn asunder."[9] Like Du Bois, who was also raised in a largely white Massachusetts town and attended public schools with white children, Baldwin lived with this two-ness throughout her life.

Despite the worsening racial climate, Maria Baldwin was praised by whites for her ability, dignity, and achievements as an educator. She was a member of several white-dominated organizations and a frequent speaker at meetings and celebrations, often as the sole African American lecturer before almost exclusively white audiences. White progressives in Cambridge and Boston saw Baldwin's achievements as a sign of the racially liberal climate of New England and the continuity of the abolitionist tradition—and, perhaps, as evidence of what they perceived as their own tolerance. Baldwin's accomplishments were admirable, but her life encompassed much more than her outstanding career as a teacher and principal in a school for the white middle-class children of Cambridge. She was also a central figure in the black community, active in numerous organizations and movements for civil rights and social justice. In addition to her key role in the founding of the Woman's Era Club and the League of Women for Community Service, she was an active member and later president of the Boston Literary and Historical Association, a member of the Niagara Movement (once women were allowed to join), and one of the Committee of Forty which helped establish the National Association for the Advancement of Colored People.

Baldwin was part of a small, closely connected Boston and Cambridge network of educated black professionals who denounced the growing violence against black people and the denial of black rights in the South, and who demanded full civil rights and social equality in the South as well as in the North. This educated black elite, similar to black groups and networks in other cities, included W. E. B. Du Bois, William Monroe Trotter, Archibald Grimké, George and Josephine St. Pierre Ruffin, Florida Ruffin Ridley, and Clement and Gertrude Morgan. There were disagreements and divisions in this group, which the sociologist Adelaide Cromwell called "the other Brahmins" of Boston, but all were civil rights activists who demanded full equality and justice for all African Americans and were leaders of black resistance to the growing racism of the late nineteenth and early twentieth centuries.[10] As well as Du Bois, the leading black intellectual of this generation, the group also included writers, lawyers, newspaper editors, and leaders of black cultural and political organizations. Maria Baldwin's life was intertwined with the lives of these black New Englanders. Her success in the white world was seen as proof of black ability, but it was also an example of the kind of non-racist society they all wanted to achieve.

Baldwin was a significant figure for both white and black publics, but her work as an activist seeking justice in a deeply divided society was unmentioned in the many testimonials to her by white observers. The black community, which celebrated her achievements as an educator, was well aware of the barriers she had to overcome and her engagement in the black freedom struggle. Historical memory of her, however, has been based on accounts by white contemporaries who never spoke of her involvement in black political organizations, and on a few brief biographical sketches by black historians who largely avoided mentioning the racism she faced or her involvement in black resistance.[11] Maria Baldwin was a public figure whose activities were noted in the major Cambridge and Boston newspapers, in the black press, in the records of the organizations she belonged to, and in the memoirs of her contemporaries. Piecing together this documentation of her accomplishments in both the white and black worlds of Boston and Cambridge reveals a complicated woman who lived the contradictions of a country that defined itself as valuing justice, respect, and freedom but that in practice sanctioned inequality, racial oppression, and violence.

It is more difficult to find a record of her own words, particularly expressions of her private views and feelings. Her voice is found in only a few published writings, in transcriptions of speeches in the white press, and in the detailed minutes of black organizations. Historians have noted the absence of personal papers from black women of her generation.[12] African American scholars have argued that the lack of documents capturing the inner life of black women in this period is a reflection of the

extreme racism of the times, which led women to protect themselves by hiding their true feelings. In Darlene Clark Hine's
words, they shielded "the truth of their inner lives and selves
from their oppressor."[13] In Baldwin's case, a desire to protect herself may have played a part in the lack of written self-reflection,
but physical exhaustion could have been an equally significant
reason. Baldwin was a teacher and principal, a well-known
figure and participant in a number of clubs and organizations,
frequently called upon as a public speaker. There must have
been little time for private personal writing. She was, however,
remembered as a remarkable writer of letters. One of her contemporaries described "her great gift as a letter-writer" who found
correspondence "a medium for her genial turn of thought and
lightness of touch. At her best she reminded you of Lady Mon-
tague in wit and repartee and of Madame Sevigne in freshness
of charm, and gayety of heart."[14] Unfortunately, only a few of her
letters have survived. She had no children; nor did her brother,
Louis, or her sister, Alice. After Alice died, there were no family
members to inherit and preserve her personal papers. If she left
any private writings, they have been lost.

Uncovering and documenting the accomplishments and
challenges of Maria Baldwin's life means piecing together the
fragments of evidence that remain. In this account I have tried to
present those fragments in the context of the social and political
events of her time. Because personal writings that might have
revealed Baldwin's responses to these developments have not
survived, in most cases we see only the public person. While the
sources for Baldwin's life—particularly those revealing her own
understanding and feelings about the events she experienced—
are slight, we know much more about the group of black activists
of which she was a part and whose histories are intertwined with
her own. Their stories illuminate both the complexity of racial
identity and the varieties of black struggle, raising questions
of class, accommodation, and resistance that can be explored
only by considering the historically shaped circumstances that
defined the cultural and social worlds in which they lived. I do
not presume to have captured the inner experience of Maria

Baldwin, but I hope enough is here to suggest the complex life of a remarkable person of integrity who worked, persevered, and achieved respect and admiration in two worlds defined and divided by the myth of race and the power of racism.

~ CHAPTER ONE ~

A New England Girlhood

Many nineteenth-century African American public figures offered stories of their family's origins, but very little is known of Maria Baldwin's family history. Accounts of Baldwin's life make no reference to either of her parents' pasts. Except for her brother, Louis, and her sister, Alice, there is no mention of any other family members—no grandparents, aunts, uncles, cousins—and no account of how or why her parents arrived in Cambridge, Massachusetts, in the mid-1850s. Maria Baldwin was born on September 13, 1856, the first child of Peter and Mary Baldwin.[1] Their documentation as Maria's parents on the 1856 birth record seems to be the first mention of either of them in any historical source. On Maria's birth record her mother, Mary's, birthplace is given as Baltimore, a detail confirmed in Mary's death notice, which gives Baltimore as her birthplace and also the birthplace of her parents, James and Catherine Blake. As a border state with a large commercial center, Maryland had a much higher percentage of free people of color than did the states of the deep South. By 1860, 75 percent of African Americans in northern Maryland, which included the city of Baltimore, were free. While Maryland may have had the largest percentage of free black people in the South, this did not mean African Americans were free of discriminatory laws and hostile treatment by whites. Nonetheless, freedom did mean the opportunity to earn money and, for some, the possibility of seeking a better life farther north.[2] How Mary Blake came to leave Maryland and, in 1856, at the age of nineteen, be found living in Cambridge, Massachusetts, the wife of

Peter Baldwin and mother to a newborn daughter, is unknown. Perhaps Mary Blake and Peter Baldwin met and married in Baltimore, or perhaps Mary came north to Boston to find work and met Peter Baldwin there. There is evidence that Mary Baldwin maintained connections with Maryland. In the 1860 US census, Peter and Mary Baldwin are listed as living at 25 Washington Street in Cambridge in a household with two other women, Mary L. Weeks, twenty, and Harriet Weeks, eighteen, both born in Maryland and most likely kin or close friends of Mary Baldwin—herself then only in her early twenties.

Even less is known of Peter Baldwin. On Maria's 1856 birth record his occupation is given as mariner and his birthplace as Stonington, Connecticut. But while the 1860 Cambridge city directory also lists his occupation as mariner, and the 1860 US census identifies him as a seaman, his birthplace in the 1860 census is listed as the West Indies. In the 1870 census, his birthplace is once again listed as Connecticut. On his death certificate, both his birthplace and his parents are "unknown." If Peter Baldwin was an immigrant seaman from the West Indies, he most probably came alone. If he was born in Stonington, Connecticut, there should have been some reference to family. Perhaps he met young Mary Blake in the port city of Baltimore and the two of them then moved to Boston. But why Boston? And what did it mean to be a black seaman?

Although in the nineteenth century seafaring was seen as difficult and low-status work for white men, African American seamen had a much higher status in the black community. In the early years of the nineteenth century, African American seamen participated in an international maritime culture that offered much greater equality and respect than did life in the United States, South or North. For African American men, work as a seaman offered more pay, greater mobility, and more social equality than almost any of the jobs available to them on land. Before 1850, about 20 percent of American seamen nationwide were black. Of the occupations listed for 575 black workers in Boston in 1850, the largest number, 142, were identified as seamen. The next-largest group were 115 laborers.[3] In his study of African American seamen, Jeffrey Bolster claims that in the first half of the nineteenth century, seafaring was "crucial to blacks' economic survival, liberation strategies, and collective identity-formation."[4]

While black seamen may have had high status in the African American community, they did not escape racism, on the part of both white captains and crew and authorities in southern ports. By the middle of the nineteenth century, when Peter Baldwin went to sea, conditions for black seamen were worsening. Most southern states had passed Negro Seamen Acts, calling for the arrest of any free black seaman who debarked in a southern port. The jailed seamen faced brutal conditions and had to pay the costs of their own imprisonment. Ships themselves became more strictly segregated, and in general, work as a seaman became less steady and more dangerous in the years leading up to the Civil War.[5] The percentage of black workers identifying themselves as sailors fell from 29 percent in 1850 to 19 percent in 1860.[6] Nonetheless, Bolster argues, "by tapping an international maritime culture that allowed them to 'feel as men' in the presence of co-workers and to 'presume upon their equality,' several generations of black men partially circumvented the racist norms of American society."[7] Peter Baldwin's experiences as a young seaman may have offered him opportunities to expand his talents and build a confidence in himself that he carried with him the rest of his life. And it probably offered him economic advantages as well. Work as a seaman was arduous, but there were no expenses while at sea, and the pay was equal to that of skilled laborers, who held jobs that were largely closed to black men.[8] The 1860 census lists Peter Baldwin as the owner of the house at 25 Washington Street, Cambridgeport, valued at $2,000. His personal property was worth $500. Somehow, by 1857 Peter Baldwin had amassed enough capital to buy a house, a rare accomplishment for an African American in nineteenth-century Boston or Cambridge.[9]

THE BLACK COMMUNITY

Whatever their path, there were good reasons why a young African American couple might have settled in Massachusetts. In Boston and Cambridge, the Baldwins found what has been called the most welcoming place for African Americans in the antebellum United States. In the mid-1850s, when Peter and Mary Baldwin were starting their life together, millions of people of African descent were still held in slavery in the American South, while in the free North, racist practices and beliefs were rampant. But in the thirty years before the Civil War, Boston became one of the major centers of abolitionist activity among both whites and African Americans. Massachusetts as a whole had a very small black population, less than 1percent of the total population of the state. Boston's black population remained somewhat higher but was still less than 2 percent of the total between 1820 and 1880.[10] Although the Boston African American community was small, it was a center of abolitionist organizing and activism. In 1829 the Boston African American activist David Walker published his "Appeal to the Colored Citizens of the World, but in Particular, and Very Expressly, to those of the United States of America," calling for the abolition of slavery and demanding full social and political equality. Two years later, in 1831, the white abolitionist William Lloyd Garrison founded the newspaper *The Liberator* and the Massachusetts Anti-Slavery Society, which later merged with the Massachusetts General Colored Association.[11] *The Liberator* became an important source of information and support for the black community with African Americans the majority of its subscribers.[12] As Elizabeth Pleck has written, "In the expansion of legal rights, the atmosphere of interracial association, and the militancy of the community leadership, black Boston was almost without equal."[13]

Although Boston offered advantages compared to other US cities, that did not mean it was not deeply marked by racism. There was no legal protection from racial discrimination in housing, employment, hotels, restaurants, or professional organizations. The primacy of conceptions of race—of white superiority and black inferiority—solidified and strengthened from the 1820s through the 1860s, in the North as well as the South. While the Boston black community was militant in its advocacy of civil rights and full citizenship, it was not always unified in terms of political strategy. In *Black Boston*, George Levesque argues that there was an underlying tension within the antebellum Boston African American community between the desire for complete social and legal equality on the one hand and pride in separate institutions that celebrated black identity on the other. In Levesque's view, demands for both integration and separatism were shaped by the entrenched racism in the North as well as the ominous shadow of the slave system of the South. The struggle against racism meant "opposition to everything that smacked of exclusion." Yet at the same time, writes Levesque, "the community—as an asylum and as a testimonial of achievement—was a psychic necessity and a source of pride." Both stances—the demand for complete integration on the one hand and pride in black institutions on the other—were "simply different means to a common end."[14]

In Boston, the black community was particularly split around schools and the church. In the antebellum period, African American integrationists argued that the very existence of separate black churches encouraged whites to practice segregation in other settings such as schools, transportation, restaurants, theaters, and shops. Frederick Douglass, for example, urged African Americans to leave black churches and join predominantly white congregations as a sign of social equality. In response, supporters of black churches argued that not only was it highly dubious that African Americans would be welcomed in white churches, but also black churches provided a refuge from racist white society and were central to fostering a sense of common black identity and encouraging collective resistance to racism. The majority of African Americans in both Boston and Cambridge belonged to black congregations.

Schooling in Boston was also a contentious issue. Although the public schools of most cities and towns throughout Massachusetts were integrated—no doubt in part because there were so few black children—Boston had a long tradition of segregation. In the early nineteenth century, in response to racist incidents in the public schools, the black community itself supported the establishment of a separate school for black children. This became the Abiel Smith School on Beacon Hill. By the 1840s, though, African

American activists saw the school as an expression not of separatism but of segregation. They began a campaign to integrate
the Boston public schools. The campaign culminated in a legal
case, *Roberts v. City of Boston*, in which it was argued that five-
year-old Sarah Roberts had the right to attend her local school
rather than walk many blocks to the all-black Smith School. In
1850 the Massachusetts Supreme Court ruled against Roberts
and affirmed that segregation was legal, a decision immediately
condemned by African Americans and their allies. This was the
same year that the US Congress passed the Fugitive Slave Act,
which allowed slave owners to send slave hunters after escaped
slaves even in the free states of the North. The Fugitive Slave
Act outraged white as well as black northerners. It was a sign of
whites' growing acceptance of black civil rights in the North as
well as the increasing strength of the abolitionist movement that
five years later, in 1855, the Massachusetts General Court banned
segregated schools throughout the state. Boston schools were
then integrated, seemingly without incident.

The integration of public schools in Boston was a victory,
but both black and white abolitionists were shaken by the US
Supreme Court's 1857 *Dred Scott* decision, which asserted that
people of African descent could never be citizens of the United
States. The decision intensified the sense of emergency caused
by the Fugitive Slave Act among both the African American community and their white allies. *Dred Scott* seemed to justify the
need for violent resistance advocated by radical abolitionists like
John Brown, but it also encouraged the growth of the antislavery
but more moderate Republican Party. Even though the extent
of its commitment to full citizenship for all was questioned by
many African Americans, the Republican Party seemed to offer
the best hope for change within the existing political landscape.

Peter and Mary Baldwin must have been aware of the currents
of opinion and struggles within the Boston African American
community, and there is strong evidence that Peter Baldwin was
a supporter of the Republican Party. The couple settled not in
Boston but across the Charles River in the city of Cambridge.
Their daughter Maria was born in 1856; in 1857 Peter bought the

house at 25 Washington Street in the Cambridge neighborhood of Cambridgeport where their second daughter, Alice Gertrude, was born in 1859. Cambridge was a small city. In 1860, Boston, with a population of 177,000, was the fifth-largest city in the United States. Cambridge had a population of 26,000 and had been formally incorporated as a city only in 1846. By 1860 the city was gradually growing together from three original villages: Old Cambridge, centered on Harvard College; East Cambridge on the Charles River, home to a growing number of factories and small businesses; and Cambridgeport, halfway between the other two. Several bridges across the Charles connected Cambridge to the much larger city of Boston. When Peter and Mary Baldwin settled in Cambridgeport, it was a sprawling neighborhood of crowded streets providing housing to a mixed population of native-born whites, immigrants, and a small number of African Americans, who made up about 1 percent of the city's total. Although the black population of Cambridge was small—rising from 141 in 1850 to 354 in 1860—it included a number of politically active abolitionists. We have no evidence of the political involvement of Peter or Mary Baldwin in these years, but they must have been aware of the Cambridge abolitionists as well as those in the larger Boston black community. In the mid-1850s there was no black church in Cambridge, although more liberal churches associated with the abolitionists could include black parishioners.[15] In contrast, by 1848 there were four black churches in Boston for a black population of around two thousand. That year the black Twelfth Baptist Church, which quickly became a center of abolitionist organizing, was established. Peter and Mary Baldwin may have found a religious and political home in one of these black Boston churches.

The outbreak of the Civil War in April 1861 would have been a momentous event for the Baldwin family, as for others in the Boston and Cambridge black community. The goal of abolition, once seen as the obsession of a few radicals, was now within reach. Peter Baldwin's activities during the war are not known. Like most other black New Englanders he supported the Republican Party, even though Lincoln and the Republicans had vacillated on the question of slavery. It was only on January 1, 1863, almost two years after the outbreak of war, that Lincoln issued the Emancipation Proclamation. Despite the hesitancy of Lincoln and the Republicans, the proclamation solidified black support for the party. Black Bostonians showed their support of the Union in a variety of ways, perhaps most dramatically in the participation of African American soldiers in the army's black regiments and in the navy. In Boston, the formation of the black Fifty-fourth and Fifty-fifth Regiments was a powerful symbol of citizenship and achievement. There is no record of Peter Baldwin's service in any of the black regiments, and although over 1,300 men enlisted in the navy at Charlestown Navy Yard, Baldwin's name is not among them. He may well have continued to work as a seaman during the war, while Mary Baldwin would have been occupied with raising her two daughters and maintaining the household. Just as the war was ending, in 1865, when Maria was nine and her sister Alice was seven, their brother Louis was born.

Maria Baldwin, known as Mollie, a nickname that intimate friends continued to use throughout her life, must have entered Cambridge's public schools in the early years of the war.[16] In her only description of these years, "A Night Watch," published in a section titled "Reminiscences" in the African American women's journal *The Woman's Era*, she describes an incident she experienced as a child in a city she calls Bainbridge, a thinly disguised Cambridge. It was a night "during the latter part of the Civil War" when news reached the black community that a mob was approaching. People already knew of the mob in New York that had "left the New York streets one mass of trampled human bodies." This is almost certainly a reference to the July 1863 New York draft riot. The incident, instigated by Irish American men, began in opposition to the draft but soon turned into a race riot in which over a hundred African Americans were killed. The Boston mob was much smaller than that in New York, but the tense racial climate and the antagonism of Irish Americans created a terrifying situation. In Boston the rioters meant to capture the weapons in the Cooper Street armory. When a large crowd tried to force its way inside, troops fired into the crowd, killing several rioters.[17] There was no violence in Cambridge, although the mayor mobilized the city's Home Guard to protect the state arsenal there. The black community of the city remained on edge. Baldwin described the scene: "Men gathered in groups on the street and talked in grave low tones, then separated to make ready their guns and pistols." She sat in a darkened room with her mother and younger sister, dressed and ready to flee from a white mob: "I took fast hold of [my mother's] dress and lay straining my eyes in the darkness to keep her outlines. I was in an agony of fear lest somehow I should lose her." Then they heard the sound of horses' hooves and black men running through the streets, "the frantic joy of their voices breaking the terrible silence. 'The soldiers! The soldiers! They've come to protect us!'"[18]

In "A Night Watch," Maria Baldwin captured the vulnerability of an African American family, her mother's terror, and her own helplessness. She would have been about eight years old when the riot occurred. Her father, Peter, is unmentioned; perhaps he was at sea. Baldwin's reminiscence reveals both her personal experience of the murderous racism faced by African Americans in the North—where they were comparatively safe—and also her confidence that the soldiers would protect them. These themes— both an acute lived knowledge of racism and at the same time a belief in the possibility of justice and protection under the law— would mark Baldwin's life. It is telling that this is the incident she chose to write about in *The Woman's Era*, an event so far from the experience of the cultivated whites she came to know.

THE POST OFFICE

The end of the Civil War was a tumultuous time for members of New England's black community. In many respects they could look back on four decades of achievement. In Boston, African Americans, though only 2 percent of the city's population, had created political alliances with white abolitionists, been central actors in antislavery politics, and served as armed soldiers in the first black regiment in the US Army during the Civil War.[19] But full equality and opportunity had not been secured. Although the story of black northerners in the years between 1865 and 1876—the years of Reconstruction in the South—is not as well known as in the period before and during the Civil War, the historian Stephen Kantrowitz argues that after the war, Boston African Americans continued to be engaged in political struggles for civil rights and full citizenship and that they "in no sense considered their work accomplished in 1865, not even with the Thirteenth, Fourteenth, and Fifteenth Amendments, which ended slavery, established national citizenship, and prohibited civic discrimination based on race."[20] Despite these accomplishments, black New Englanders continued to face racism and discrimination, particularly in employment.

African Americans in the North had achieved legal equality and some political power, but they did not have economic security. Discrimination against black workers at all levels was at the heart of racial inequality in Massachusetts, as it was throughout the nation. In Boston as elsewhere, African Americans were disproportionately found in poorly paid service jobs and casual labor. In 1870, fewer than 3 percent of African American men had the talent, luck, and support to succeed in the professions or business. Eighty-five percent held menial jobs.[21] The situation after the war remained similar to that described by the African American activist Dr. John Rock in 1860. "Nowhere in the United States," he said, "is the colored man of talent appreciated. Even here in Boston, which has a great reputation for being antislavery, he is by no means treated like other talented men." Rock cited widespread white prejudice and hostility and the segregation of restaurants, theaters, and hotels. But most important, he spoke of discrimination in terms of work, which he saw as increasing over the years: "Fifteen or twenty years ago, colored men had more than an equal chance in menial employment; today we are crowded out of almost everything, and we do not even get the patronage of our friends." The situation was if anything worse for better-educated young black men, who were not given any opportunity to show their talents. "Who is taking our boys into their stores at a low salary, and giving them a chance to rise?" Rock asked. "Who is admitting them into their workshops or their counting-rooms? Who is encouraging those who have trades? With the exception of a handful of abolitionists and a few black Republicans, there are none."[22]

In this hostile environment, access to secure government jobs was even more important to African Americans than it was to whites. The patronage system, in which elected officials controlled appointments to government jobs, meant that political allegiance and loyalty offered a route to these desirable civil service positions. In the years immediately after the Civil War, northern black Republicans were able to take advantage of this system. Furthermore, as Stephen Kantrowitz notes, African Americans in Boston were "able to insert themselves into the Republican Party's councils, help determine the outcome of elections, and even achieve office themselves."[23] Racial patterns of settlement in Boston meant that the black population was concentrated in Ward 6, on the back side of Beacon Hill and the West End of Boston. Black men made up 14 percent of the voting population of the ward, a significant number. African American leaders such as Dr. John Rock and George Ruffin mobilized the black electorate to vote solidly Republican. In return for their loyalty, white Republicans backed African American candidates for the state legislature, and in the years following the Civil War, several African American Republicans were elected to the state legislature. Black Republican loyalty also meant at least a limited entry into the patronage system and access to government employment.

One of the African Americans appointed to a government position was Peter Baldwin, who first appears in the civil service list as a letter carrier in the Boston post office in 1869. The US post office, which became a significant source of political patronage in these years, was integrated in 1865, when legislation proposed by Senator Charles Sumner of Massachusetts was passed stating that "no person, by reason of color, shall be disqualified from employment in carrying the mails."[24] Appointment to a position in the US post office was desirable for a number of reasons. First, the position was a mark of responsibility and respect. Letter carriers were government employees trusted with the duty of handling and delivering private documents at a time when letters were the major means of long-distance communication. And the postal uniform itself had symbolic importance. As Philip Rubio notes, the uniform "signified citizenship, manhood, and personhood in a country that had only a few years before denied that blacks had any 'rights which the white man is bound to respect,' in the words of the infamous 1857 Supreme Court *Dred Scott* decision."[25] Adelaide Cromwell, in *The Other Brahmins*, claims that in the late nineteenth-century African American community, postal workers had "greater status" than even doctors or lawyers.[26]

After the Civil War, a small number of black postmen were hired in Massachusetts cities. In New Bedford, William Carney, a highly respected Civil War veteran who had served with the Fifty-fourth Massachusetts Regiment and was the first African American to be awarded the Medal of Honor, was hired as a letter carrier. By the late 1860s, almost a dozen black men were employed in the Boston post office, among them some of the most respected figures in black Boston, including James Trotter, William Dupree, and William Nell. Trotter and Dupree were former second lieutenants in the renowned Fifty-fifth Regiment and were among the first African American officers in the US Army. James Trotter, who had been born into slavery in Mississippi, was freed by his master and made his way north, where he attended school and eventually became a teacher. After the war, he and his family settled in the integrated Boston suburb of Hyde Park. In the 1880s, Trotter was appointed to the federal position of recorder of deeds in Washington, DC. Trotter's son William Monroe Trotter would graduate Phi Beta Kappa from Harvard, found and edit *The Guardian* newspaper, and become a leading advocate of black civil rights and racial equality. William Cooper Nell had been a leading abolitionist in Boston. A follower of William Lloyd Garrison, he published articles in *The Liberator* and helped found the Freedom Association. He later was a close associate of Frederick Douglass and for a time published Douglass's paper *The North Star*. After the passage of the fugitive slave law in 1850, Nell became actively involved with the Underground

FIGURE 2. William Carney of New Bedford, one of the first African American postmen. Courtesy of Carl J. Cruz.

Railroad. A scholar, he produced some of the first studies of African American soldiers in the Revolutionary War and the War of 1812. In 1858, in response to the *Dred Scott* decision, Nell helped organize the first Crispus Attucks celebration, commemorating the first African American to die in the Revolutionary War. One of the first African Americans appointed to a position in the Boston post office, which he held until his death in 1874.[27]

That Peter Baldwin was among this small group of black men who gained positions at the post office almost certainly is a sign of the respect in which he was held and of his involvement with black Republicans, even though there is no existing record of his political activities. It may be significant that although he had been identified as West Indian in records in the 1860s, beginning in the 1870 census, the year after he first appears as a postal worker, Peter Baldwin's birthplace is once again given as Connecticut. Of course, work at the post office meant much more than respectability and status in the black community. Baldwin's annual salary in 1869 was $800, and the work was a secure civil service position. By comparison, the daily wage for non-farm laborers in New England in 1870 was approximately $1.50 a day. For a six-day workweek, an annual salary would be $470.[28] And that assumes black men would be hired in the first place and have steady work throughout the year, which is highly unlikely. Not only did the post office pay twice as much as casual labor, the employment of more than four fifths of all African American men, but also the position was guaranteed. A family man with a secure wage could live in a comfortable house, plan for the future, and support his children's education.

Through his position at the post office, Peter Baldwin acquired the capital to give his family financial security. But he provided social capital as well. Stephen Kantrowitz has described Boston's African American community as a "dense, complex social world in which people distinguished themselves less by wealth or descent than by accomplishment and bearing."[29] Peter Baldwin's origins remain obscure, but he clearly had accomplished a great deal in a racially hostile world. Work at the post office gave him a position of further respect and responsibility. The African American journalist and novelist Pauline Hopkins, who knew Maria Baldwin well, described both of Baldwin's parents as "well-known and highly respected citizens" of Cambridge.[30] Through his association with black Republicans, Peter Baldwin must also have come to know some of the leading political actors in black Boston, among them George Ruffin, and his wife, Josephine, who would become central figures among Boston's black social reformers and defenders of black civil rights.

In 1858, when he was twenty-three and she was sixteen, George Ruffin married Josephine St. Pierre, the daughter of John and Eliza St. Pierre of Boston. The entry in the Boston registry of marriages does not give John and Eliza's birthplaces, but it does note that they were "people of color."[31] Other sources describe John St. Pierre as a clothes dealer in Boston of mixed African and Native American ancestry and Eliza Mahinnick St. Pierre as a white Englishwoman born in Cornwall.[32] Several accounts claim that Josephine St. Pierre's parents sent her to elementary school in Salem rather than have her attend the segregated Boston public schools, which suggests their support of the growing campaign to integrate the schools in the 1840s and 1850s.[33]

Although he did not attend college, George Ruffin began to study law in his twenties and was eventually accepted at Harvard Law School. In 1869 he became the first African American to graduate from Harvard Law. He was active in the Republican Party and in 1870 was elected to the Massachusetts state legislature. In April 1871 Ruffin presented a resolution to the legislature demanding that the US Congress act to protect the life, liberty, and property of black people in all parts of the United States. He described the violence directed toward black southerners and denounced the southern Democratic Party, declaring, "They will go into no canvass, make no political platform, fight no battles at the polls, which has not as its object the degradation of the Negro." If Congress failed to act, Ruffin argued, "the reign of terror will continue and become intensified in this portion of our land, and the blood of murdered men will be laid at its door."[34] Although Ruffin's resolution was not passed by the Massachusetts legislature, it is evidence of his awareness of the racist violence in the South.

Ruffin's public condemnation of white racism and demand for full equality was typical of black leadership in Boston. Stephen Kantrowitz points out that demands of the politically active black community in Boston for true social equality in all spheres

and "full and unhedged citizenship" had their roots in the abolitionist movement, where both black and white radicals sought to
overthrow slavery and where cross-race friendships did on occasion take root. Black Bostonians, Kantrowitz argues, imagined
that as they won rights and achieved prosperity, demonstrating
their abilities and equal worth, "the whole ideological architec-
ture of racial hierarchy would collapse under the weight of its
own absurdity."[35] Ruffin may have had his doubts that the racial
hierarchy would soon collapse, but he was able to work with
whites at the same time that he maintained his strong anti-racist
stance. He was later elected to the Boston Common Council in
1876 and 1877 and was an active member of the Twelfth Baptist
Church, which had been a center of abolitionism before the Civil
War and continued to preach a social gospel of racial justice and
civil rights similar to that of radical white Unitarian churches.[36]
In 1883 Ruffin was appointed a municipal judge, the first African American judge in Massachusetts. He served for only three
years, however, before dying in 1886 of Bright's disease.

George and Josephine Ruffin had five children, the oldest born
in 1859, one year after their marriage, and the last ten years later,
in 1869. The only girl, Florida, known as Flora, was born in 1861.
Peter Baldwin and George Ruffin must have known each other
through black Republican circles, and the families probably saw
each other socially. As children, Flora Ruffin and Maria Baldwin became friends and remained close throughout their lives.
Young Maria Baldwin must have been impressed by George Ruffin, a lawyer and judge, but also by Flora's mother, Josephine St.
Pierre Ruffin, one of the best-known African American women
in late nineteenth-century Boston. Despite the responsibility
of raising five children, Josephine continued to be active in the
public world. As a young married woman she had performed
across New England giving dramatic readings. An 1864 article
in *The Christian Recorder*, an African American paper, referred
to her as "Madam Ruffin, the great dramatic reader."[37] During
the Civil War she became more politically active, helping to
recruit soldiers to serve in the black regiments and participating
in the New England Woman's Auxiliary Association (NEWAA),
a white-dominated organization formed to assist families and

soldiers in the black regiments.[38] In the late 1870s, she was active in the Boston branch of the Kansas Relief Association, which sought support for the "Kansas Exodus," the African Americans who fled the South at the end of Reconstruction for a new life in Kansas.

Josephine St. Pierre Ruffin was increasingly involved with white-dominated women's organizations after the war: she was a charter member of the Massachusetts School Suffrage Association, an early member of the Massachusetts Woman Suffrage Association, and a member of the Women's Industrial and Educational Union. In these settings she became acquainted with leading white women reformers, many of whom had been active in the abolitionist movement.[39] Ruffin later described how she had been "welcomed into the Massachusetts Woman Suffrage Association by Lucy Stone, Julia Ward Howe, Ednah Cheney, Abbey Morton Diaz and those other pioneer workers who were broad enough to include 'no distinction because of race' with 'no distinction because of sex.'"[40] The welcome that white women reformers offered to Ruffin and Ruffin's participation in white-dominated organizations in the 1870s and 1880s must have suggested the possibility of an integrated world to her young daughter Flora and to Flora's good friend Maria Baldwin.

Flora Ruffin was five years younger than Maria Baldwin, but in Flora's memory of her youth, she and Maria were members of a small group of politically conscious African American friends. Flora Ruffin Ridley later remembered these days as "a time when the names and deeds of the Higginsons and Hallowells and Forsters and Mays and Putnams and Parkers and Garrisons and Channings formed a part of daily home talk," when "with Maria Baldwin and other girls, we committed and recited the poems of Whittier and Longfellow," and "when at any time in our journeys up the Joy Street hill across the Common to reach the only line of cars to the high school or across the old Cambridge bridge to reach the Baldwin home, we might come face to face with these upholders of abolition."[41] Given the five-year difference between them, it is not clear how accurate this picture is, but Ridley's account captures her own and Maria Baldwin's identities as educated New Englanders and inheritors of the

FIGURE 3. Flora Ruffin.

abolitionist tradition, typical of the politically active network
of black Bostonians, but a very different legacy from that of the
majority of African Americans of their generation. Conversations in the Ruffin home, the family's interactions with whites,
and the uncompromising anti-racist stance of the Ruffins and

other members of the small black Boston elite must have made an impact on young Maria Baldwin. Her education included not only the formal curriculum of a New England public school but also the political activism and conversations she heard around her in her youth.

A NEW ENGLAND EDUCATION

If Maria Baldwin enjoyed a financially secure childhood and the social capital of her father's connection to the Boston black elite, she also acquired the cultural capital of a New England public school education. In the years after the Civil War, when Maria was growing up, the idea that the state should provide free and compulsory public education became broadly accepted in the United States and was particularly strong in Massachusetts, home of Horace Mann and the common school movement. In 1852 Massachusetts became the first state in the union to make school attendance compulsory for all children aged eight to fourteen, and after 1855 all public schools in Massachusetts were integrated. As a child, Maria Baldwin attended the Sargent Primary and Allston Grammar schools in Cambridge. The African American journalist and novelist Pauline Hopkins saw Baldwin as shaped by the morality and integrity she had learned from the "plain, straightforward curriculum of the New England public school." There, said Hopkins, she acquired "grace of mind and body together with comprehensive Christianity and orderly deportment from her cultured teachers, many of them descendants of the best New England stock."[42] Maria Baldwin herself left no record of her experiences in school. There is no way to know the racial dynamics of these classrooms or if she was treated differently because she was black. The Cambridge public schools did not record children's race, so it is not even possible to trace the numbers of black children in the schools in the years of Baldwin's childhood. But her love of Dickens and Tennyson and her pride and comfort in her work as a teacher and principal support the claim of Pauline Hopkins that she was deeply influenced by the cultural values she encountered in the Cambridge public schools.

Although the Cambridge schools did not record race or ethnicity, the US census did inquire about race, and so we know that the Baldwin family lived in a racially mixed neighborhood in Cambridgeport. The 1870 census page for Washington Street, where their house was located, is divided almost equally between white and black (including "mulatto") families.[43] Occupations include barber, dressmaker, hotel waiter, seamstress, carpenter, cabinetmaker, laborer, watchman, and, for Peter Baldwin, letter carrier. Mary Baldwin, like most of the married women in households, is listed as "keeping house." The Baldwin family included three children, Maria, fourteen; her sister Alice, eleven; and their five-year-old brother Louis, born at the end of the Civil War in 1865. Like the rest of Cambridge, the Cambridgeport neighborhood grew rapidly after the war. Attracted by cheap land and the expansion of the railroads and local public transportation, industries moved into Cambridge, offering jobs to both immigrants and internal migrants from rural New England and the South. The population of Cambridge more than doubled in Maria Baldwin's childhood and youth, increasing from around 19,000 in 1856, the year of her birth, to 47,000 in 1875, the year she graduated from the Cambridge teacher training program. The black population also continued to rise, reaching 921 in 1875, but it was still less than 1 percent of the population of Cambridge.

All three of the Baldwin children graduated from Cambridge High School: Maria in 1874, Alice Gertrude in 1875, and Louis in 1882. At this time, the majority of Americans achieved only an eighth-grade education. If high school graduation was not the norm for whites, in Massachusetts as elsewhere the percentage of African Americans who were high school graduates was smaller still. Cambridge had established a single public high school in 1848. In 1864 the school had grown and moved to a new building located near Harvard College. It was at that time "one of the best equipped and most elegant schoolhouses in the State," according to a later observer.[44] When the Baldwin siblings were students, Cambridge High School offered two courses of study, classical, which prepared male students for college, and English. Maria, Alice, and Louis all completed the English course.[45] It is impossible to determine the number of African Americans who graduated from Cambridge High School in these years since the school did not record race, but given the limited black population of the city, the number was doubtless quite small.

For both African Americans and whites, high school attendance depended on a family's financial resources, as of course did college. In the 1870s and 1880s it was expected that the children of the small Boston and Cambridge black elite would graduate from high school; exceptional young men like William Monroe Trotter went on to Harvard. For young black women, high school graduation and, for a few, preparation for a teaching career seem to have been the highest goals. In 1874, when Maria Baldwin graduated from Cambridge High School, very few colleges were open to white, let alone black, women, but young women could prepare for a teaching career by attending a normal school or teacher training program.[46] Although the great majority of normal school students were young white women, Massachusetts state normal schools did accept a handful of black students. Charlotte Forten, the well-known black diarist, attended Salem Normal School in the 1850s, and Maria Baldwin's friend Flora Ruffin graduated from the Boston Normal School in 1880.[47] Cambridge did not have a separate normal school; instead it offered a one-year teacher training course. Immediately after she graduated from high school, Maria Baldwin entered the teacher training program, held at the newly built Agassiz School. Her sister Alice graduated from the high school one year later and also enrolled in the teacher training program.

Maria and Alice Baldwin received an education in the most modern approaches to pedagogy. The Cambridge School Committee was proud of the training school, which had opened in 1870 "with a very large class of young ladies."[48] According to the 1870 report of the school committee, the training school was intended not just to provide a group of potential teachers for the Cambridge primary schools but "to do much more than this and be an important benefit to every instructor in the city" by offering a model of excellent teaching. Teachers throughout the city were invited to observe the practices at the training school. The training students assisted experienced primary school teachers and also received lessons in theory and practice from the principal.

As the school committee noted, "Particularly at the present time, when efforts are being made to introduce a freer and more various system of instruction into the Primaries, does the value of such a training become conspicuous."[49]

The Cambridge School Committee's mention of "freer and more various systems of instruction" doubtless was a reference to the ideas of European educational reformers such as Pestalozzi, Froebel, and Herbart, who were becoming increasingly well known and influential in the United States in the years after the Civil War. Deeply influenced by Rousseau's ideas of childhood, these theorists advocated pedagogies appropriate to children's emotional and developmental needs. The best known of these new pedagogical practices in Massachusetts were the reforms being put into place in the Quincy public schools under Colonel Francis Parker, who was appointed superintendent of schools in 1875. Parker immediately introduced a number of progressive reforms emphasizing children's emotional and cognitive development, their need to explore the natural world, and the importance of teaching writing as the expression of ideas rather than the recapitulation of memorized facts. He also instituted a training school for future teachers, which the educational historian Michael Katz has called "perhaps his most important single innovation."[50] But Parker's training school in fact followed the program that Cambridge had introduced a few years earlier. Cambridge school officials were apparently well aware of this fact. The 1880 Cambridge School Committee report emphasized that "the principles, and for most part the methods, which have given extended fame to the Quincy primary schools, as marking a new departure in education, had for several years previously formed an essential part of the instruction in our Training School, and had been and still are in successful operation in the primary schools under the special direction of the principal, and in the other schools under the tuition of her pupils."[51] This "new departure," with its emphasis on the unique qualities of each child, was the foundation of Maria Baldwin's education at the Cambridge training school. She was one of fourteen young women who graduated from the program in June 1875. Maria and her younger sister Alice, who followed her to the training school, were the only two graduates of color.[52]

Events in Maria Baldwin's life between 1875, when she completed the training course, and 1881, when she was finally offered a full-time teaching position at the Agassiz School, are difficult to sort out. After completing their training, both Maria and Alice applied for positions in the Cambridge public schools. In 1878 the *Cambridge Chronicle* reported that Maria Baldwin had been appointed a substitute teacher at the Agassiz training school, but neither of the sisters was offered a full-time position.[53] In her biographical entry on Baldwin in *Notable American Women*, Dorothy Porter claims that, "unable to find employment at home," Baldwin began teaching in a segregated black school in Chestertown, Maryland. The exact dates are not certain, since no records of the names of the teachers at the school seem to have survived. It appears probable that she had a personal connection to the town, since her mother and her grandparents, James and Catherine Blake, were from Maryland. The 1870 US census lists a number of black families in Chestertown with the surname Blake. Whether these Blakes were relatives or not, there probably was some connection to bring young Maria from her home in Cambridge to teach in this small town on the Eastern Shore of Maryland.

There are conflicting accounts of the circumstances of Maria Baldwin's move to Chestertown. According to various sources, Baldwin wrote to Cambridge School Committee member Horace Scudder, a respected figure who wrote children's books as well as a widely used textbook on US history, and later was editor of the *Atlantic Monthly*, asking his help in obtaining a position in Cambridge. One account claims she appealed to Scudder before she went to Chestertown and that Scudder advised her that instead of teaching in Cambridge, "it was clearly her duty to go south and work for those with more limited educational opportunities."[54] In his lengthy 1903 *Cambridge Chronicle* article on the Cambridge black community, the white novelist Linn Boyd Porter presents a different scenario, claiming that Baldwin first taught in the segregated school in Chestertown and only later wrote to an "eminent member of the board, a well-known literary man" (presumably Scudder), seeking a place in Cambridge. According to Porter, the school board member "kindly advised her to continue her work in the South, where he thought she would be more useful than in a white community."[55] Scudder was a member of the Cambridge School Committee between 1877 and 1882, so the exchange between them must have occurred during those years. Whenever the correspondence with Scudder took place, it seems clear that when Maria Baldwin sought a teaching position in the Cambridge public schools, she was either ignored or told to look elsewhere for a place in a black school.

Baldwin taught only briefly in the segregated school in Chestertown, and there is no account of her time there in existing documents of her life. Her return to Cambridge may have been a rejection of segregated rural life in Chestertown, but it also may have been for personal family reasons. On March 13, 1880, her father, Peter Baldwin, suddenly died. According to his death record, the cause was cardiac disease.[56] His death must have been a blow on all levels. He was only in his mid-fifties, a responsible, well-respected man, the sole support of his wife and their two younger children. There is no evidence that Mary Baldwin worked outside the home. Maria's younger sister Alice was twenty-one, a graduate of Cambridge High School and its teacher training school, but she also had been unable to find a teaching position in Cambridge and does not seem to have been employed. Her brother Louis was still in high school. At twenty-four, Maria Baldwin was now responsible for the family. When school ended in Chestertown in the spring, she may have returned to Cambridge to be with them. But when the school year began in the fall of 1880, she still had no place in the Cambridge public schools.

THE AGASSIZ SCHOOL

In the fall of 1881, more than a year after Peter Baldwin's death and five years after she had successfully completed Cambridge's teacher training program, Maria Baldwin was finally offered a full-time position at the Agassiz School. Despite the sometimes self-congratulatory white view that Cambridge was a tolerant city without race prejudice, there were no other teachers of color in the Cambridge public schools. A 1917 article in *The Crisis* asserts that it was the "agitation of the colored leaders, under the time of Mayor [James Augustus] Fox," that led to Maria Baldwin's appointment.[57] Both Benjamin Brawley in *Negro Builders and Heroes* and Dorothy Porter in her biographical entry on Baldwin in *Notable American Women* agree that she was hired because of pressure from Cambridge's black community.[58] These black leaders would have known the Baldwin family well and must have understood that after Peter Baldwin's death his daughters Maria and Alice were now the sole possible financial supports of the Baldwin family. A teaching position for them was not simply a matter of racial justice; it was vital for the family's survival.

A December 4, 1880, letter to the *Cambridge Chronicle* from William Hazel, a black Cambridge citizen, suggests the anger of the black community at the failure of the school committee to appoint qualified teachers of color, despite the fact that two young women of color had successfully completed the training school. Hazel writes, "It is now five years since the first young colored women graduated from our training school, having completed the prescribed course of study, passed a successful examination and received as a reward of their diligence a diploma setting forth in unequivocal terms that they were 'competent to teach in the public schools of Cambridge.'" Although they applied for teaching positions, "they have been persistently ignored by the school authorities," even though more recent white graduates of the training school had been hired. While the two young women's petitions "have been repeatedly denied," Hazel notes that the school committee need only look "across the river to the city of Boston to find one of the youngest and most successful teachers in the person of a colored lady." This is doubtless a reference to Maria Baldwin's close friend Flora Ruffin, who had just graduated from the Boston Normal School and who, when she began working as a special assistant teacher at the Phillips School in Boston in October 1880, became the second African American teacher in the integrated Boston public schools. Hazel pointedly notes that municipal elections were coming up and this issue was a question of justice. "The question," he concludes, "will not be allowed to be set aside until it has been fairly and satisfactorily determined."[59]

A few days after Hazel's letter appeared in the *Cambridge Chronicle*, a letter was sent to Francis Cogswell, the Cambridge superintendent of schools, again demanding that the school committee hire "one or more of the young colored women who are applicants for the position of teacher in our public schools." Cogswell was so concerned about this letter that he included a section titled "Colored Teachers" in the 1880 Cambridge annual school report, in which he summarized and tried to respond to its demands. Cogswell does not identify the writer, but since this letter was written only two weeks after William Hazel's letter to the editor of the *Cambridge Chronicle*, it seems likely that it was written either by Hazel or by someone closely associated with him. And although the "two young colored women" are not named, there is no doubt that the reference is to Maria and Alice Baldwin.

Cogswell's discussion of "colored teachers" in the 1880 annual school report reveals his class bias as much as his assumption of race privilege. He acknowledges that "a prejudice exists towards the colored race," but, he insists, "it does not exist, to any extent, among the more intelligent part of the community." Among these "more intelligent" citizens, Cogswell claims, there was no personal animosity toward appointing "either of the two colored graduates of our Training School to the position of teacher." In fact, he claims to be "perfectly willing to have my own daughter under the tuition of either of them, not doubting that she would be well taught and kindly dealt with." But if these two young women were responsible and capable teachers who had successfully completed the city's teacher training course, then why hadn't they been hired? Cogswell denies any personal responsibility. The decision was made "simply because, in my opinion, our committee have felt that the prejudice still existing among that part of the community most dependent upon free schools for the education of their children was too strong to justify their appointment." So it wasn't because of the two young women's lack of ability or achievement but rather because of the assumed prejudice of poor white families. But Cogswell then equivocates: "It may be that our committee are behind public sentiment" and that "the time has come when the experiment of appointing them can be successfully tried here in Cambridge."[60]

Nine months later the experiment was begun when Maria Baldwin was offered a provisional position at the Agassiz School. The agitation of the black community may finally have swayed white officials. Political pressure put on school boards to hire certain candidates on the basis of ethnicity was hardly unusual in late nineteenth-century Cambridge or Boston. It was commonly believed that Irish American politicians used their influence to secure positions in the police department, schools, and other municipal and state agencies. Black political leaders obtained patronage positions as well. Peter Baldwin himself almost certainly gained his job at the post office through the political influence of black Republicans. But in addition to the protest of the black community, the new mayor, James Fox, who began his term in January 1881, may have supported her. And according to Linn Boyd Porter's 1903 *Cambridge Chronicle* article, two white women who were school board members, Mrs. Phebe M. Kendall and Miss Sarah S. Jacobs, also supported her hiring.[61] It was typical of Maria Baldwin herself that her own account, given to journalist Pauline Hopkins, omitted any hint of this conflict. She said simply: "I was given at first an 'overflow' class to teach, with the assurance that I would be kept while that class continued to be a necessity. I was, in short, a temporary teacher. Mr. Francis Cogswell, Superintendent of Schools, said he could not tell how long I would stay but the next year I was called to the same place, and was continued in my position by the Board."[62] Baldwin's account says nothing about the five years during which the school board refused to hire her, the tragedy of her father's death, the mobilization of black Cantabrigians to defend her, or why she was offered only the overflow class, and mentions nothing at all about race.

Once she was hired, Maria Baldwin received the same salary as other teachers. In her first year at the Agassiz School, she was paid $400 a year, which seems to have been the usual starting salary for teachers. For example, Emma Child, another new teacher at the Agassiz that year, also made $400. Throughout her career Baldwin's salary matched the salaries of white women teachers and principals.[63] Her sister Alice, however, was not offered a position in Cambridge. Perhaps Alice did not show the same promise as a teacher, or perhaps she had a sharper and more combative personality, or perhaps two black teachers were too much for the superintendent and school board to accept. But with only Maria's salary, the Baldwin family now had to survive on half the income Peter Baldwin had earned at the post office.

The Baldwin family had always been close. After Maria was hired at the Agassiz School, she continued to live with her mother, her sister, and her brother Louis. Besides her salary, the family's only other resource was the house at 25 Washington Street. In 1882, two years after Peter Baldwin's death and a few months after Maria Baldwin was hired at the Agassiz School, Mary Baldwin sold the house, and the family moved to a smaller rented house on nearby Clark Street. Then, only four years after their father's death, the siblings experienced another loss. In 1884 their mother died of cancer at the age of forty-seven. For the next few years, Maria, Alice, and Louis lived together in the Clark Street house. But in 1888 they moved into a much larger house at 196 (previously 91) Prospect Street in Cambridge. All of the houses that the Baldwins lived in were located in the multiracial neighborhood of Cambridgeport within six blocks of one another, but the Prospect Street house was by far the most comfortable and spacious. It was a home appropriate for a proper and successful teacher at the Agassiz School.

Although the Agassiz was a public school, it drew upon a neighborhood of well-to-do professionals and Harvard professors. There were some private schools in Cambridge attended by the children of the wealthy elite, but the public schools, particularly the primary and grammar schools, were well respected and served a wide range of children. Since the primary and grammar

FIGURE 4. Clark Street, Cambridgeport, where the Baldwins lived from 1882 to 1888. Cambridge Historical Commission, Cambridge Engineering Department Photo.

schools served only their local neighborhoods, the composition of each school reflected the class and racial divisions within the city. Typically, neighborhoods were defined by informal racial boundaries; virtually all of the students in the Agassiz School were white. In the account she gave to Pauline Hopkins, Maria Baldwin presented her early teaching career as a time of professional growth. "For seven years," she said, "I taught in all the lower grades of the school, gaining thereby invaluable experience."[64] She clearly was an outstanding teacher. In 1889, when Miss Charlotte Ewell, the principal of the Agassiz School, retired, a former school committeeman recalled that "the superintendent [Francis Cogswell] told me it would be my duty to appoint a new principal. 'Why,' I said, 'you know as well as I do there is only one suitable person, Miss Baldwin.' 'I think so too,' he said, 'but I was not sure about the color.' 'It is not a question of color, I said, 'it is a question of the best.'"[65] This account of a color-blind response to the question of Baldwin's appointment as principal, of course, was given thirty years after the event.

We cannot know what was actually said at the time, but this account supports the claim that Cambridge was relatively progressive around race compared to most of the United States. But the acceptance of isolated individuals does not mean that racism was not pervasive, nor that successful individuals escaped the burden of always "representing the race." Maria Baldwin expressed this sense of racial responsibility in her reaction to the offer of the principalship. In the interview with Pauline Hopkins, she described the scene: "One Friday Mr. Cogswell asked me how I would like the position of principal. I immediately answered, 'Not at all.' 'Why?' he inquired. I replied, 'I am happier with the little children and prefer to remain where I am. If I failed in the position you mention it would be a conspicuous failure.'" This reference to a "conspicuous" failure surely reflects Baldwin's own acute sensitivity to racism. If she failed in the public position of principal, the failure would be more than her own; it would be seen as a failure of the race. But Cogswell did not accept her refusal. The next day he called on Baldwin at her home. He reiterated that the school committee had every confidence in her and wanted her to accept the position. He also argued that she was "neglecting an opportunity to show Cambridge more than you have already done," again recognizing the racial symbolism of her position. Baldwin remembered herself as "confused and somewhat dazed" by the offer. But with the support and encouragement of the former principal, Miss Ewell, she finally agreed to take the position as a trial. Baldwin told Hopkins: "That afternoon I told Mr. Cogswell that I would accept for two weeks, and for thirteen years I have been principal of the school, being appointed in October, 1889. There are eight associates and three hundred and fifteen pupils. In October, 1902, I round out twenty happy years spent teaching in the public schools of Cambridge."[66]

As principal of the Agassiz School, Baldwin was the leader of one of the most respected schools in Cambridge. Her appointment was a matter of great pride in the black community. In a December 1889 speech defending black Americans' abilities, the black journalist and later head of the Boston branch of the

NAACP Butler Wilson used Maria Baldwin's appointment as principal to defend "black potential and worth."[67] Her success was also mentioned by whites as evidence of racial tolerance in Cambridge. In his 1903 article on race in Cambridge, for example, Linn Boyd Porter cited the fact that "a woman of nearly pure African blood" was serving as the principal of "a grammar school in a fashionable district, with six white teachers and several hundred white pupils under her charge."[68] The Cambridge superintendent of schools reported that it was not uncommon to receive "requests from mothers living outside the Agassiz school district that their children may be transferred to Miss Baldwin's school."[69]

Although her career encompassed the years of John Dewey's educational experiments and early writings, Baldwin did not make reference to him. Dewey emphasized the importance of recognizing each individual child and of creating rich classroom environments that children could explore. The Cambridge teacher training program Baldwin had attended embraced similar ideas. But Baldwin herself was eclectic in her approach. She believed in valuing each child's strengths and needs, but she also believed that all children should memorize poems, that teachers should read aloud from the classics of English literature, and that there should be clear rules of conduct and authority.[70] She doubtless agreed with Horace Scudder's call for teaching the classic literature of England and New England, although perhaps not his assumption that American identity was defined by British, Protestant, and by implication white culture.[71] But if Baldwin advocated the memorization of classic poetry and read aloud from Charles Dickens, she also valued the individuality of children and treated them with respect. In a later interview in the *Cambridge Chronicle* she reflected that she always tried "to keep on friendly, intimate terms with the children. . . . They work so much better when they realize that the teacher is their friend than under the old-fashioned system which made them consider all the school authorities their enemies. That system is absolutely dead." And she recognized that children had different and unique abilities, not all of them captured by the formal curriculum. "The greatest problem of school work," she declared, "is how to allow the individual to develop whatever talent he may have and still conform to the school standard. Some day I hope that a solution will be found."[72]

Accounts of Baldwin as a teacher and principal mention her calmness, love of literature and history, easy authority, and humor. Few written records of her work as principal have survived, but a sense of her warmth and authority is captured in a school report she wrote about ten-year-old Edward Cummings: "He is a most lovable little boy and we are glad that he is part of our little community."[73] Both her care for the boy, who became the celebrated poet e. e. cummings, and her confidence in and vision of the school as a community of which she was the leader, shine through here. Former students remembered her with affection and respect. Elizabeth Thaxter Hubbard recalled her time at the Agassiz School: "The principal . . . was a remarkable colored woman by the name of Miss Maria Baldwin. All the children loved her and she had complete control of them at all times. I never heard her raise her voice. She taught us a great love of poetry, reading to us each morning and having us learn a lot of it."[74] Mary Haskell also remembered the memorization and recitation of poetry: "Poem after poem was memorized and we stood alone, often, to recite, learning to enunciate clearly and to shade the voice pleasingly, and, above all, to stand quietly erect with a pleasant face while doing so. Visitors to our room were entertained by solo recitations of fine poetry. Many of these poems are today fresh and a comfort to me."[75] Alice Whiting recalled: "I can see her now, entering the schoolroom, bearing under her arm *David Copperfield*, which she read delightfully and which we never tired of hearing. She had a remarkable sense of humor and her eyes always seemed alive with sparkle and animation."[76] Something of her humor and presence is captured in one teacher's description of the daily conclusion of the morning assembly: "Disperse ye rebels," Baldwin would say, "with those dancing eyes."[77] "Disperse ye rebels" is supposedly what a British officer called out to the Minutemen before the battle at Concord and Lexington that began the Revolutionary War.

~∽ CHAPTER TWO ∽~

The Woman's Era

Maria Baldwin's appointment as principal of a respected public school attended by the children of the white elite of Cambridge was a significant accomplishment in the hostile racial climate of the late nineteenth century. The Supreme Court's 1896 *Plessy v. Ferguson* decision ruling that segregation was constitutional marked the culmination of two decades of the erosion of the civil rights of people of color to equal treatment under the law. Segregation and white violence in the South and increasing discrimination in employment in the North created an even more rigid caste society. The historian Deborah Gray White has called the lynching and mob violence of the late nineteenth century "the most savage and barbaric manifestation of white on black violence since slavery." Migration to western and northern cities did not protect black people from white violence. As White notes, "unprosecuted white lawlessness" against African Americans was the norm even outside the apartheid system of the South.[1] Historians have pointed to the contradiction that the 1890s—labeled the Progressive Era by white historians—is commonly viewed as the nadir of the African American experience. An additional irony is that the years of the nadir were also known as the "woman's era," marked by the emergence of black women intellectuals and writers, the founding of African American women's clubs, and the growing militancy of politically active black women.[2]

The 1890s saw the coming of age of a remarkable generation of African American women. The previous generation, born in the 1820s or earlier, which included such charismatic leaders as Harriet Tubman, Sojourner Truth, Fannie Jackson Coppin, and Frances Harper, was now followed by a younger group of women born just before or during the Civil War, among them Ida B. Wells-Barnett, born in 1862; Anna Julia Cooper, born in 1858; and Pauline Hopkins and Maria Baldwin, both born in 1856.[3] These women were intellectuals and political activists, working for women's rights as well as fighting racism and racist violence. They lived during what Hazel Carby in her seminal study *Reconstructing Womanhood* calls "the first flowering of black women's autonomous organizations and a period of intense intellectual activity and productivity."[4] These years saw rapid social changes in the United States as more women entered paid employment and gained access to higher education, the suffrage movement demanding full citizenship for women gained momentum, public spaces opened to women, and cultural views of women's sexuality began to shift. As Martha Jones comments, "The disappointments of the nadir and the optimism of the woman's era were entangled with one another in the lives of African American activists."[5] Like other African American women, Maria Baldwin had to negotiate this complex territory of race and gender.

THE OTHER BRAHMINS

Unlike most African American women of her generation, Maria Baldwin spent her professional life in a white setting. After her appointment as principal of the Agassiz School, she became recognized as a public figure of some note, moving between white and black worlds.[6] Baldwin clearly was successful in dealing socially with white Cambridge and Boston reformers. According to the African American historian Hallie Q. Brown, writing shortly after Baldwin's death, Baldwin was acquainted with the leading figures of white Boston, as shown by her "autograph letters from such noted persons as Elizabeth C. Agassiz, Alice Freeman Palmer, Thomas Wentworth Higginson, Mrs. Ole Bull, Alice M. Longfellow, Ednah Cheney, and Edward Everett Hale."[7] In 1892 Higginson, a well-known figure who had been a passionate abolitionist, served in the Union Army as commanding officer of the otherwise all-black First South Carolina Volunteers, and was a strong supporter of woman's suffrage, held a "small dinner party" for Baldwin at his Cambridge home. According to one of the white guests, after Baldwin left that evening Higginson said, "I feel that she is bound to be one of the living forces in our Cambridge, for she has to a remarkable degree the gift of fruitful service."[8]

Baldwin may have impressed white reformers like Thomas Higginson, who saw her as dedicated to the "fruitful service" of caring for the white children of Cambridge, but her deepest political commitments were to black issues, and her closest friends and supporters were found in the African American communities of Boston and Cambridge, particularly among the black elite. As was true for whites, African Americans inhabited a social world marked by class differences. But what class signified for late nineteenth and early twentieth-century black communities was somewhat different from what it meant for whites. As Deborah Gray White notes, "At least through the first quarter of the twentieth century, middle-class status in black society was associated as much with 'style of life' as with income."[9] High social status in black communities reflected education, employment, and social networks as much as it did wealth. Nonetheless, in Boston as in other cities, there did exist a small black elite based on wealth, which Adelaide Cromwell has called "the other Brahmins."[10] Elizabeth Pleck estimates that at the turn of the twentieth century, about twenty families constituted this wealthy Boston African American upper class. These families lived on Beacon Hill or in the South End; they attended the symphony, some sent their sons to Harvard or MIT, and in some cases they had white servants.

When she was growing up, Maria Baldwin became acquainted with this group through the Ruffin family. George Ruffin, the first black graduate of Harvard Law School and the first black judge in Massachusetts, was a central figure in this elite. After his death in 1886, his widow, Josephine St. Pierre Ruffin, remained active in a number of social reform organizations and was recognized as a leader of black Boston society. Her daughter Flora followed her mother's lead. Like many other young women, including her friend Maria Baldwin, Flora became a teacher. While one of her brothers graduated from Harvard and another from MIT, Flora attended Boston Normal School and then found a teaching position, becoming the second black teacher in the Boston public schools. Boston city directories between 1882 and 1886 identify her as a teacher at the Grant School, still living with her family at 170 Cambridge Street in Boston. But in the late 1880s, Flora Ridley's path began to diverge from that of Maria Baldwin. At the age of twenty-seven she married Ulysses Ridley, a prosperous African American Boston tailor. That ended her teaching career, since married women were not allowed to teach in the Boston public schools. An 1894 *Boston Globe* article titled "Sets in Colored Society" claimed that there were two competing "fashionable sets" in black Boston, one centered in the West End and one in the South End. The leaders of the West End set were "the Ruffins and the Ridleys."[11] But Josephine St. Pierre Ruffin and Flora Ridley were not just socialites; they were also committed to racial uplift and opposition to racism.

The political activism of Josephine St. Pierre Ruffin and Flora Ruffin Ridley was not unusual. While they seem to have shared with white Brahmins a sense of their own cultural superiority, the black elite of Boston, like those of other American cities, also maintained a strong commitment to racial justice. As Willard Gatewood has noted, while the black elite were proud of their refinement and respectability, they also "figured prominently in numerous civic, social uplift, and civil rights causes and attempted to utilize their access to the white power structure to temper the more blatant forms of white prejudice."[12] A significant percentage of the black upper class was biracial, what Gatewood calls "a mulatto elite."[13] They mixed with whites in churches, clubs, and workplaces much more frequently than did most other black people in these years. By the end of the nineteenth century, there were some indications of unease among African Americans at the way this elite socialized with whites.[14] For example, one young black woman wrote to the African American leader

Mary Church Terrell in 1896 that some people of color "so merge themselves in the affairs and functions of the whites that it seems to sap all independence and strength from the colored people, especially the better class."[15] By contrast, Gatewood argues that the black elite were not traitors to the race or imitators of whites, but could more accurately be seen as "a culturally and often racially composite people capable of blending black culture with the white culture they knew so well."[16]

As a high school graduate, a teacher, and later a principal, Maria Baldwin was accepted into this social circle of black lawyers, writers, and successful businessmen and their wives, who were often powerful political figures themselves. There is no specific mention of white forebears in contemporary descriptions of Baldwin. Pauline Hopkins described her as "a dark mulatto" with well-defined features and "an intelligent and refined countenance," while one white reporter described her as a woman "of nearly pure African blood."[17] But if she was not biracial by descent, she, like her closest African American friends, certainly blended black and white culture in her intellectual and social life. Deborah Gray White has described what she calls "cultural passing," which she argues was a strategy of some educated African American women who "embraced white culture, or 'passed' culturally, as a means of boosting their own sense of worth, and, ironically, as a way of legitimating their 'race woman' status."[18] But for Maria Baldwin, the embrace of white culture and classic literature seems more a reflection of her experience as a black New Englander—one of a handful of black youth born in New England, educated in predominantly white public schools, and steeped in New England high culture. Struggling against a deeply racist society and proud of her blackness, she also embraced what she saw as the moral strength of traditional New England values, which she claimed as her own.

In the 1880s, Baldwin became part of a loosely organized group of politically active black professionals in Cambridge and Boston. In these years, she became acquainted with Archibald Grimké, one of the leaders of this group, who was then a young lawyer in Boston. Grimké had been born into slavery in South

Carolina in 1849, one of three sons of Henry Grimké, a white plantation owner, and Nancy Weston, an enslaved black woman. Henry Grimké's sisters were Angelina and Sarah Grimké, the well-known white abolitionists. After the Civil War, when Angelina and Sarah learned of their three nephews, they helped support their education and invited them into their reformist circles. Archibald Grimké's brother John remained in the South, while his brother Francis went into the ministry. After graduating from the Princeton Theological Seminary, Francis Grimké was appointed minister of the Fifteenth Street Presbyterian Church in Washington, DC, married the well-known diarist Charlotte Forten, and became a respected leader of black Washington society. Archibald Grimké graduated from Harvard Law School in 1874 and settled in Boston, where he had a long and distinguished career as a lawyer, journalist, and political activist. At first, like George Ruffin and most other black leaders, Grimké strongly supported the Republican Party. In July 1883, a number of black Republicans, including Grimké and Butler Wilson, founded a newspaper, *The Hub.* Although it proclaimed itself "the official voice of black Boston," in reality *The Hub* was a partisan paper intended to mobilize support for the Republican Party among black Massachusetts voters.[19] In the late 1880s, like several other black Boston activists, Grimké grew disenchanted with the racial politics of the Republicans and sought ways to work for racial justice outside the two established political parties. He was one of the founders of the Colored National League, formed in Boston in October 1887 as an organization unaffiliated with either the Republican or the Democratic Party.[20]

In the mid-1870s, Grimké was central in establishing the Banneker Literary Society, a black literary and cultural group. The Boston Banneker Society may have been modeled after the Banneker Literary Society in Philadelphia, which was founded in the 1850s, one of a number of African American cultural and political organizations founded throughout the North in the nineteenth century to provide forums for education and debate for black Americans, who were largely excluded from white societies and associations. The societies were named after the

FIGURE 5. Archibald Grimké. Moorland-Spingarn Research Center, Howard University Archives, Howard University.

eighteenth-century natural scientist Benjamin Banneker, who had come to symbolize black talent and achievement. Maria Baldwin, who graduated from Cambridge High School in 1874 and began teaching at the Agassiz School in 1881, probably joined the Banneker Society sometime in the late 1870s or early 1880s as a young woman in her early twenties. According to the historian Dorothy Porter, Baldwin became the secretary of the club, and "numerous papers which she read at the Banneker Literary Society meetings indicated her broad knowledge of literary and

historical subjects."[21] Her active participation in the club indi-
cates both her intellectual curiosity and her ambition, but also
her connection to the world of the Boston black elite. Archibald
Grimké, who was a leading member of that elite, remained her
friend and supporter throughout her life.

Baldwin's appointment as principal of the Agassiz School
in 1889 made her the most prestigious black educator in New
England. She had moved into the house at 196 Prospect Street the
year before. By 1890 she had begun to open her house as a meeting place for various groups from the black community, among
them a literary gathering she established for African American
Harvard students. There were only a handful of black students at
Harvard at this time, and despite their talents and achievements,
they inhabited a separate social world. The college did not allow
black students to live in dormitories with white students; they
had to board with local African American families.[22] It may have
been her awareness of this separate world that led Baldwin to
organize regular evening meetings for the black students at her
home. Among the students attending the meetings were William
Lewis, Clement Morgan, William Monroe Trotter, and W. E. B.
Du Bois. Lewis later wrote that his first recollection of Baldwin
was at a meeting at her house on Prospect Street, where she read
from Tennyson's poem "In Memoriam."[23] A graduate of Amherst
College and Harvard Law School, Lewis served three terms on
the Cambridge Common Council and in 1903 was appointed
assistant US attorney general by President Taft. Clement Morgan
attended Boston Latin School and graduated with honors from
Harvard, where he was a commencement speaker. After completing Harvard Law School, he set up a successful law practice
and became involved in local Cambridge politics. He was elected
to the Cambridge Common Council in 1895–96 and to the board
of aldermen in 1897–98.[24] Both he and his wife, Gertrude, were
strong supporters of black civil rights, and both became good
friends of Maria Baldwin's. William Monroe Trotter was the son
of James Trotter, who had served as an officer in the Fifty-fifth
Massachusetts Voluntary Infantry in the Civil War, was one of
the first black postmen, and was later appointed recorder of

deeds in Washington, DC. Monroe Trotter, who graduated Phi Beta Kappa from Harvard, was one of the founders and a long-time editor of *The Boston Guardian*. W. E. B. Du Bois, the leading black intellectual of his generation, received both his BA and PhD from Harvard, and was both a scholar and an activist. He was for many years the editor of the NAACP's magazine *The Crisis*.

Du Bois, who remained Maria Baldwin's friend and ally throughout her life, later wrote of the meetings at 196 Prospect Street and his impressions of her in *The Crisis*: "She was already a school teacher—already the quiet, almost diffident personality, with a beautiful brown face and speaking eyes and with a low voice full of earnest inquiry." Du Bois described the weekly meetings at Baldwin's house as a "sort of salon . . . but palpitating with spirit." He remembered himself as a passionate and opinionated young man: "Most things I knew definitely and argued with scathing, unsympathetic finality that scared some into silence." But Maria Baldwin was not intimidated. Du Bois recalled her as "always serene, just slightly mocking, refusing to be thundered or domineered into silence and answering always in that low, rich voice—with questionings, with frank admission of uncertainty which seemed to me then as exasperatingly weak." But the young men increasingly viewed her with respect. Du Bois remembered "her courage—her splendid, quiet courage astonished us, and so she came to larger life and accomplishment. She fought domestic troubles and bitter never-ending insults of race difference. But she emerged always the quiet, well-bred lady, the fine and lovely Woman."[25] Du Bois's brief portrait of Maria Baldwin, while laudatory, also reflects his own conventional and sentimental views of women.[26] She was a public school teacher, a high school graduate with a diploma in teacher training. Her initiative in founding and leading a literary group for young men from one of the most exclusive colleges in the country shows a sense of racial solidarity, confidence, and activism not usually associated with the image of a nineteenth-century "quiet, well-bred lady."[27]

Baldwin's active participation in the Boston Banneker Society and her creation of the literary group for black Harvard students are examples of her engagement with black cultural and political worlds. Like other northern African Americans, Baldwin was alarmed by the spread of segregation and increasing racist violence in the South. A number of organizations emerged in the North to combat the attack on black rights, the best known of them the Afro-American League, organized by T. Thomas Fortune in 1889, which sought to publicize the oppression and violence facing black Americans and to challenge southern state laws in the federal courts. The small Boston branch of the Afro-American League included Josephine St. Pierre Ruffin among its members.[28] The league helped publicize the increasing white violence in the South. In 1892, 161 African Americans were lynched—the largest number ever recorded. By that summer, mass meetings were being held across the North to denounce lynching and to call on Congress to pass laws specifically targeting lynching and establishing a bureau to investigate the crimes. In Boston, several public meetings were held where leaders of the black community—including Josephine St. Pierre Ruffin—demanded action.[29]

Lynching was an all too frequent and unpunished crime in the South, but the lynching of three black men in Memphis in March 1892 caused particular outrage. The issue here was clearly economic. Thomas Moss and the two other victims had opened a cooperative venture called the People's Grocery which had taken business away from a white-owned store. When their store was attacked by whites, the black men defended themselves. In response, they were arrested and jailed. That night a white mob stormed the jail, dragged the men out, and lynched them. Moss was a close friend of the Memphis journalist Ida B. Wells, who was horrified by the crime. Wells—known as Wells-Barnett after her marriage in 1895—had been born into slavery in 1862 in Mississippi and grew up in the South during Reconstruction. When she was sixteen, both her parents died of yellow fever. Although still in high school, Wells took a position as a teacher in order to support her younger siblings and keep the family together. She later became a journalist and co-owner and editor of a black Memphis newspaper. In response to the lynching of Thomas

Moss and the two other men, Wells undertook a speaking tour of the North and eventually published a pamphlet, *Southern Horrors: Lynch Law in All Its Phases*, a powerful condemnation of lynching that provided detailed evidence of the underlying economic and political reasons behind the demonization and socially condoned murder of black men in the South. In the white South she was denounced as a dangerous radical, and in Memphis the office of her newspaper was burned. She was threatened with death if she returned to Memphis. But African Americans, particularly African American women, were galvanized and inspired by Wells's uncompromising exposé and denunciation of racist crimes. In New York City, African American women organized a testimonial on her behalf in late 1892. Black women from across the Northeast attended. Wells later called the event "the greatest demonstration ever attempted by race women for one of their own number."[30] In the audience that night was Josephine St. Pierre Ruffin.

THE WOMAN'S ERA CLUB

Maria Baldwin was not present at the New York testimonial to Ida B. Wells, but like Josephine St. Pierre Ruffin and many other African American women, she was inspired by Wells's example. In February 1893, a few months after the New York testimonial, Josephine St. Pierre Ruffin, Flora Ridley, and Maria Baldwin brought together a small number of African American women to found a new group called the Woman's Era Club.[31] Ruffin was elected president, Maria Baldwin vice president, and Flora Ridley secretary. Josephine St. Pierre Ruffin was probably the best-known black clubwoman in Boston, a member of several white-dominated women's organizations. Her daughter Flora Ridley was deeply interested in black history. In March 1890, Ridley held a meeting in her home to consider the formation of a society to collect Negro folklore. W. E. B. Du Bois, then a student at Harvard, was among those present. Although the society apparently did not survive, Ridley retained her commitment to black issues.[32] In her 1894 account of the Woman's Era Club, she described the events that led to its founding: "In February last, at the time Miss Wells was creating so much interest in her crusade against lynch-law, it was a good time to carry out the club idea, call the women together and organize, not for race-work alone, but for work along all the lines that make for women's progress. The result was that a club was formed with a membership of twenty."[33] Later in life Ruffin provided a starker account of the impact of the racist violence and political suppression of black rights in the South. In a 1937 speech she described the despair felt by the black community at the "stories and pictures of horrible lynchings, of ghastly depredations by Ku Klux night riders" that were coming out of the South. But she also remembered the inspiration she and other Boston women took from the abolitionist movement: "The little group of colored women had mingled too closely and seen and felt too strongly the power of that small invincible group of abolitionists that had pitted itself against the world and mighty civilization not to be inspired by its courage and ready to take a lesson from it."[34] Membership in the club soon grew. Meetings were held twice a month in the Blue Room of the Tremont Temple in downtown Boston; one was a business meeting and the other was for "literary pursuits, lectures and similar educational features."[35]

Boston's Woman's Era Club was part of a wider movement among African American women. The early 1890s saw the founding of a number of other clubs, among them the Woman's Loyal Union in New York City and the Chicago Women's Club. In Washington, DC, the Colored Women's League, founded by Mary Church Terrell and Anna Julia Cooper among others, brought together a number of smaller clubs. These clubs were grounded in a tradition of black women's active participation in their communities, but while black women's self-help organizations had existed for many years, the clubs that emerged in the 1890s expressed a new sense of collective power among black women.[36] The clubs may also have reflected a growing dissatisfaction with the aggressive masculinity that marked both black and white culture at the end of the nineteenth century.[37] For example, Boston's Colored National League, founded in 1887 by a group of black activist men, among them Archibald Grimké, was formally open to women but had a strong masculine bias. At its first meeting, one of the male officers of the new organization claimed that the league would become a nucleus around which African Americans could "rally for the purpose of making a manly stand."[38] Women did join the league; Josephine St. Pierre Ruffin served as a member of its executive committee for a time, and Pauline Hopkins was an active member. It is not known if Baldwin formally belonged, but she was present at some meetings. There were a few women members, but men dominated. In July 1888 the Colored National League offered a group of women the opportunity of leading a "ladies night," which only seems to highlight their exclusion from the regular meetings. Ruffin was chair for this evening, and both she and Maria Baldwin read papers; the topic of Baldwin's was "the part that woman is to play in the great uplifting of the race," a pointed topic for the men of the Colored National League.[39]

White women's clubs in the late nineteenth and early twentieth centuries have often been seen as expressing middle-class values of respectability and the traditional womanly virtues of charity and domesticity. Black women's clubs shared these values, but they were also concerned with broader issues of racial justice.[40] Although the black women's clubs echoed the concern with social housekeeping of contemporary white women's clubs—seeking to improve family life, support kindergartens and schools, encourage mothers, and instill middle-class values in the poor—they were also highly political sites of race politics. Elizabeth McHenry has argued that at a time when there were few opportunities for women of color to gain access to higher education, black women's clubs offered a setting where women could "acquire and practice the skills they needed to confidently and effectively enter public and organizational life."[41] In 1900, the African American clubwoman Fannie Barrier Williams called the clubs "schools" in which "race problems and sociological questions directly related to the condition of the Negro race in America are the principal subjects for study and discussion."[42] We can imagine the impact of these conversations on members like Maria Baldwin as African American women met and taught one another while exploring and analyzing issues of race and politics.

With the founding of the Woman's Era Club, Baldwin began to work more actively for racial justice. Her activism and that of the Woman's Era Club were not unique. As Crystal Feimster points out, the Woman's Era Club was only one of a number of early African American women's clubs that "published articles, pamphlets, novels, and a range of essays that challenged the racist and sexist presumptions concerning rape and lynching."[43] Baldwin's first public action was a pamphlet, *A Columbian Year Contrast*, which she co-authored with Josephine St. Pierre Ruffin and Flora Ridley. The Chicago Columbian Exposition, held in 1893 to commemorate Columbus's first landing in North America four hundred years earlier, had celebrated the glories of American civilization. But as Ida B. Wells documented in her pamphlet *The Reasons Why the Colored American Is Not in the World's Columbian Exposition*, it was also deeply racist.[44] Inspired by Wells's critique, Ruffin, Ridley, and Baldwin contrasted the grandiose claims of the Columbian Exposition with the realities of lynching. They described a lynching in Denmark, South Carolina, that had occurred just before the exposition: "Only one week before the opening of the exhibition which is to commemorate our greatness, occurs a crime, which, if committed in a semi barbarous country, would arouse the civilized world, but which in America, because of the frequency of such crimes receives little more than passing notice and comment."[45] Like Ida B. Wells, Baldwin, Ruffin, and Ridley questioned the meaning of freedom in a country where such crimes were ignored or even condoned.

Baldwin and the other members of the Woman's Era Club were committed not only to racial justice but also to the common interests of women. From its inception, the club defined itself as committed to women's rights. In her account of its founding, Flora Ridley emphasized that while the immediate impetus was the campaign against lynching and for full civil rights for black people, the organization had a broader vision. The women of the club wanted to work "hand in hand with women, generally for humanity and humanity's interest, not the Negro alone but the Chinese, the Hawaiian, the Russian Jew, the oppressed everywhere as subjects for our consideration, not the needs of the colored women, but women everywhere are our interest."[46] This concern with women's rights was not unique to the Woman's Era Club. As Martha Jones points out, the woman question was a central issue within black political and religious groups throughout this period, just as it was in white reform organizations.[47] The Woman's Era Club was supported by progressive white clubwomen, many of whom were already acquainted with Josephine St. Pierre Ruffin through her work in Boston reform circles. Several white women reformers attended the first meeting, among them Ednah Cheney, who had been active in the abolitionist movement and supported freedmen's schools after the Civil War; Abby Morton Diaz, also a member of the New England Women's Club and former president of the Women's Industrial and Educational Union; and the British women's rights campaigner Laura Ormiston Chant. Applauding the founding of the club, Chant noted that such organizations were important because a woman needed the opportunity to exercise her mind; otherwise she might become "a mere machine" to her children. Moreover, she argued, not all women were meant to be mothers. "Clubs will make women think seriously of their future lives, and not make girls think their only alternative is to marry."[48]

The motto of the Woman's Era Club was "Help to make the world better." By 1894 the club had a membership of 104 and was welcomed into the Massachusetts General Federation of Women's Clubs.[49] Although the Woman's Era Club supported women's rights, its main activities involved issues central to African American women. The club undertook a number of initiatives focused on racial justice and racial uplift, including a series of Sunday afternoon public meetings and a sewing circle to support St. Monica's Home for Sick Colored Women and Children; it also provided the New England Hospital for Women and Children "a collection of the best books and photographs of colored authors," including works by W. E. B. Du Bois and Paul Laurence Dunbar.[50] The women saw themselves as the inheritors of the tradition of New England abolitionism. The African American journalist Pauline Hopkins, who was a member of the club, described a visit the group made to the home of the white abolitionist poet John Greenleaf Whittier one Fourth of July. Hopkins remarks how, after touring the house, the clubwomen gathered in the garden and "sat beneath the old apple trees where Mr. Whittier was wont to sit with Charles Sumner and Mr. Garrison planning measures which should sway a nation." Josephine St. Pierre Ruffin delivered some remarks, Hopkins provided a sketch of Whittier's life, and his poem "Barbara Frietchie" was read. The women then visited the Quaker meetinghouse where Whittier had worshipped and visited his grave, where they laid a wreath. Hopkins's account of the visit vividly captures the club's veneration of the abolitionists and their sense of pride as New Englanders, a pride shared by Maria Baldwin.[51]

Like other members of the Woman's Era Club, Baldwin engaged the major cultural and political issues that concerned progressive black women nationally. She clearly was familiar with the work of Ida B. Wells. But Wells was not the only black woman activist in the early 1890s; she was part of a broader collective movement of African American women writers and intellectuals. In addition to Wells's *Southern Horrors*, both Frances Harper's *Iola Leroy* and Anna Julia Cooper's *Voice from the South* were published in 1892, the year before the founding of the Woman's Era Club. While Wells's pamphlet was a call to political action, *A Voice from the South* and *Iola Leroy* were deeply pedagogical, meant to raise consciousness among black readers.[52]

An abolitionist and writer, Frances Harper was of the older generation of African American women activists. There is no evidence that Maria Baldwin was personally acquainted with her, but Baldwin may well have read *Iola Leroy*, which Hazel Carby has called "a textbook for the educated black person in the crisis of disenfranchisement, lynching, and the Jim Crow laws."[53] Harper's novel suggested that educated black people should create their own institutions and work among their own people. Baldwin may have found the story of Iola Leroy, the novel's heroine, who returns to the South at the end of the novel in order to teach black children, disquieting. Baldwin, after all, had left the children of the segregated black schools of Maryland and, with the support of the leaders of the Cambridge black community, attained a position teaching the white children of Cambridge. She may have found Cooper's *Voice from the South,* the first work analyzing the intersection of racism and sexism published in the United States, more appealing.

Anna Julia Cooper was a powerful political writer who analyzed and denounced racism but also argued for women's rights. As Deborah Gray White comments, Cooper fought for the black woman's "personal independence, for intellectual and moral development, for physical culture, for political activity, and for a voice in the arrangement of her own affairs, both domestic and national."[54] There is no mention of *A Voice from the South* in accounts of Maria Baldwin's public lectures, but she was personally acquainted with Cooper, who was almost her exact contemporary and was also an educator. Cooper later served as principal of the celebrated M Street High School in Washington, DC, probably the most highly regarded black secondary school in the United States. It seems very likely that Baldwin read *A Voice from the South* and *Iola Leroy* as well as Wells's *Southern Horrors.* All three works offered African American women readers like Maria Baldwin models of political engagement and activism. For Baldwin in particular, who had been raised in the tradition of New England high culture dominated by white writers and reformers, these three writers would have suggested an identity that could encompass her race, gender, and politics without compromise.

THE WOMAN'S ERA

Soon after the founding of the Woman's Era Club, the membership decided to publish a monthly journal, *The Woman's Era.* The first issue appeared in March 1894. Though published only from 1894 to 1897, *The Woman's Era* was, according to Beverly Guy-Sheftall, "probably the best vehicle of the articulation of the political aspirations of black women during the period."[55] Maria

Baldwin, occupied with the demands of the Agassiz School, does not seem to have been involved in the production of the journal, but her friend Flora Ridley was a central figure. In her "Greeting" in the first issue of *The Woman's Era*, Ridley pointed to the need for a journal that could provide "a medium of intercourse and sympathy between the women of all races and conditions." As a mark of its commitment to women's rights, the first page of the first issue included a tribute to the recently deceased veteran white suffragist Lucy Stone. But Ridley emphasized that the most important goal of the journal was reaching out to the "educated and refined . . . colored woman," who suffered from "the limitation of her surroundings and the circumscribed sphere in which she must move." Although Ridley, like her mother, Josephine St. Pierre Ruffin, was among the most privileged of black women, she was well aware of the evils of segregation and race prejudice. For the educated black woman, she wrote, this meant "the impossibility of mingling freely with people of culture and learning, and so carrying on the mental growth begun in schools and colleges." It "shuts her in with her books but shuts her out of physical touch with the great world of art, science and letters which is open to all other ambitious women."[56] *The Woman's Era* sought to provide a forum and create a community among these ambitious women. In a public lecture, "Opportunity and Privileges of Club Life," sponsored by the Woman's Era Club, Ridley later defended the organization against its detractors. "It is true the club is all talk," she told her audience. "It was created to furnish opportunities to talk."[57]

If the Woman's Era Club and other black women's clubs gave women a chance to articulate and discuss their ideas, *The Woman's Era* journal provided a venue to address cultural and political issues before a broader audience. One of its goals was to celebrate the achievements of black women such as Maria Baldwin. Like Josephine St. Pierre Ruffin, Baldwin was a member not only of the Woman's Era Club but also of a predominantly white women's organization, in Baldwin's case the Cantabrigia Club, which included the most socially elite women of Cambridge. In 1893 she read a paper, "A Poet's Hold on the People," before the group. The account of her presentation in the *Cambridge Chronicle* was effusive, describing it as "an admirable effort, full of original thought, of scholarly refinement and stimulating suggestions, clad in the cleanest and most beautiful language. As the president said, when the quick burst of applause, at the end, had subsided, 'If we have not interrupted Miss Baldwin with frequent applause, it has been because we were listening with breathless interest for the next thought.'"[58] *The Woman's Era* also celebrated this speech and made a point of mentioning Baldwin's membership in the Cantabrigia Club, noting that its membership numbered nearly four hundred and included "all of the many distinguished ladies of Cambridge."[59]

As well as celebrating the accomplishments of individuals like Maria Baldwin, *The Woman's Era* published a range of articles of interest to middle-class black women, including advice on household maintenance and social news, particularly of the elite of New York, Boston, and Washington. It also offered suggestions for cultural improvement. One column, titled "Reading," was written by Sarah Tanner, principal of the Bordentown Industrial School and wife of African Methodist Episcopal bishop Benjamin Tanner.[60] In June 1895, Tanner recommended studying the great works of Western literature as a way of enriching one's life: "Read the best novels and romances, authors like Sir Walter Scott, George Eliot, Thackeray, Dickens and Hawthorne. Do not read about authors and imagine you have read the authors themselves, but with great care study the masters of the art of literature, authors like Milton, Dante, Shakespeare, Bacon, Goethe, Cervantes, Schiller, and others."[61] These suggestions, which echoed Maria Baldwin's own taste for classic authors, support the idea of "cultural passing" described by Deborah Gray White. But *The Woman's Era* also celebrated the work of African American writers. In her column "Literature Notes," Medora Gould discussed the work of well-known white writers of the day such as Longfellow, Hardy, Kipling, and Tennyson, but she also advocated the work of African American authors including Victoria Earle Matthews and Gertrude Mossell. She had particular praise for the poet Paul Laurence Dunbar, probably the most popular

African American poet of the late nineteenth century. One editorial in *The Woman's Era* claimed that Dunbar's success suggested that "more poets, more artists, more musicians" would emerge among African Americans, leading the world "to acknowledge them and the people from whom they spring."[62]

The Woman's Era was concerned with more than social and cultural issues. It also addressed political questions of interest to the black community. A consistent theme was the rights of black Americans as citizens: they were black, but they equally were Americans. An editorial in the first issue of *The Woman's Era*, for example, denounced proposals to send African Americans back to Africa, arguing that "it is a physical and legal impossibility to deport the colored people." But the editorial then fell into the contemporary panic over immigration, contrasting loyal and hardworking black Americans with what it described as "the riff-raff of other countries who owe no allegiance to man or God, who are opposed to any government that compels them to work for a living and to observe and not encroach upon the rights of other men." The editorial called for restrictions on immigration based on the idea "that this land is for Americans black or white and that other men are welcome and can come here only by behaving themselves and steering clear of plots and schemes against the people and the citizens who are here by right."[63] The editors of *The Woman's Era* celebrated both their race and their nationality as Americans, but in this case at the cost of demonizing others, here "foreigners," imagined as anarchists and atheistic "riffraff."

Another editorial addressed the complicated question of separate institutions for black people. After all, a paper published by black women could itself be seen as encouraging the kind of "race lines" that marked southern institutionalized segregation. The editorial noted that there was "a growing class of our people who doubt the wisdom in starting any enterprise along race lines; there are those who withhold their support from [*The Woman's Era*] because they do not believe in 'colored papers.'" The editorial argued in the journal's defense: "Right here let it be said that the *ERA* is not 'colored.' It is a paper whose managers and editors are colored, but the paper is open to all. . . . We do not believe in accentuating race lines, but we do believe in being more accurately represented than we are or ever can be in any paper that has no colored man or woman on its editorial staff." *The Woman's Era* sought a day when all institutions would be open to people of all races, but in the meantime, it was important to have a venue in which black voices could be heard. The editorial concluded: "God speed the day when there will be no color in newspapers, when the *Age* and the *Planet* and the *ERA* will all be employing white as well as black. In the meantime, let us not be content with being served up as others choose. We are about old enough to speak for ourselves."[64]

That the day of "no color" had not arrived, and that white people could not yet fully be trusted, was made clear in 1894, when Laura Ormiston Chant, the British reformer who had attended the initial meeting of the Woman's Era Club, actively worked to block a resolution against lynching at the National Conference of the Unitarian Church. In response, Flora Ridley drafted an open letter to Chant, which was published in *The Woman's Era*. In her letter, Ridley explained why the campaign against lynching was so important in the context of the racism that permeated the United States. Speaking as herself a "colored woman," she described the stance of the Woman's Era Club:

> We have endured much and we believe with patience; we have seen our world broken down, our men made fugitives and wanderers or their youth and strength spent in bondage. We ourselves are daily hindered and oppressed in the race of life; we know that every opportunity for advancement, for peace and happiness will be denied us; that in most sections Christian men and women absolutely refuse not only to live beside us and to eat with us, but also to open their churches to us; we know that our children, no matter with what tenderness that they may have been reared, are considered legitimate prey for insult; that our young girls can at any time be thrust into foul and filthy [railway] cars and, no matter their needs, be refused food and shelter.[65]

Black women had borne and continued to bear this oppression, Ridley wrote, but now they were raising their voices "against the horrible crimes of lynch law as practiced in the South" and calling on "Christians everywhere to do the same or be branded as sympathizers with the murderers."[66] According to Ida B. Wells-Barnett, Ridley's eloquent letter was widely circulated in England; Wells-Barnett herself published it as an appendix to her own autobiography. In an August 1894 editorial, *The Woman's Era* noted that Mrs. Chant had not replied to Ridley's letter: "To the many colored women who have been enthusiastic listeners to Mrs. Chant's talks, this will come as a blow, but it is not the first of the kind we have received."[67]

BUILDING A NATIONAL MOVEMENT

The events of the early 1890s—the campaign against lynching led by Ida B. Wells, the publication of works by Frances Harper and Anna Julia Cooper, the founding of *The Woman's Era*, and the formation of black women's clubs in cities across the country— were signs of a shift in consciousness and political engagement among educated black women. Maria Baldwin and the women of the Woman's Era Club were aware that they were part of a broader movement. Soon after they began publishing *The Woman's Era*, the leaders of the club began to discuss the idea of a national meeting of black clubwomen. In the second issue, Maria Baldwin published a letter proposing a national conference. She wrote, "Just at this stage of the higher activity among colored women, I know of nothing that would prove more stimulating than a congress of their clubs." She noted that newspapers seldom included accounts of black women's clubs, which meant that each club worked in isolation. What black clubwomen needed was "the sympathy, the encouragement, the larger wisdom that comes from intercourse with others who are pushing on towards the same ideal." Baldwin argued that the Woman's Era Club could provide the leadership for a convention and that Boston was the ideal site for such a meeting: "I know of no other city where the attitude of the press and that of the general public would be as respectful; nor where the impressiveness of such a gathering would receive such recognition."[68] This statement may have reflected the relative racial tolerance of Boston compared to other cities, but it also can be seen as an expression of Baldwin's own optimistic and idealized view of race relations, of what she so wanted Boston to be.

A "Call of Meeting of '95" was sent to black women's clubs across the country, inviting them to come together in Boston in the summer of 1895 "for consultation, for conference, for the personal exchange of greetings." Participants from the Woman's Era Club were listed at the end of the "Call": Josephine St. Pierre Ruffin was president of the "Committee of Arrangements" and Maria Baldwin was chairman of the executive board.[69] Although she was listed as chairing the executive board and had suggested the national meeting, Baldwin did not speak at the 1895 conference, nor was she involved in the subsequent national woman's club movement. Unlike most other members of the Woman's Era Club, Baldwin held a demanding public position that required a great deal of her time and energy. Both Josephine St. Pierre Ruffin and Flora Ruffin Ridley, who were not employed, were centrally involved in organizing the first national meeting and were major figures in the formation of a national organization.

The national conference was eventually held in Boston in July 1895, in large part because of the efforts of the Woman's Era Club. But the immediate impetus for the conference was a widely circulated letter written by John Jacks, a white Missouri journalist, in which he attacked Ida B. Wells and claimed that black women in general were "prostitutes, liars and thieves."[70] An editorial in *The Woman's Era* noted that although the idea of a conference had been discussed for some time, it became more pressing because of "a letter . . . written by a southern editor, and reflecting upon the moral character of all colored women."[71] In the view of clubwoman Fannie Barrier Williams, "the letter, in spite of its wanton meanness, was not without some value in showing to what extent the sensitiveness of colored women had grown."[72]

The conference was held in Berkeley Hall in Boston on July 29, 30, and 31, 1895. Delegates from about twenty-five clubs were present. They were provided lodging by members of the Woman's Era Club.[73] Anna Julia Cooper, author of *A Voice from the South,* along with two other women, stayed with Maria Baldwin and her sister Alice in their house on Prospect Street in Cambridge; as *The Woman's Era* commented, "It would be hard to get together a group of brighter women than these." Maria and Alice Baldwin entertained their guests with visits to historic New England sites. According to *The Woman's Era,* this "group of pleasure trips planned by the Misses Baldwin . . . included pilgrimages to Concord and to Plymouth, and trips down the harbor and drives through the country." Even though Maria Baldwin was not listed in the program as a speaker, it seems almost certain that she attended the July conference. Her close friends Flora Ridley and Josephine St. Pierre Ruffin were central figures at the conference, and both Ruffin and Baldwin's house-guest Anna Julia Cooper presented addresses there.[74]

A lengthy article in the *Boston Globe* described the opening session "of the first national convention ever held by colored women in this country." The platform was "decorated with palms and potted plants," and a portrait of the white suffragist Lucy Stone was prominently displayed, while a table held "a number of books from the pens of colored women."[75] The portrait of Stone, a supporter of the Woman's Era Club, highlighted the commonality of black and white women reformers, while the prominent display of books written by black women celebrated the coming of age of black women intellectuals.

Josephine St. Pierre Ruffin set the tone of the conference in her introductory address. She began by stating that it was important for "women in general" to meet together and confer but argued it was especially important that "we, bearing peculiar burdens, suffering under especial hardships, enduring peculiar privations, should meet for a 'good talk' among ourselves." Ruffin noted the desire of the women who had gathered in Boston to provide moral guidance and help for children and families in poverty, concerns similar to those of white clubwomen. But she also emphasized the need to prepare black children "to meet the peculiar conditions" in which they would find themselves, and the need for black clubwomen to "make the most of our own, to some extent, limited opportunities." She argued that all over the country there was "a large and growing class of earnest, intelligent, progressive colored women, who, if not leading full, useful lives, are only waiting for the opportunity to do so." In order to combat racist and sexist views of black women and to support the many young women looking to live meaningful lives, black women needed to organize and demonstrate their capabilities. Ruffin pointedly contrasted the respectability and moral qualities of African American women with the brutality and barbarism of white lynchers. Ruffin was well aware of the fine line between solidarity and separatism in terms of both race and gender. She noted that although "our woman's movement" was "a woman's movement in that it is led and directed by women," it was meant "for the benefit of all humanity, which is more than any one branch or section of it." She argued that black clubwomen sought "the active interest of our men," and that they were "not drawing the color line." She concluded: "We are women, American women, as intensely interested in all that pertains to us as such as all other American women; we are not alienating or withdrawing, we are only coming to the front, willing to join any others in the same work and cordially inviting and welcoming any others to join us." There is no way of knowing how the audience responded to Ruffin's remarks about the commonality of black and white women's interests, but they must have appreciated her description of themselves as "earnest, intelligent, progressive colored women."[76]

Eleven papers were delivered at the conference. In attendance were some of the most accomplished and powerful African American women in the country. Two of the best known, Anna Julia Cooper of Washington and Victoria Earle Matthews of New York, gave presentations. Cooper, of course, was the well-known author of *A Voice from the South*. Matthews, a self-educated journalist, was one of the founders of the Woman's Loyal Union, a black woman's club, and would later establish the White Rose Mission for black girls in New York City.[77] Cooper spoke on "The Need for National Organization," while Matthews presented a scholarly defense of black intellectual accomplishment in "The Value of Race Literature."[78] Both Cooper and Matthews

FIGURE 6. Josephine St. Pierre Ruffin. From the New York Public Library, https://
digitalcollections.nypl.org/items/510d47da-733a-a3d9-e040-e00a18064a99.

presented perceptive analyses of the impact of racism on black
women. That they would be chosen to speak at the conference
is an indication of the seriousness and level of political engagement of the women organizers and their confidence in those who
attended. Accounts of this conference bring to mind the political
activism of black women in the 1960s and 1970s more than the
social housekeeping of white women's clubs of the time.

At its business session, resolutions were drafted to condemn
the convict labor system in Georgia, lynching, and the continued
spread of segregation.[79] And finally the convention voted to form

a new national organization, to be called the National Federation of Afro-American Women. Margaret Washington, wife of Booker T. Washington, was elected president, Victoria Earle Matthews of New York chair of the executive committee, and Flora Ridley secretary. This group represented not only different sections of the country but also the different political stances that were developing among African Americans in general. While Margaret Washington shared the cautious and practical approach of her husband, and Matthews was increasingly drawn into his circle, Flora Ridley offered the much sharper critique and condemnation of white racism that was emerging in the cities of the North. Josephine St. Pierre Ruffin, the guiding spirit of the convention, had only an honorary position in the new organization. Also left out of the leadership were representatives of the powerful women's clubs of Washington, DC, who had already formed an umbrella group of clubs called the National League of Colored Women.

In her first statement in *The Woman's Era*, Margaret Washington gave credit to Josephine St. Pierre Ruffin for calling the 1895 conference which had led to the formation of the National Federation of Afro-American Women. In response, the Woman's Era Club made a point of expressing their support of Washington. A note in *The Woman's Era* commented that "putting aside Mrs. Washington's personal fitness for the position and the advantages for the work which her position as a co-worker with her husband will give her, this choice will go further than anything else in uniting the intelligent women of the North and South." Somewhat condescendingly, the author of the piece argued that Margaret Washington's leadership of the national organization would encourage southern clubs to learn from "the culture and race work such as already exist in the North." With Washington as leader, "no colored woman who has the interest of her race at heart can find excuse not to enlist."[80]

Despite these statements of goodwill, there is evidence of almost immediate conflict among the clubwomen. When a second national meeting of black women's clubs took place six months later at the Atlanta Exposition, Margaret Washington attended, but Josephine St. Pierre Ruffin was missing. That there may have been some bad feeling about convening a second national meeting only six months after the first is suggested by an editorial in *The Woman's Era* which described the Atlanta conference as a notable one but reminded its readers that "it was not, however, the first congress; that held in Boston last July enjoys that distinction."[81] Perhaps Josephine St. Pierre's absence from Atlanta was fortuitous. It was at the Atlanta Exposition in September 1895 that Margaret Washington's husband, Booker T. Washington, delivered his infamous speech defending segregation, claiming that "in all things that are purely social we can be as separate as the fingers, yet one as the hand in all things essential to mutual progress."[82] Washington's speech was welcomed by whites, especially white southerners but was viewed with alarm by black northerners like Josephine St. Pierre Ruffin, Flora Ridley, and Maria Baldwin, who were committed to complete integration and full civil rights for all African Americans.

Even before the Atlanta Exposition speech there were obvious differences between the political stances of Margaret Washington and the women of the Woman's Era Club. For example, in her first statement of the goals of the National Federation of Afro-American Women, Washington made no mention of fighting lynching or racism. Instead, she focused on the obligation of enlightened women to help "the masses." She wrote: "True, honored womanhood, enlightened motherhood, and happy, comfortable homes can only be secured by concerted effort on the part of the women of our land. Individual effort has accomplished some good in this direction, but the mighty effect upon the masses unreached will be the result of our future united effort."[83] But future effort would not always be united. Growing differences in political strategy and interests would mark not just the women's club movement but African American political and intellectual life in general in the years to come.

The National Federation of Afro-American Women lasted for only one year. In the summer of 1896 a meeting was held that brought together representatives of the NFAW and the Washington, DC–based National League of Colored Women with the intention of creating a unified organization embracing all the black women's clubs in the country. The formation of the new organization was reported in *The Woman's Era:* "On the 22nd day of July, 1896, at Washington, D.C., the two large bodies of colored women known respectively as the National Federation of Afro-American Women and the National League of Colored Women united their forces and became the National Association of Colored Women. This union resulted in one of the largest and most significant organizations of women in the world." Neither Josephine St. Pierre Ruffin nor Flora Ridley took leadership of the new organization. Instead, Mary Church Terrell of Washington, DC, was elected president.

There is no evidence that Maria Baldwin was involved in the National Association of Colored Women. She may well have been too absorbed in her work at the Agassiz School, but she may also have been alienated by the internal conflicts and the less activist approach of the new organization. *The Woman's Era* had envisioned the National Association of Colored Women as combining the drive for social betterment with anti-racist organizing. Attacking segregation seemed particularly pressing, given the Supreme Court's May 1896 *Plessy v. Ferguson* decision upholding southern segregation laws. An editorial in *The Woman's Era* late that year set out what the editors expected of the new organization: "To attack the chain gang system of the South, the separate car law, to do rescue work in the alleys and slums of our great cities, and for the plantation woman and child, the founding of homes for our indigent, and to show greater interest in the fallen and wayward." *The Woman's Era* reminded its readers that "these are some of the things clubs in the association are pledged to consider this year and decided improvement along these lines should be shown at the next annual meeting."[84] But from the beginning, the National Association of Colored Women took a more conservative stance than had the Woman's Era Club.

The National Association of Colored Women's motto was "Lifting as we climb." One interpretation of the motto was that as middle-class black women rose, they were also raising up poor and working-class black people. The clubwomen were the actors, doing both the climbing and the lifting. Mary Church

Terrell, president of the NACW, emphasized the obligation of enlightened black women to provide moral guidance to the poor. In her article "The Club Movement among Colored Women of America," Fannie Barrier Williams, a close ally of Terrell's, argued that the task of black clubwomen was to reach out to the "underprivileged" and described the clubs as "agencies of rescue" that encouraged "better homes, better schools, better protection for girls of scant home training, better sanitary conditions, better opportunities for competent young women to gain employment."[85] At the same time, although she did not directly condemn lynching or the growth of segregation, Williams acknowledged the scars of slavery and the wounds of racism. For her, one of the goals of the black women's clubs was to remind black women that they were "something better than a slave or a descendant of an ex-slave." For Williams, "the National Association of Colored Women has certainly meant all this and much more to the women of the ransomed race in the United States."[86]

Williams's defense of the NACW masked growing tensions within the organization between those who wanted to emphasize social uplift of the underprivileged and those who wanted to join a more militant struggle for racial justice and rights. In the beginning these differences were muted and individuals with different views worked together. In May 1896, for example, Josephine St. Pierre Ruffin wrote to the veteran white Boston reformer Ednah Dow Cheney about the upcoming visit of clubwomen Mary Church Terrell and Victoria Earle Matthews, hoping that Cheney would be able to meet them.[87] In another letter, she asked Cheney to preside at a lecture Fannie Barrier Williams was to give in support of *The Woman's Era* and to encourage white women's clubs to sell tickets for the lecture.[88] Terrell, Matthews, and Williams were all considered more conservative than Ruffin. Despite these early examples of collaboration, the differences between the women of the Woman's Era Club and the leaders of the National Association of Colored Women soon became evident.

One example of these differences is the fate of *The Woman's Era* itself. The Woman's Era Club had published *The Woman's Era* from its inception in 1894; in reality, production of the journal seems to have fallen almost exclusively to Josephine St. Pierre Ruffin with the help of her daughter Flora Ridley. After two years, the burden of producing *The Woman's Era* was becoming too much for Ruffin to bear. In March 1896 she wrote to Ednah Cheney, "I am struggling to carry along until the first annual meeting of the national federation of colored women's clubs, when it is hoped and expected that some arrangements may be made for better, more reliable support of the organ of this union of work among the colored people."[89] In May of that year she apologized to Cheney for not writing sooner: "As usual my hands are full to overflowing—a little more so just now getting out the May Era."[90] A few months later, *The Woman's Era* became the official publication of the National Association of Colored Women, which then took over responsibility for its content and publication. The very next year the NACW closed down the journal and replaced it with the *National Association Notes*, which, under the editorship of Margaret Murray Washington, took a more conservative tone supportive of the ideas of Washington's husband, Booker T. Washington. Josephine St. Pierre Ruffin was not pleased. In November 1897, only a few months after Margaret Washington began to edit the *National Association Notes*, Ruffin issued an appeal for funds to reestablish *The Woman's Era* as a more general political publication, to be focused initially on "prison reform in the South." The goal of the journal's campaign would be to "wipe out a national stain, a withering curse, 'The Convict Lease System.'"[91] The appeal failed, and *The Woman's Era* never resumed publication.

Ruffin's struggles to restart *The Woman's Era* and to meet the needs of the Woman's Era Club were particularly difficult because she was working without the help of her daughter Flora. In 1896 the young Ridley family left Boston and purchased a house in the nearby town of Brookline, probably the first African American family to own a home there.[92] Flora Ridley was the mother of a small child, and the move to a white neighborhood must have added to her responsibilities and concerns. Then, in early 1897, the Ridleys experienced a personal tragedy. Flora Ridley gave birth to a son, who died in infancy, a loss that must have been devastating. In a letter to Ednah Dow Cheney in March 1897, Josephine St. Pierre Ruffin wrote of the difficulty of managing the affairs of the Woman's Era Club without the help of her daughter, who, she wrote, was unable to take on club work at that time.[93] Ruffin continued to dedicate herself to the Woman's Era Club and in 1899 was reelected president. This time neither Flora Ridley nor Maria Baldwin was an officer.[94] Ruffin stopped participating in the national black women's club movement in 1899 after a conflict with Mary Church Terrell over the leadership of the National Association of Colored Women. When Terrell defeated Ruffin in a contested presidential election, Ruffin withdrew from the national meetings for many years.[95]

THE WASHINGTON'S BIRTHDAY ADDRESS

Maria Baldwin did not become active in the National Association of Colored Women and seems to have retreated from involvement in the Woman's Era Club as well. But she continued to be deeply engaged with political issues and became a central figure among the educated black elite of Boston and Cambridge. She was involved with a number of organizations and clubs. One of these was the Omar Circle, or Omar Khayyam Circle. The writer of Baldwin's obituary in the *A.M.E. Church Review* described it as "a club in which the works of that old Persian poet were studied or read as a prelude, which finally the club turned to Dante and others of the epic choir. Membership here was made up mainly of former Harvard and other New England college men."[96] According to the later recollection of Almira Park, who seems to have been a member of the group, the club also included women. The Omar Circle, she wrote, "met at the cozy home of the president and founder, Miss Maria Baldwin, Cambridge school teacher and beloved member of the community." There, by the "cheerful fireside" of the Prospect Street house, "such notables as Dr. W. E. B. Du Bois, Atty. William H. Lewis (both recently out of Harvard), George W. Forbes, Amherst grad., William Monroe Trotter, Harvard '95 and the first colored Phi Beta Kappa scholar (he stood fifth in a class of 400), Miss Nellie Smith,

Boston school teacher, musician, thespian, writer and easy public speaker. . . . Charles Gould Steward, Harvard '96, writer and poet . . . discoursed learnedly on the poets, including the hard to understand Omar Khayyam." Several of these men had been members of the reading group for Harvard students Baldwin had organized, and the Omar Circle may have been an expanded version of that original group. But, Almira Park remembered, it also drew "lesser lights who sat at the feet of these gifted ones and drank in all that the great ones talked about."[97] The Omar Circle does not seem to have been a political club, but it included key figures who would become the leaders of black resistance in the early twentieth century.

Maria Baldwin clearly held a central position among the black elite and, as the successful principal of the Agassiz School, seems to have been greatly respected by white progressives as well. A sign of her standing in these years was doubtless the invitation from the Brooklyn Institute of Arts and Sciences to deliver its annual Washington's Birthday address in 1897. In these years, the Brooklyn Institute was a major New York cultural venue; being selected to give the Washington's Birthday address was a great honor. Baldwin was the first woman and first African American to be invited. *The Woman's Era* proudly stated, "We know of no one better fitted by intellectual and spiritual insight, and by power and grace of expression to deliver this address."[98] The title of Baldwin's lecture was "The Life and Service of the Late Harriet Beecher Stowe."

It is not clear whether the Brooklyn Institute or Baldwin herself chose Stowe as the topic for the address. Stowe, who had died recently, in July 1896, was still revered in the black community. With the growth of more militant black movements in the second half of the twentieth century, Stowe, and particularly the figure of Uncle Tom in her antislavery novel *Uncle Tom's Cabin*, would become the focus of intense criticism and debate, but at the time of her death and for some years after, she was still seen as a key figure in the abolitionist movement, and *Uncle Tom's Cabin* was recognized as a powerful protest against slavery. W. E. B. Du Bois, for example, lauded Stowe's contributions, writing in

1911, "To a frail overburdened Yankee woman with a steadfast moral purpose we Americans, both black and white, owe our gratitude."[99] Stowe's identity as a New Englander as well as her passionate condemnation of slavery would have had a strong appeal to Baldwin.

Baldwin delivered her lecture on February 22, 1897. The *Brooklyn Daily Eagle* noted that this was "the first time in the history of the Brooklyn Institute" that the annual Washington's Birthday lecture was given by a woman.[100] The *Eagle* described Baldwin as "a colored woman . . . a type quite as extraordinary in one way as Booker T. Washington is in another. Her English is pure and felicitous, her manner reposeful, and her thoughts and sympathies strong and deep." The *Eagle* published a lengthy account of Baldwin's presentation. The address touched on familiar themes in Baldwin's life: her deep belief in what she saw as traditional New England virtues and her faith in black strength and progress in the face of racism. She began by noting that Harriet Beecher was born in that "happy transitional period of New England character when Puritan hardness was yielding to the sweet influence of a humaner conception of righteousness." She then outlined the main events of Beecher's early life—teaching in her sister Catherine's school in Connecticut, her move to Cincinnati with her father, the Reverend Lyman Beecher, and her marriage to Professor Calvin Stowe of the Lane Seminary. It was in Cincinnati that Stowe learned firsthand of the horrors of slavery. Baldwin noted: "Mrs. Stowe must often have seen some poor fugitive passing from one station to another of the underground railroad. Scarcely a week passed that some fresh outrage was not reported and letters from a brother in New Orleans revealed the horrors of the system of chattel slavery in the far South."[101]

Baldwin described how in 1850, when the fugitive slave law was passed, "the North found itself in guilty complicity with the thing it hated." It was then that Stowe began publishing her novel as a magazine serial: "Chapter and chapter of the moving tale poured forth, its author waxing strong with the conviction that the great work for the slave was hers to do." *Uncle Tom's Cabin*, said Baldwin, "had been conceived in a moment of rare spiritual

fervor; it was sustained at that height till the end. It is not difficult to find in literature passages that glow with exalted feeling,
but there are few instances in which an entire book catches and
holds emotion at its highest." In her concluding remarks, the
Eagle reported, "Miss Baldwin said that Harriet Beecher Stowe's
steady faith in the possibilities of the negro was as a spur in the
toilsome path he is engaged in climbing." The Reverend Lyman
Abbot then commented on Baldwin's presentation: "Only a
woman can understand a woman," he said, "and, therefore, you
will not expect me to add to this interpretation of Mrs. Stowe by
one of her sisters. We will agree that for broad comprehension of
the issues involved, for delicacy and refinement, cultivation of
manner and spiritual elevation the interpreter has been worthy
of the person interpreted." The account in the *Eagle* concluded,
"When she had done the applause was so hearty that twice she
had to rise and acknowledge the enthusiasm."[102] Later that year,
Baldwin, along with Booker T. Washington, was elected an honorary member of the Brooklyn Institute of Arts and Sciences.[103]

After the success of her Brooklyn Institute address, Maria Baldwin was increasingly in demand as a speaker before white orga-
nizations. She presented her lecture on Harriet Beecher Stowe
to a number of Cambridge and Boston groups. In April 1897 the
Cambridge superintendent of schools invited her to deliver the
address to an audience made up of the Cambridge City Council,
Cambridge teachers, the school committee, and invited guests.[104]
She also presented it to the Cantabrigia Club, to the Cambridge
YWCA, and as part of the municipal free lecture course at the
Bowdoin School in Boston. She spoke on other topics as well. At
the 1898 annual meeting of the Massachusetts Teachers' Associa-
tion, she lectured on "The Working Value of Educational Ideals."
The other two speakers were Harvard professors.[105]

That same year she was invited to join the prestigious Twentieth Century Association of Boston, which had been founded in
1894 by a group of well-known white social reformers. From the
beginning it included both men and women members, among
them progressives such as Thomas Wentworth Higginson, Harvard professor Edward Cummings, and Wellesley professors

Emily Balch and Vida Scudder. The names of the members are those of the Boston Protestant establishment. There are very few obviously Italian, Irish, or Jewish names on the membership lists. In 1896 Rabbi Samuel Hirshberg was elected—although later he is referred to as "the Reverend" Hirshberg.[106] The association grew quickly, holding public lectures by well-known political and academic figures, conferences, and luncheon talks on social, economic, and political issues. It also ran a speakers' bureau composed of members of the association prepared to lecture on issues of the day. By 1901 the association had 450 members.[107] In addition to Baldwin, there were a handful of other African American members, among them the radical journalist William Monroe Trotter and Baldwin's close friend Flora Ridley.

Maria Baldwin's achievements were celebrated in the black community as an example of what could be accomplished by African Americans even in the face of widespread racism. In her series "Famous Women of the Negro Race" in the *Colored American Magazine*, for example, Pauline Hopkins chose Baldwin as the main focus of her article on notable black women educators. Hopkins lauded Baldwin for her many accomplishments, particularly her success as a speaker. On the lecture platform, Hopkins wrote, Baldwin was "a pleasant picture, dignified in her carriage and polished in her address; her full, softly modulated, contralto voice easily reaching the most distant corners of a hall."[108] For Hopkins, Baldwin's lecture on Harriet Beecher Stowe at the Brooklyn Institute demonstrated the intelligence and achievements of African Americans to disbelieving whites. The lecture, Hopkins wrote, "was a distinctive triumph, in which Miss Baldwin stood alone beneath the searching light of public curiosity, and in some instances, we doubt not incredulity, among the educated whites unacquainted with her ability. She rose to the occasion grandly and fulfilled our fondest hopes, covering herself and us with new honors."[109] Thus for Hopkins, Baldwin's successes were not just individual but represented the capabilities of the race. Baldwin was doubtless aware of this sentiment. As with the African American women writers described by Anne-Elizabeth

Murdy, Baldwin's accomplishments were seen "as evidence of the entire race's intelligence, humanity, and educability."[110]

For liberal whites, Baldwin's eloquence, dignity, and accomplishments were proof that African Americans could be valuable members of society; at the same time, their acceptance of her seemed to show that the values of the abolitionists lived on in Boston and Cambridge. Baldwin's success in both black and white worlds meant that she walked a fine line between a non-threatening respectability and her political beliefs. In the years immediately following her Brooklyn Institute lecture, those beliefs grew more radical and critical. Although her addresses to white organizations tended to be measured and apolitical, she began to participate in meetings and activities over issues that were more controversial, such as the late nineteenth-century expansion of US power abroad that led to the Spanish-American War. African Americans were divided in their reactions once war broke out in 1898. Some, like Booker T. Washington, supported the war and argued that African American men should volunteer to serve so as to demonstrate their courage and loyalty to their country, while others, such as Ida B. Wells-Barnett, argued that black men should not serve the United States until the United States granted them full citizenship.[111]

Although there were differences within the black community about how to respond to the war, black activists in Boston quickly pointed out the hypocrisy of the US government's claim that it was defending the values of freedom and democracy in light of its treatment of black Americans. Federal officials took no action as violence against black people in the South continued, segregation spread, and black political rights were destroyed. The 1898 lynching of Frazier Baker, a black postmaster, by a white mob in South Carolina was only the most dramatic southern lynching in these years. The failure of the US government to respond to this crime—an attack on a federal employee that led not only to his own death but also to the death of his young child—galvanized the Boston black community. Bloodshed in Phoenix, South Carolina, and Wilmington, North Carolina, in November 1898, where whites brutally repressed black voting rights, graphically demonstrated the political nature of white racist violence.

Maria Baldwin, like other Boston black activists, denounced lynching and southern white violence and was suspicious of the nationalistic and imperialistic sentiments that led to the Spanish-American War.[112] In May 1899, Baldwin, along with Flora Ridley and Mary Evans Wilson, who later became a central figure in the Boston branch of the NAACP, helped organize a meeting in Boston's Chickering Hall to protest lynching. Both black and white women—including the eighty-year-old Julia Ward Howe—spoke out against lynching and denounced US actions in Cuba and the Philippines.[113] That same month, Baldwin spoke at large anti-imperialist meetings in Cambridge and Boston. She was the only woman mentioned in the account of the Cambridge event in the *Cambridge Chronicle.* According to the *Chronicle,* the speakers were unanimous in condemning US military actions in the Philippines, and at the close of the meeting a number of resolutions were adopted, beginning: "IN THE NAME OF LIBERTY. . . . We believe that the war in the Philippine Islands is without justification, and is contrary to the principles of our republic, and that the conquest of alien people in distant lands is a wicked and unrighteous proceeding, dangerous to American institutions." The *Chronicle* quoted Baldwin as saying that while "the American people are disarmed by the thoughts of the schools, hospitals, etc., in the Philippines, there is abundant evidence that Filipinos prefer their liberty and independence to all these."[114]

The foreign interventionism of the United States government was widely criticized by black Boston activists, who viewed it in the context of unconstrained racist violence at home. In October 1899, the Colored National League sent an extraordinary open letter to President McKinley demanding the federal government take action against lynching. The letter, first read publicly by Archibald Grimké at an open meeting in the Charles Street Church in Boston, began by stating that African Americans' rights as "American freemen," guaranteed by the Constitution, were being denied to them throughout the South "by mobs, by lawless legislatures, and nullifying conventions, and conspiracies." After documenting the most recent racist attacks on black people in the South, including the lynching of Frazier Baker, the letter compared the government's complete silence in response to the lawlessness and racist violence of the white South with its rhetoric justifying the Spanish-American War on the basis of Spanish "criminal aggression." The president, the letter continued, should "pause, if but for an hour, in pursuit of your national policy of 'criminal aggression' abroad to consider the 'criminal aggression' at home against humanity and American citizenship." The black man "has wrongs such as have never in modern times been inflicted on a people and yet he must be dumb in the midst of a nation which prates loudly of democracy and humanity, boasts itself the champion of oppressed peoples abroad, while it looks on indifferent, apathetic, at appalling enormities and iniquities at home, where the victims are black and the criminals white."[115]

ONENESS OF THE HUMAN RACE?

The Colored National League's open letter to President McKinley captured black anger and despair over the growth of an apartheid society enforced by violence in the South, the failure of the government to protect the constitutional rights of black citizens, and growing racism in the North. Although Baldwin was well aware of these issues and spoke out against them, she still retained her optimistic hope that a more tolerant and just society was possible in the United States. Increasingly recognized and respected as an outstanding educator by both whites and African Americans, in 1899 she was invited to teach at the annual summer program at Hampton Institute and Normal School in Virginia. The focus of the summer institute was on education for African American children in the segregated schools of the South. Topics such as the need to combat racist violence, the meaning of "hand work," the need to know the whole child, and the importance of academic subjects were addressed. The institute demonstrates the way vocational and academic education, which came to be seen as opposing approaches to black progress, were intertwined in the practice of black educators. There were over three hundred participants at the 1899 institute, most from the South, although some came from New York, New Jersey, and Massachusetts. Most were classroom teachers, but principals, doctors, journalists, lawyers, and others also attended. There was a model school for observation of methods and optional courses in vocational subjects such as agriculture and in manual training such as knife and bench work, as well as cooking and sewing. Major morning sessions included academic subjects such as English, physics, arithmetic, nature study, and history, taught by Maria Baldwin, described as "the successful and well-known colored principal of the Agassiz School in Cambridge."[116]

In January 1900, six months after her summer school course, Baldwin published an article in *The Southern Workman*, at that time a leading journal for black intellectuals. This issue included a story by the poet Paul Laurence Dunbar, an essay by Archibald Grimké on Frederick Douglass, and Baldwin's article "The Changing Ideal of Progress." In her short piece Baldwin considered the dominant ideals that characterized the world of her day, in particular whether the primary goal was success for the individual or for the whole society. She described a possibly fictitious exchange at a "small gathering not long ago" between a seventy-five-year-old man who deplored what he saw as a lowering of "the spiritual tone of society" and a young man who argued that the ideals of his generation were not lower but had changed from the individual to the social, and that "the aspiration of the individual for knowledge, for culture, for moral perfection has been transformed into a passionate dream of social regeneration." Baldwin worried that the young man's vision meant trampling "upon those instinctive longings for pre-eminence in our march of progress." But she was also concerned that the needs of ordinary individuals could be overlooked. "Surely," she wrote, "this is not the fulfillment of the word of the first great individualist, Christ. This is not in accordance with his insistence upon the dignity and worth of a human soul."[117]

Baldwin seldom mentioned Christianity in her public presentations; her own religious beliefs were grounded in the broad humanism and social activism of radical varieties of Boston Unitarianism. Her reference to Christ's insistence on "the dignity and worth of a human soul" captured her own understanding of Christian ethics as based on social justice. In the end, Baldwin agreed with the young man. For her, a politics based on the idea of "the social" implied the "oneness of the human race" and thus challenged conceptions of racial hierarchy. But it also implied that the individual can find true fulfillment and expression only within an inclusive conception of society. The individual needs society, "for it is there he must realize his own aspirations; there he must hear the divine tone that has come to him only in whispers; there see fully the vision of moral beauty; there feel the strength of the ties that link him with the Infinite." Once again, she expressed her cautious optimism that racism could be overcome and that respect and understanding could exist between the races. She wrote, "Quietly, but surely, there is growing a social consciousness. All the activities of life are being profoundly influenced by this deepening sense of the oneness of the human race. Ever longer sets the tide of feeling against isolation, against segregation, of biases or of interests. A strong conviction of interdependence is weakening the barriers between caste and caste, between race and race." In "The Changing Ideal of Progress" Baldwin expressed again her optimism that race differences could be overcome by a shared recognition of "the oneness of the human race."[118] Her belief in cross-race cooperation and friendship was almost immediately tested.

Both Maria Baldwin and Josephine St. Pierre Ruffin had worked with white women in white-dominated organizations in Boston and Cambridge for years, seemingly without incident. But at the turn of the twentieth century, they had interactions with southern white women that were increasingly problematic. White women in the South had been slow to form women's clubs, but in the 1890s they began to establish clubs and pursue reform efforts similar to those of middle-class women in the West and North. In 1898 the white Georgia clubwoman Rebecca Lowe was the first southerner elected president of the General Federation of Women's Clubs. A few months later, in January 1899, a group of prominent Georgia women founded a club they called the Georgia Educational League with the goal of supporting educational opportunities for the poor.

In April 1899 Lowe visited Boston, where she met with local clubwomen and may have met Josephine St. Pierre Ruffin, president of the Woman's Era Club, which since 1895 had been a full member of the Massachusetts Federation of Women's Clubs.[119] A few weeks later, in May 1899, the Georgia Educational League, which had at first focused on the needs of poor white girls, announced that it would support the establishment of kindergartens for black children. The response to this announcement was consternation among Georgia whites, who could not imagine that white women would support an educational project for black children. In letters published in the *Atlanta Constitution* and the *Boston Daily Globe*, Mrs. Frank Gale, head of the kindergarten division of the Georgia Educational League, defended the decision, making clear that the league's goal was "moral training for the negro race" to counter their "moral degeneracy." In her letter to the *Atlanta Constitution,* she emphasized that the league was not advocating academic study: "It is useless to undertake educating the negro children in any except two directions . . . the religious line [and] industrial training. To teach the negro children social equality would be ruinous. . . . To educate them in the classics would be and is proving as ruinous; it unfits them for work."[120] In a May 30 letter to the *Boston Daily Globe*, Gale reiterated that the focus of the league's work with black children would be moral training. She contrasted this approach with the "thousands of dollars (northern capital)" spent on black education, which had succeeded only in "making expert criminals." Instead, the goal of early education for black children would be to raise "the standard of morality" among the black population. If something was not done, Gale wrote, "we are destined to face more appalling crimes than have yet been perpetrated," a reference to the late nineteenth-century white moral panic over the assumed danger of white women being raped by black men.[121] The league planned to establish kindergartens for black children out of "the first great law of human nature, self-protection." She concluded, "The awful crime of outraged virtue, which is a constant menace to every southern woman, urges us to this effort."[122]

Two weeks later, on June 16, a group of black women educators responded in an open letter to the Georgia Educational League, also published in the *Boston Daily Globe*. The women began by stating that they, as educators, were writing "in the name of the many colored women of Boston and vicinity" to acknowledge the "splendid work for the moral education of the negro" outlined by Gale in her May 30 letter. But they immediately added that they could not "approve of the intimation that the schools for the negro have failed in moral training." They cited the great work done by black teachers "in the woods and plantations" of the South, as well as the self-sacrificing teachers from the North who had taught in black southern schools. None of these schools had kindergartens, and the Boston women strongly supported their introduction. But, they insisted, these kindergartens should be supervised by educators from the existing black schools and colleges of the South. The writers offered to help raise funds for such a project and to work with the Georgia Educational League. The letter bore the names of eleven women including Florida Ruffin Ridley, who signed herself "President Students Aid Association"; Josephine St. Pierre Ruffin, "Woman's Era Club"; and Maria L. Baldwin, "Principal, Agassiz School, Cambridge."[123]

The June open letter from the Boston women made clear their objection to the idea that black Georgia children were in special need of moral training, but it was framed in conciliatory language and contained an offer to work cooperatively with the white Georgia clubwomen. That same month Josephine St. Pierre Ruffin sent her own open letter to the Georgia Educational League. She began by praising the willingness of the league to "undertake the moral training of the colored children of Georgia," but she immediately noted that this was the first public acknowledgment by southern women of any responsibility for the welfare of black children, who were, she wrote pointedly, "the children of their former slaves." In contrast, Ruffin celebrated the northern women who taught in the freedmen's schools immediately after the war and who continued to teach in the South in an atmosphere of white contempt and persecution. Given their failure to help black children in the past, Ruffin wrote, southern white women should now ask their husbands for the funds to support kindergartens. She concluded, "If, when you have entered upon it, you need the cooperation, either by advice or other assistance, of the colored women of the North, we beg to assure you that they will not be lacking—until then, the earnest hope goes out that you will bravely face and sternly conquer your former prejudices and quickly undertake this missionary work which belongs to you."[124]

Despite Ruffin's sharp letter and the Boston women's criticisms of the southern women's assumption of black immorality, at some point between June and November 1899 the two groups seem to have reached an agreement. A November article in the *Boston Daily Globe* reported that for the first time, white southern women and "their colored allies in Boston" had agreed to work in harmony by supporting kindergartens for black children. According to the *Globe*, the Georgia women responded positively to the offer of help from "a number of colored women associated in clubs" and even invited the Boston black women to join the Georgia Educational League. It is not clear that any of the Boston women actually joined, but according to the *Globe*, they did form their own Association for the Promotion of Child Training in the South and donated $20 a month to pay for a kindergarten teacher in an Atlanta school. The officers of the Boston Association were listed as a Mrs. F. Ruthy of Brookline (almost certainly a misstating of Flora Ridley), president; Mrs. J. St. Pierre Ruffin, treasurer; and Miss Maria Louisa Baldwin, "Principal of the Agassiz grammar school, Cambridge," secretary.[125]

The reaching out to the Georgia Educational League by the Boston black women may have reflected the desire for a common social consciousness and a "deepening sense of the oneness of the human race" that Maria Baldwin expressed in her *Southern Workman* article, which would be published only a few months later. But if so, this view was soon challenged. In 1900, Josephine St. Pierre Ruffin attended the national convention of the General Federation of Women's Clubs (GFWC) as a delegate from both the Woman's Era Club and the New England Federation of Women's Clubs. Some of the officers of the GFWC, which was composed of white women's clubs, apparently had not realized that the Woman's Era Club was a black women's club when they admitted Ruffin as a delegate. Once they realized that Ruffin was representing a black organization, the program committee refused to allow her to speak before the convention.[126] Rebecca Lowe of Georgia, the president of the GFWC, and the members of the Georgia delegation, who may have had Ruffin's strong and uncompromising letter in their minds, led the move to unseat Ruffin as a delegate. The incident was widely publicized. According to a report in the *Chicago Tribune*, when one of the members of the credentials committee "attempted to snatch [the badge] from Mrs. Ruffin's dress," Ruffin avoided her "and fled with her badge."[127] She may have retained her badge, but Ruffin did not succeed in speaking at the conference. And although her treatment was criticized by northern progressives, in 1902 at their next national convention the federation, bowing to the southern women's demands, adopted a whites-only membership policy. Southern white clubwomen wanted no part of militant and articulate black women like Josephine St. Pierre Ruffin. As the historian Mary Jane Smith comments, Ruffin's "public scolding of Georgia's white clubwomen" showed "the potential threat to southern white clubwomen. If larger numbers of black women like Ruffin joined the General Federation, southern white women would no longer be able to argue to their club colleagues, without challenge, that they knew what was best for southern blacks and southern race relations."[128]

The experiment in interracial collaboration around the Georgia kindergartens does not seem to have lasted very long. In early 1901, Baldwin wrote to the veteran white reformer Ednah Dow Cheney for advice about a Georgia school that the Association for the Promotion of Child Training in the South was supporting. Baldwin was already acquainted with Cheney, who had known Josephine St. Pierre Ruffin for years, been an early supporter of the Woman's Era Club, and was a member of the Free Religious Association in Boston, which Baldwin had joined the year before. Baldwin wrote to Cheney that although the spirit of the Georgia school seemed high, the Association for the Promotion of Child Training in the South was concerned about the attitude of the Georgia clubwomen who had promised to work with them. "Instead of the cooperation of southern white women," Baldwin wrote, "they have given us lately no help. The adequately equipped school that they promised does not exist and I cannot even get an answer from them to a letter inquiring as to their future assistance." One question was whether she should discuss this situation with "persons who have given us help in the belief that they were uniting colored women and white in a worthy movement." For many supporters "it was this aspect that appealed most strongly." The other question Baldwin raised was whether the association should go on with the project alone, without the help of white women, or abandon it.[129] Cheney's response has been lost, but it seems she suggested that the association send an expert to evaluate the school before proceeding. Baldwin asked George Towns, professor of pedagogy at Atlanta University and a good friend of W. E. B. Du Bois, to investigate. Towns gave the school a strong recommendation. Baldwin sent his report to Cheney with a brief letter pointedly noting that since Towns was a professor at Atlanta University, "his opinion should therefore be worth something."[130] No further letters about this issue have survived, but Baldwin's acerbic comment about Towns does seem to show that she found Cheney's response condescending. The experiment in interracial collaboration was not a success.

In her article in *The Southern Workman*, Maria Baldwin spoke of her confidence in the "deepening sense of the oneness of the human race" that was eroding segregation and bias, but her own and Josephine Ruffin's experiences with southern white clubwomen challenged that belief. It is not clear how long the Association for Child Training in the South continued to be active. It is not mentioned again in Boston newspapers or in accounts of Baldwin's life. The world of organized women's clubs seems to have lost its attraction for both Ruffin and Baldwin. Ruffin left the NACW in a conflict with Mary Church Terrell in 1899, and by the early twentieth century, both Ruffin and Baldwin appear to have stepped down from central positions in the Woman's Era Club as well. According to the account of her life in Julia Ward Howe's *Representative Women of New England*, in 1903 Ruffin declined reelection as president of the Woman's Era Club "because of the pressure of other work."[131] There is no evidence of Baldwin's further participation, and the club itself continued to exist for only a few more years.[132] Baldwin's hope for "a growing social consciousness" and racial harmony would be tested even more severely in coming years, not only by deepening racism and white-on-black violence, but also by a growing militancy in the black community as a whole, the emergence of new organizations, and conflicts among African Americans themselves. In this changing world, Maria Baldwin, like many other African Americans, looked for more focused and direct ways to challenge racism and work for full citizenship.

‿ CHAPTER THREE ‿
Contending Forces

On November 15, 1899, the African American writer Pauline Hopkins read from the manuscript of her novel *Contending Forces* to the members of the Woman's Era Club.[1] *Contending Forces,* which was published the following year, provides a vivid picture of the African American community in Boston and the political debates that consumed it at the turn of the twentieth century. In the novel, the two settings where pressing political questions such as lynching, disenfranchisement, segregation, and race itself are debated are the male-dominated American Colored League and the women's sewing circle, where a group of black women regularly discuss issues of race and politics. The fictional American Colored League was clearly modeled on the Colored National League of Boston, to which Hopkins belonged.[2] The women's sewing circle recalls the sewing circle for St. Monica's Home for Sick Colored Women and Children, which included several members of the Woman's Era Club. Hopkins herself was a member of the Woman's Era Club, and *Contending Forces* must have been of great interest to the other members, among them Maria Baldwin, who as a leading member of the club was almost certainly present when Hopkins read from her novel.

Given the small world of the educated activist black community in Boston, Maria Baldwin was doubtless already acquainted with Pauline Hopkins, who was her close contemporary. Both Baldwin and Hopkins were born in 1856—Baldwin in Massachusetts, Hopkins in Maine. Like Baldwin, Hopkins, who moved to Boston as a young child, was a high school graduate educated in integrated Massachusetts public schools, and grew up in a politically sophisticated and activist community. But unlike Baldwin and many other gifted young black women of the time, Hopkins did not become a teacher. Instead, she became involved in the theater—as both a performer and a playwright. By her late twenties, though, she had left the world of the theater and was supporting herself as a stenographer with a secure civil service job at the Massachusetts Bureau of Statistics. In 1899 she left her job and turned to writing. In 1900 she began to publish both short stories and journalism in the newly established *Colored American Magazine*.[3] That same year her novel *Contending Forces* was published by the Colored Co-operative Publishing Company of Boston.

Though a work of fiction, *Contending Forces* provides one of the few contemporary depictions of activist black Boston at the turn of the twentieth century.[4] The major characters are clearly based on real people. The eloquent figure of Will Smith, educated at Harvard and in Germany, closely resembles W. E. B. Du Bois; Mrs. Willis, the leader among black Boston clubwomen, "well-read and thoroughly conversant with all current topics," recalls Josephine St. Pierre Ruffin.[5] Booker T. Washington is the model for Dr. Arthur Lewis, the president of a southern black industrial school. The beautiful mulatto heroine Sappho is a stenographer like Pauline Hopkins herself.

The only mention of an African American woman teacher in *Contending Forces* is the account in the chapter "The Sewing Circle" of a political conversation among the group of black women who meet with Mrs. Willis. At one point the schoolteacher Anna Stevens, who is described as having a "very studious temperament," recounts the sermon of a white minister who "thanked God that the mulatto race was dying out, because it was a mongrel mixture which combined the worst elements of two races. Lo the poor mulatto! despised by the blacks of his own race, scorned by the whites! Let him go and hang himself!" Anna Stevens is so outraged at this racist slur that, Hopkins writes, "she forgot the scissors and bit her thread off viciously with her little white teeth."[6] There were very few black teachers in Massachusetts public schools in these years, and Maria Baldwin was by far the best known. She and Flora Ridley were the only teachers in the Woman's Era Club, and Ridley had left teaching when she married in 1888, so this portrait of the studious teacher quietly outraged by the racism of the white minister may well be based on Maria Baldwin.

There are different possible meanings to the term "contending forces" in Hopkins's novel. One character, Luke Sawyer, a black man whose family has been murdered by a lynch mob, names "conservatism, lack of brotherly affiliation, lack of energy for the right, and the power of the almighty dollar which deadens men's hearts" as "the contending forces that are dooming this race to despair!"[7] But another meaning was becoming clear to the Boston black community: the conflict between the views represented by the characters Dr. Arthur Lewis (Booker T. Washington) and Will Smith (W. E. B. Du Bois).

At the turn of the twentieth century there were a variety of responses among African Americans to the increasingly oppressive and violent racism in the United States. These included self-help and economic success, racial solidarity and separate black institutions, working within the two dominant political parties, integration in all spheres, and political demands for the vote and full citizenship. Individuals moved among these possible responses or combined them in sometimes seemingly contradictory ways.[8] By the end of the nineteenth century, a number of organizations had emerged with the goal of combating the racist violence and deterioration of black rights in the South. The most influential of these was the Afro-American League, but other local groups also existed, among them Boston's Colored National League. These associations developed approaches that were the basis for later civil rights organizations, but they all were small, had financial difficulties, and failed to attract a mass base. In 1898 the Afro-American League, the best known of these groups, was replaced by the Afro-American Council. Both T. Thomas Fortune and Ida B. Wells-Barnett continued to participate in the Afro-American Council, as did Josephine St. Pierre Ruffin.[9]

The emergence of Booker T. Washington as a national figure after his Atlanta Exposition speech in 1895 changed the African

American political landscape. Washington was born in 1856—the same year as Maria Baldwin—but unlike Baldwin, he was born into slavery in the South. In his autobiography *Up From Slavery* he describes his extraordinary struggle to gain an education and eventually to found the Tuskegee Institute. A supporter of the Afro-American League, he kept his involvement quiet and maintained a nonthreatening and conciliatory public persona. His emphasis on economic progress and pragmatic accommodation with the white majority gained him the trust of white philanthropists and made him the best-known and most powerful African American leader of the late nineteenth century. His cautious approach made sense to many African Americans in the South, where white violence was ever present and black civil rights had virtually vanished by the turn of the twentieth century, although even there, as August Meier notes, "it must be emphasized that such ideas were usually regarded as being a tactic in the struggle for ultimate citizenship rights."[10] Washington had ties to Boston, particularly to white philanthropists and the small black business community. After his Atlanta Exposition address, Washington frequently visited Boston, invited by the white elite of Boston and Cambridge. In 1896 he received the first honorary degree ever given to an African American by Harvard.[11]

Although Washington was celebrated by Boston whites, he was met with suspicion by the leaders of the city's black community, who had long demanded full civil and political rights, the integration of all public institutions and spaces, and the condemnation of white racism—a stance that came to be identified with Du Bois. The historian William Gatewood argues that the northern black elite in general was hostile to Washington on class grounds as well as on the basis of racial politics. They were more sympathetic with the Harvard-educated Du Bois and felt very comfortable with Du Bois's idea of an educated "talented tenth" who would provide black leadership.[12] By the late 1890s, when *Contending Forces* was written, black Bostonians were organizing to oppose Washington's ideas. When Washington arranged a dinner with his Boston critics in the spring of 1898, he faced sharp criticism from them.[13]

In *Contending Forces,* Hopkins shares black Boston's growing suspicion of Washington. Dr. Arthur Lewis, who is clearly modeled on Washington, is presented as a respected figure, but Hopkins is critical of his conservative and accommodationist stance. Dr. Lewis's speech before a black audience recalls Washington's 1895 Atlanta Exposition speech, in which he described African Americans as "the most patient, faithful, law-abiding, and unresentful people that the world has seen." In *Contending Forces,* Dr. Lewis admonishes his audience, "If we are patient, docile, harmless, we may expect to see that prosperity for which we long, in the years to come, if not for ourselves then for our children."[14] Replacing Washington's terms "patient and faithful" with Dr. Lewis's "docile and harmless" seems pointed, particularly in comparison with the speech given by the passionate Will Smith, the novel's romantic hero, based on Du Bois, who directly condemns white racism: "If the Negro votes, he is shot; if he marries a white woman, he is shot; if he accumulates property, he is shot or lynched—he is a pariah whom the National Government cannot defend. But if he defends himself and his home, then is heard the tread of marching feet as the Federal troops move southward to quell a 'race riot.'"[15] In this passage, the forces shaping black people's lives are racism and violence condoned by the US government itself. The answer for Will Smith, as for Du Bois, is to demand full citizenship and civil rights.

In the years immediately following the publication of *Contending Forces,* the conflict between Washington and his radical critics became sharper and more public. Boston and Cambridge, where black citizens could vote, where the schools were at least nominally integrated, and where black people kept alive the memory of the abolitionists, were at the center of anti-Washington agitation.[16] The educated black Boston elite held fast to the goal of achieving not only full political and civil rights but institutional and social integration as well. These leaders were often more likely to have white ancestry than other African Americans and were members of white-dominated organizations. They were much less likely to belong to separate black institutions and churches or to participate in the informal networks that supported the majority of black people who were excluded from employment and met discrimination and hostility even in northern cities like Boston. But the elite's demands for civic and social equality were negotiated in a social and political world in which rigid conceptions of race permeated all aspects of life and where ideas of racial hierarchy and white superiority were increasingly seen as "scientifically" proven.

Maria Baldwin, more than most African Americans, lived this tension. She inhabited both black and white worlds, symbolizing African American achievement to both communities. Her closest friends were found among the educated black elite, but she also seems to have moved easily in white settings. She lived and worked in one of the least oppressive cities for black people in the country. In the context of the profound racism of US society in these years, Cambridge was unusually open to individual black achievement. In his 1903 article "Color Line Not Drawn and Merit Recognized" in the *Cambridge Chronicle*, Linn Boyd Porter wrote that in Cambridge, "the color line has never been closely drawn and honor has not been withheld from the colored men and women." Porter lists the African Americans who had played and continued to play an active role in the city in the years since the Civil War. Where else, he asks, could you find "a black alderman, sitting in a board with 10 white colleagues and elected by voters 96 per cent of whom were white? Two negro representatives in the Legislature, chosen by constituencies in which the colored vote was relatively small? A negro chief of a fire department in which he was the only man of color? A black policeman, patrolling streets occupied mostly by white residents, for 19 years in succession? A negro at the head of the city department of bacteriology? A negro member of the public library trustees, with all white associates? A black commander of a white post of the Grand Army? And—a woman of nearly pure African blood acting as principal of a grammar school in a fashionable district, with six white teachers and several hundred white pupils under her charge?"[17] Celebrating the achievements of single individuals, of course, does not mean that deep patterns of discrimination were absent. In 1903 Maria Baldwin was still the only African American teacher in the Cambridge public schools.

In the years after her triumph at the Brooklyn Institute, Baldwin was frequently invited to speak to white organizations in Massachusetts, particularly on women's issues and education. In these settings, where she was usually the only African American, she presented a measured and nonthreatening persona. She continued to give her sympathetic lecture on Harriet Beecher Stowe, first as one of the speakers in the Cambridge Cooperative's 1902 lecture series and subsequently to an audience of two hundred at the Women's Baptist Social Union of Boston in 1903.[18] Her praise of the white abolitionist surely was intended on some level as a lesson for her white audiences that interracial cooperation on behalf of racial justice was still possible. She also began to speak on educational issues, framing the work of the woman teacher within the discourse of women's rights and the suffrage movement. In 1901 she spoke at the New England Woman Suffrage Festival at Faneuil Hall on "The Teacher in Social Reform." According to the account in the *Cambridge Chronicle*, Baldwin observed that teachers were no longer "satisfied with the narrow learning and life that formerly sufficed." Instead, they sought to involve themselves in public service. Baldwin expanded on this theme in an address she gave to a meeting of the Massachusetts Federation of Women's Clubs in October 1901, in which she reflected on the responsibility of teachers to contribute to the "social good." She warned that "teaching, detached from social ends, had the temptations of narrowness, loss of enthusiasm and despotism, arising from dealing with less developed minds." But as women had organized for their right to suffrage, she argued, women teachers had also begun to be aware of their own responsibilities: "The time will come that wherever people are gathered together to consider what will advance the social good, there will the teacher be found."[19] In October 1902 she spoke at the annual meeting of the Essex County Teachers' Association; in February 1903 she gave a lecture, "The Parent and the Teacher," to the Newton Education Society; in December 1903 she was one of the speakers at the annual meeting of the Massachusetts Teachers' Association; and in 1904 she presented a paper, "The Parent and the Teacher," to the Cantabrigia Club. None of the accounts of these presentations suggests that she mentioned race at all.

BELIEF IN A CREED

Like many Boston and Cambridge progressives of her time, Baldwin sought a community that would provide spiritual support. She claimed to have been brought up in a faith, but it is not clear whether this meant membership in an established church. There were no black churches in Cambridge during Baldwin's early childhood. It is possible that her parents belonged to a black church in Boston, several of which, like the Twelfth Baptist Church, were committed to abolitionism and racial justice. In the 1870s, when Baldwin was a teenager, two black churches were established in Cambridge—St. Paul's African Methodist Episcopal Church in 1873 and Union Baptist Church in 1879. Both were located in Central Square, where the Baldwin family lived, and they may have attended one of them.

Historians have pointed to the importance of the black church in the years of the nadir. In a hostile society it became what Evelyn Higginbotham has called a "forum of discussion and debate, promoter of education and economic cooperation, and arena for the development and assertion of leadership."[20] Black churches in Boston and Cambridge certainly played these roles, but membership was relatively low in Massachusetts compared to other areas of the country in the late nineteenth century. In 1890, 16 percent of African Americans in Massachusetts claimed membership in a church, for example, compared to 52 percent of North Carolina African Americans.[21] Among the black New England elite, literary and social clubs seem to have provided the network of support that black churches offered in other areas. And it was not unusual for members of the black Boston elite to belong to white-dominated churches. According to John Daniels in his 1914 study of black Boston, African Americans attending white churches were "the most uncompromising of those members of the race who insist on the importance of equal privilege and who profess to be opposed to all racial segregation."[22] Josephine St. Pierre Ruffin and Flora Ridley were part of that group. Although in the mid-1870s George and Josephine St. Pierre Ruffin had attended the black Twelfth Street Baptist Church, after George Ruffin's death in 1886, Josephine joined the white-dominated

Trinity Episcopal Church in Copley Square, where her son George was a member of the choir. Flora Ruffin Ridley and her family were also members of Trinity Episcopal.[23] For a time in the 1890s, Maria Baldwin seems to have worshipped at the Hope Congregational Church, located on Harvard Street near her home in Cambridge. Hope Congregational was predominantly white, but Baldwin's friends Clement and Gertrude Morgan, who were black, also attended. Through the church, Baldwin and Clement Morgan both were involved in charity work for St. Monica's Home for Sick Colored Women and Children.[24]

Baldwin also sought community and a spiritual home in non-traditional white-dominated settings. She was a member of the Boston Society for Ethical Culture and the Free Religious Association, closely related groups which stood outside of traditional Christian denominations. Both were part of the wider movement of free thought, which rejected the idea of a monotheistic God, embraced the scientific method, evolution, and progress, and defended independent thinking and intellectual freedom.[25] The Boston Society for Ethical Culture, founded in 1884 by Clara Bisbee, though similar in beliefs to Felix Adler's well-known Society for Ethical Culture, was a separate organization and had no formal ties to the national society.[26] It seems to have been a small local group. The early black historians Benjamin Brawley and Dorothy Porter both state that Maria Baldwin served one term as president of the Boston ethical culture society, but neither provides the date.[27] Other evidence suggests that this was probably during the late 1890s. In 1900, Maria Baldwin joined the better-known Free Religious Association, which shared many beliefs with the ethical culture movement.

The inheritor of Boston abolitionism and Transcendentalism, the Free Religious Association had been founded in Boston in 1867, influenced by the radical ministry of Theodore Parker. Among its members were Ralph Waldo Emerson, Charles Eliot Norton, Lucretia Mott, Lucy Stone, Julia Ward Howe, Rabbi Isaac Wise, and Thomas Wentworth Higginson. In an 1880 editorial in *The Index*, the journal of the Free Religious Association, the organization described itself as "standing squarely outside of Christianity" with the goal of "uprooting every conservative prejudice by which reform is checked. Uncompromising, fearless, radical, it will put forth faith in ideas, and work for them openly, regardless of all consequences. Its only policy will be strong thought and plain speech."[28] The association's membership never rose beyond a few hundred, but *The Index* seems to have been widely read and was influential in radical religious circles. It is not clear why Baldwin left the Boston Society for Ethical Culture for the Free Religious Association, but the fact that Thomas Wentworth Higginson served as president of the association between 1894 and 1899 may have influenced her decision to join. In June 1900, Baldwin spoke to the association about her decision, saying she had "left the faith she was brought up in because she found that a good life counted for nothing unless it is allied to belief in a creed."[29] This use of the term "creed" here seems to mean a commitment to social justice that she did not find in "the faith she was brought up in." She said nothing about her involvement with the Boston Society for Ethical Culture.

The addresses presented at the 1902 annual meeting of the Free Religious Association provide a sense of its religious and political positions and something of its membership. Speeches were given by the radical Unitarian minister Charles Gordon Ames, the Harvard sociologist Edward Cummings, and reformers William Lloyd Garrison Jr. and Julia Ward Howe, among others.[30] The association supported progressive causes such as women's suffrage and endorsed a statement calling on the president and Congress to address the war in the Philippines and "replace the present measure of coercion with a policy of conciliation and good will" and to "secure for the people of the Philippine Islands self-government after the fashion of really free nations."[31] There was no mention of lynching, unions, immigrants, or the tension between Protestants and Catholics, and there do not seem to have been any other prominent African American members besides Maria Baldwin, whose role in the association appears to have been the familiar one of acting as a kind of tutor about race to the white members. In 1904 she presented an address to the association's annual convention on "The Duties and Rights of the Different Races in the Republic."[32] Baldwin later joined another progressive congregation, the radical Unitarian Church of the Disciples, also in Boston. The Church of the Disciples, led by the charismatic Charles Gordon Ames, included a number of other members of the Free Religious Association in its congregation, including Julia Ward Howe. According to a later newspaper account, Maria Baldwin "became a loyal member of that society, attending its services regularly and contributing her own gifts and enlightened and persuasive speech at many of its meetings."[33] The Church of the Disciples was also overwhelmingly white, and Maria Baldwin, with her "enlightened and persuasive speech," may well have raised issues of race there as she did in the Free Religious Association.

The members of the Boston Society for Ethical Culture, the Free Religious Association, and the Church of the Disciples, like the white audiences for her lectures, probably had little knowledge of the parallel black world in which Maria Baldwin moved. In fact she had ties to a complex web of individuals and factions within the African American community. Baldwin was seen as a moderate because of her connection to the white progressive community in Boston, her position as principal of a largely white public school, and her unthreatening presentations to white audiences. But she was active in black organizations and had long-standing connections with almost all the major figures in black Boston, including the leading opponents of Booker T. Washington. She had known both W. E. B. Du Bois and William Monroe Trotter when they were undergraduates at Harvard and members of the reading circle for Harvard students that she held at her home on Prospect Street. Du Bois was the leading African American intellectual and would become probably the best-known critic of Washington's views of education and politics. The fiery journalist and activist Trotter founded and was the editor of *The Guardian*, which became a relentless and often polemical voice in opposition to Washington. But if Baldwin had connections to these radical figures and the established black Boston elite, she also had ties to Washington's followers, most intimately though her brother, Louis.

LOUIS AND ALICE

For over twenty years, Maria Baldwin shared a home with members of her family. After their mother's death in 1884, the three Baldwin siblings—Maria, Alice, and Louis—continued to live together, first in the small house on Clark Street and then after 1888 in the much larger house on Prospect Street. That year Maria was teaching at the Agassiz School. Her sister, Alice, had not found a position as a teacher; if she had paid work, it is not noted in the Cambridge city directories. Her brother, Louis, had graduated from Cambridge High School in 1882 and was seeking to find his way in life. As a high school graduate, Louis was better educated than most of his contemporaries, black or white. He was one of twenty-four young men who graduated from the English course at Cambridge High School in his year. Nationwide, only 2 to 3 percent of the population were high school graduates, and the percentage of African American high school graduates was much lower.[34] His graduation from high school only two years after his father's death was a significant accomplishment. Unlike his two sisters, Louis Baldwin did not become a teacher but was involved in publishing, politics, and business. The Cambridge city directories list his first occupation after he graduated as porter, then in subsequent years as bookkeeper and salesman, and finally in real estate. But his first love was politics. When he was twenty, he was named the corresponding secretary for the newly founded Blaine and Logan Club, organized by "the colored citizens of Cambridge" to support the Republican slate of James Blaine and John Logan in the 1884 presidential election.[35] He was a member of the Republican Club and a Republican precinct inspector for Ward 2 in the 1889 Cambridge elections. That year he also ran for a seat on the Cambridge Common Council. The *Cambridge Press* described him as "a young man who received his education in the schools of our city, and who has been an active and earnest worker in all measures pertaining to the welfare and general good of the public," concluding that "his election to the Council would secure to the citizens, an honest, straightforward, faithful servant of the people."[36] Despite the endorsement of the *Press,* young Louis Baldwin failed to win election that year.

While Cambridge politics remained a major focus of Louis Baldwin's energies, he also participated in the black community more broadly. In May 1890 the *Cambridge Chronicle* reported on the formation of an equal rights association at a meeting of "Massachusetts colored men." Two Cambridge men were elected officers: Dr. W. C. Lane as vice president and Louis Baldwin as secretary.[37] He was also involved with two black newspapers in Boston, *The Courant* and *The Republican,* which were associated with some of the best-known members of the black community.[38] The editors of *The Courant* were Butler Wilson, later head of the Boston branch of the NAACP; George Forbes, a graduate of Amherst and well-known civil rights leader; and Josephine St. Pierre Ruffin, the leading black Boston clubwoman and of course well known to Louis's sister Maria. *The Republican,* as its name suggests, was a partisan paper supporting the Republican Party. Louis Baldwin also continued to pursue local politics. In 1891 he ran again for the Cambridge Common Council and this time was elected as one of the councilmen from Ward 2, which included the small black community in Cambridgeport.

Alice Baldwin had lived with her family since graduating from the Cambridge teacher training program. Nothing is known of her life during these years; perhaps she continued to apply for teaching positions in Cambridge but was refused, or perhaps she took responsibility for the household after her mother's death. But in 1891, the same year when Louis was elected to the Common Council, Alice left Cambridge to take up a position at the newly established Howard High School in Wilmington, Delaware, recruited by Howard's charismatic principal Edwina Kruse. The Baldwin sisters were already acquainted with Kruse. Two years earlier, in August 1889, they had held a reception for Kruse when she visited Cambridge.[39] Alice must have been pleased with the invitation to join the faculty of Howard, the only black high school in the state of Delaware, and regarded as one of the best academic high schools for black students in the country. Its faculty came to include graduates of Oberlin, Radcliffe,

Pembroke, Cornell, and the University of Pennsylvania.[40] In 1895 Mary Church Terrell, soon to become president of the National Association of Colored Women, was the graduation speaker. But Wilmington was a very different world from Cambridge. Delaware was a border state, and the public schools, restaurants, hotels, and other public spaces were segregated.

Although Alice Baldwin entered a new world in Delaware, she retained her close ties to Maria and Louis. In summers, Alice, who was also known by her middle name, Gertrude, returned to Cambridge, where she stayed in the house on Prospect Street. On these visits she seems to have participated in the popular new pastime of bicycling. The August 1896 issue of *The Woman's Era* noted that "Miss Gertrude Baldwin is spending the month of August at her home in Cambridge, or rather that part of it which she does not spend on her wheel."[41] But Alice Baldwin became more and more absorbed in her new life in Wilmington in a racially divided society and a school led by powerful black women. In 1902 Alice Dunbar Nelson, the estranged wife of the poet Paul Laurence Dunbar, joined the faculty of Howard as head of the English department. Dunbar Nelson may well have already known Alice Baldwin through Maria. In 1896 and 1897, when Alice Dunbar Nelson (then Alice Moore) was living in Medford, a Boston suburb, she joined the Woman's Era Club, where she almost certainly would have encountered Maria Baldwin.[42] Like Edwina Kruse, Alice Dunbar Nelson was a powerful figure, a published writer acquainted with the black intelligentsia through her husband. Over the years, Alice Baldwin made an independent life for herself apart from her siblings, influenced by forceful women like Alice Dunbar Nelson and Edwina Kruse and more and more grounded in the black world of Wilmington.

After Alice left in 1891, Maria and Louis Baldwin continued to share the house at 196 Prospect Street. The next year the two of them bought the house with two mortgages.[43] While Alice was making a new life in Delaware, Louis pursued his political ambitions in Cambridge. The high point of his political career was the term he served as a member of the Cambridge Common Council between 1891 and 1893. In these years, Cambridge city government consisted of an elected mayor, the twenty-member Common Council elected by ward, and a board of aldermen elected from across the city. Louis appears to have been successful as a councilman. In 1893, the *Cambridge Chronicle* reported that he seemed "to have a 'cinch' on one of the Republican nominations for representative from ward 2. . . . Mr. Baldwin says he has not made up his mind what he shall do this fall, though he is willing to serve the people in any capacity they may call him."[44] In the end, rather than run for reelection to the Common Council from Ward 2, where he was well known, Baldwin ran for alderman. The fact that aldermen were elected from across the city, not from individual wards, may have played a part, but whatever the factors involved, Baldwin was not elected.

Perhaps making use of the knowledge and connections he had acquired as a councilman, Louis Baldwin turned from politics to real estate. In 1894, the year after his defeat in the election for alderman, he formed a partnership with Joseph Dorsey and established the real estate firm of Baldwin and Dorsey. Dorsey, who had graduated from Cambridge High School in 1888, was four or five years younger than Baldwin and was probably white, since Baldwin is often referred to in newspaper accounts as a "colored" real estate dealer while Dorsey's race is unremarked. The partnership worked well, and for the next few years the firm was quite successful.[45] Although he was now absorbed in a thriving real estate business and no longer a city official, Baldwin continued to be involved in Republican politics. In 1896 he was elected party secretary for Ward 2.[46] He was also involved in a controversy that year which demonstrates the complexity of his political position. A long article in the October 10, 1896, *Cambridge Chronicle* titled "Indignation Meeting" reveals the racial tensions in the city and also shows Louis Baldwin's ambiguous role as a black man attempting to succeed in a white-dominated political world. The article describes a meeting of what the *Chronicle* referred to as "about 400 of our colored friends" who met to protest the city's response to a racially charged incident. The call for the meeting described it as a protest against "the language used to the women of our race, by one of the Cambridge police officers, and endorsed by a high official in the said city." According to the *Chronicle*, "two young colored women assert that they were called vile names late one night near Mt. Auburn by several young white men. They appealed to the special police officer, who, when told what the words used were, asked 'What else are you?'"[47] The white men were summoned to court and fined. Charges were also brought against the policeman, but Mayor William Bancroft had the charges dismissed. Mayor Bancroft, a graduate of Philips Exeter Academy, Harvard College, and Harvard Law School, and later president of the Boston Elevated Railway Company, was a Republican, as was Louis Baldwin.

Speakers at the public meeting denounced Bancroft's actions as insulting to the race. As one participant argued, black men saw the incident as demonstrating the need to protect the virtue of black women: "White men, and especially white police officers and mayors of cities and other high officials have from now on got to recognize this fact, that they have got to cease insulting our colored women here in Massachusetts and must see to it that when they are insulted that the same strong arm of Massachusetts law in regard to the protection of women shall be extended the same over a colored woman as it is over a white woman." Since Mayor Bancroft was not present to respond to these charges, a move was made to appoint a committee to confront the mayor with the group's demands. At this point, according to the *Chronicle*, "amid considerable confusion," Louis Baldwin stood up and announced that he was the representative of the mayor. He said "that the mayor had refused a hearing to men who had been disrespectful and disorderly and had accused his honor of being prejudiced in favor of the officer. The mayor had not yet held the hearing in this case, but he stood ready to give a hearing if properly conducted."[48] His statement was met by hissing from the audience. After more discussion, a committee was appointed to visit the mayor. It did not include Louis Baldwin.

In 1899 Baldwin again ran for alderman, and again failed to be elected.[49] But if his political career did not succeed, his real estate business continued to thrive and he became a well-known figure in Cambridge's black community. When a reception was held to celebrate the dedication of St. Paul's African Methodist Episcopal Church's new building in Cambridge, addresses were given by "the leading colored citizens of Boston and Cambridge," among them Louis F. Baldwin.[50] In February 1900, he and his sister Maria attended a meeting of sixty prominent Boston and Cambridge citizens on "The Right of the Negro to Be Educated." The meeting, called by liberal Harvard professor Edward Cummings, was intended to elicit support for Atlanta University, an institution that included W. E. B. Du Bois on its faculty and represented the ideal of higher education for African Americans—the antithesis of Booker T. Washington's vocationally focused Tuskegee Institute. At the Cambridge meeting Horace Bumstead, the president of Atlanta University, detailed the university's accomplishments and its needs, the writer Charles Chesnutt read two of his stories, and Alice Freeman Palmer, the former president of Wellesley, spoke of the North's obligation to support education for African Americans in the South. Maria Baldwin spoke briefly.[51] After the meeting a committee was established to help secure support for Atlanta University. It is worth noting that Maria Baldwin, not Louis, was named a member of this committee, which included Harvard president Charles Eliot, Harvard professors Edward Cummings and William James, and Colonel Thomas Wentworth Higginson.[52]

Louis Baldwin may have attended the fund-raising event for the university whose best-known professor was W. E. B. Du Bois, but he increasingly seems to have been drawn to Booker T. Washington and his circle. In August 1900, the first National Negro Business Men's Convention was held in Boston. The convention, organized by Washington and his followers, led to the establishment of the National Negro Business League. It may seem anomalous that Washington would have chosen Boston as the site for the convention, given the growing hostility of radicals like William Monroe Trotter, but as Mark Schneider has noted, Washington probably knew Boston better than other northern cities because of his dealings with white philanthropists there.[53] And black Massachusetts businessmen like Louis Baldwin were sympathetic to Washington's emphasis on hard work and material success. Baldwin was a central figure at the convention. He was a member of the planning committee, served as chairman, and was then made a member of the new National Negro Business League's executive committee.[54] In its account of the convention, the *Colored American Magazine* called Louis Baldwin the "Tom Reed" of the Negro race.[55] Tom Reed, the Republican speaker of the US House of Representatives in these years, was widely recognized as a master politician.

In 1901 Louis Baldwin undertook his most ambitious project, a luxury apartment house, The Greenacre, constructed on the corner of Harris and Oxford Streets in Cambridge, only two blocks away from the Agassiz Elementary School, where Maria Baldwin served as principal. Through a complicated series of transactions, in April 1899 Louis had taken ownership of the house at 196 Prospect Street. Maria was no longer listed as co-owner of the property. In 1901 Louis sold the house, doubtless to raise

FIGURE 7. National Negro Business League executive committee, 1900. Library of Congress, Prints and Photographs Division.

cash for the Greenacre project, although he and Maria continued living there.[56] In October 1901 the *Cambridge Tribune* ran a long article on The Greenacre, described as a "magnificent new apartment house" with "the most exquisite apartments ever offered." It was "owned by Mr. Louis F. Baldwin, the senior member of the firm of Baldwin & Dorsey, the leading real estate dealers of this city, and under whose direct supervision the building is being constructed." The project consisted of nine apartments of five or six rooms each "with every modern appointment." The article extolled the mosaic floor of the vestibule, the paneled walls and ceilings, the amenities of gas and electricity, modern sanitary plumbing and ventilation. A unique feature of the apartments was that "every room is an outside room with sunny exposure." In addition to the apartments, the property also included a twelve-room house, "the whole having a value of $40,000."[57] By June 1902, the project was completed. The *Cambridge Tribune* reported on the catered open house that Louis Baldwin held for the contractors who had worked on the project and for the press. An orchestra from Boston provided music.[58] The glamour of The Greenacre and Louis Baldwin's business success seemed evidence of Booker T. Washington's argument that hard work would lead to black social and economic advancement.

THE BOSTON LITERARY AND
HISTORICAL ASSOCIATION

Louis Baldwin's success may have supported the claims of Booker T. Washington's Negro Business League, but not everyone in the African American community was convinced that Washington's path was the correct one. There was increasing suspicion of Washington and his followers and their attempts to influence black politics, what came to be called the workings of the "Tuskegee machine." Opposition to Washington continued to grow in Boston, led by William Monroe Trotter. In 1901 Trotter founded a newspaper, *The Guardian*, whose motto was "Segregation for colored is a real permanent damning degradation in the U.S.A.—Fight it!"[59] That was the year Louis Baldwin was

FIGURE 8. The Greenacre, Louis Baldwin's "magnificent" apartment house. Courtesy of the author.

overseeing the completion of The Greenacre, and it was also the year of the founding of the Boston Literary and Historical Association, established as a venue for political and cultural discussion in the African American community. On March 18, 1901, the new organization adopted a constitution and elected Archibald Grimké as president. Both Maria Baldwin and William Monroe Trotter were among those appointed to the seven-person executive committee.[60]

In the late nineteenth century, literary societies and clubs were a feature of black middle-class life. They provided a space for self-education and debate in a society that often excluded African Americans from higher education and public venues. The Boston Literary and Historical Association was only one of a number of African American societies founded in these years that, as the historian Elizabeth McHenry points out, "furthered the evolution of a black public sphere and a politically conscious society."[61] The association was probably modeled on the Bethel Literary and Historical Society in Washington, the best known of these groups, which had been established in the 1880s. Membership in the association quickly grew. Like the Bethel Society, the association held public meetings attended by hundreds of people, many of whom were not members.[62] Elsa Barkley Brown has argued that in general the black literary clubs were dominated by men, but although the Boston Literary and Historical Association was founded by men, it was also open to the contributions of women.[63] On May 13, 1901, Maria Baldwin's close friend Flora Ridley joined, soon followed by Pauline Hopkins.

From the beginning, the association invited speakers on cultural and political issues of interest to both men and women in the African American community. Speakers in the fall of 1901, for example, included Frances Harper, Anna Julia Cooper, Professor Kelly Miller, and Alice Stone Blackwell, who spoke on women's suffrage. In 1902 the association presented a symposium on the emancipation of women. The subsequent discussion of the papers, the minutes report, "was participated in by Miss Baldwin, Mrs. Scott, Messrs. Forbes, Buchanan, Smith, and Sargent."[64] The association presented lectures on a wide range of topics of interest to black Bostonians, including presentations on Phillis Wheatley, John Brown, Wendell Phillips and other abolitionists, the role of African American soldiers in the Civil War, and contemporary questions of education and politics. For many members, the Civil War was still alive in their memories. At one meeting Archibald Grimké, who had been born into slavery, recalled incidents he had seen during the war when he was a young child in South Carolina. In May 1902 Grimké presented a highly critical address on Lincoln, contrasting the president's failure to address racism with William Lloyd Garrison's stronger commitment to abolition and equality. Grimké summarized, "Lincoln was a great American and a great statesman but no friend to humanity as evidenced by the negro." The association's minutes note, "The paper was provocative of much animated discussion." Grimké's friend Maria Baldwin was sharply critical of his presentation. "Mr. Lincoln," she argued, "moved above the feeling of the public. . . . Garrison in Lincoln's place would have meant utter failure."[65] This comment reflects both Baldwin's discomfort with political confrontation and her hope that, like Lincoln, other white politicians could be motivated by a sense of justice to support the interests of African Americans. But if Maria Baldwin still placed her faith in a great leader like Lincoln, her friends and colleagues in the Boston Literary and Historical Association were more demanding of immediate social and political change. According to Elizabeth McHenry, the goal of the association from the beginning was not just to provide an arena for political discussion and self-improvement; it was intended to "launch a self-conscious attack on the prestige and racial policies of Booker T. Washington and his 'Tuskegee machine.'"[66]

An example of the growing militancy of the Boston Literary and Historical Association was the January 1903 meeting, when W. E. B. Du Bois addressed a packed audience on "The Outlook for the Darker Races." This was only a few months before the publication of *The Souls of Black Folk*, which includes the chapter "Of Mr. Booker T. Washington and Others," in which Du Bois attacks Washington's narrow and constricted view of education for black youth and his contention that if black people would only demonstrate their hard work and patience to whites, they would be rewarded for their faithful loyalty. Instead, Du Bois demands equal access to higher education and full civil rights. In his lecture before the association, Du Bois developed his famous claim that the greatest issue for the twentieth century would be the question of the "color line." He tied racism within the United States to imperialism abroad, mentioning in particular white leaders' treatment of China and the Philippines and echoing the suspicion of US actions in the Philippines shared by many other African Americans, including Maria Baldwin.

In March 1903, Maria Baldwin was elected president of the Boston Literary and Historical Association. A month later, Louis Baldwin married Mrs. Estella E. Rector, a widow, in Washington, DC. Within a few weeks, the newly married Mr. and Mrs. Louis F. Baldwin were proposed for membership in the association.

The couple may have subsequently attended meetings, but there is no mention in the minutes of their participation in the association's discussions. At the same time, Maria Baldwin was moving toward a more vocal social critique and demand for racial justice. Her increased militancy clearly reflects the growing opposition to Booker T. Washington and his politics, led not only by Du Bois but also by the militant William Monroe Trotter. In July 1903, the tensions between the followers of Washington and his critics exploded into open conflict at a public meeting held by the Boston branch of the National Negro Business League at which Washington was the featured speaker. Two thousand people attended. When Washington was introduced, fights broke out between the factions. As Trotter attempted to challenge Washington from the audience, police moved in to remove him and other protesters. The result was chaotic, with the anti-Bookerites shouting while police dragged them out of the church. Trotter was arrested for disturbing the peace. This came to be known as the notorious "Boston riot." There is no direct evidence that either Maria or Louis Baldwin was in attendance, but given Louis's active participation in the National Negro Business League, it seems almost certain that he would have been there. If Maria did not actually attend the meeting, she must have heard first-person accounts from friends and other members of the association. Two months after this dramatic confrontation, in September 1903, Trotter and a group of about fifty Boston radicals opposed to Washington organized the Boston Suffrage League to demand full civil rights for all African Americans. Trotter was elected president.

There is no evidence that Maria Baldwin joined the Suffrage League, and she certainly did not share Trotter's combative politics. But she was becoming more public in her critique of racism, at least within the black community. In March 1904, at the end of her year's term as president of the Boston Literary and Historical Association, Baldwin presented a talk on the current racial climate. Two years earlier she had spoken to the association on "The Teacher and the Parent." That lecture, which she had delivered earlier that year to the Newton Education Society, was typical of the addresses she had been presenting to white educational organizations, offering an apolitical discussion of the relationship between home and school and arguing for better parenting and the need to instill hygiene, obedience, and moral values. Race was not mentioned.[67] But the talk she gave to the association in 1904, at the completion of her year as president, was quite different.

The extensive summary of Baldwin's address in the minutes of the association reveals an analysis that is much sharper than anything she had previously publicly presented. In marked contrast to her earlier apolitical talk to the association, in her 1904 lecture Baldwin now directly addressed and condemned white racism. "We hear a great deal of the white man's burden but have you ever thought of the dark man's burden?" she wondered. She agreed that self-help was good but pointed out that people needed outside help as well. She noted the impact of insults and contempt and the pressure placed on black people to make themselves worthy and fit. But, she asked, "what was the white neighbors' reward for Negroes when they were worthy?" She used the example of the Carnegie Library in Atlanta, which was open only to whites. Referring to Du Bois, who was then a professor at Atlanta University, she pointed out that the "most cultured man, the most brilliant writer, the profoundest scholar in that town was a Negro. No one . . . could be more 'fit' to enjoy the advantages of this library than he—and yet he was barred from it because he was a Negro."[68]

Baldwin noted that it had long been claimed the "Negro nature" was "buoyant and forgiving," but, she said, "the awakening Negro nature was not so forgiving." She gave examples of southern black teachers she had recently met who were deeply alienated by the study of American history. This is almost certainly a reference to the teachers she had taught in the summer at the Hampton Institute. One teacher had told Baldwin that "she was not interested in history and took no pleasure in it. Why should we teach our children to love the country that is not ours?" According to the minutes, Baldwin "was severe in her denunciation of the Jim Crow [railroad] cars and spoke of the prejudice that is growing against the Negro and regretted the fact that the friends of the Negro are growing indifferent and that his New England friends forget his sensibilities are as keen and as susceptible to insult as those of a white man." She demanded the right to vote for all African Americans and concluded that the Negro's "contributions to the world's civilization would be in the realm of art, literature and music rather than in the fields of politics and business," a direct rejection of the values of Booker T. Washington and perhaps also of her brother, Louis, who may well have been in the audience.[69] There is no account of how he responded to his sister's address.

"LOOKS LIKE THE TRUTH"

The year 1903 was probably the high point of Louis Baldwin's life. According to the account in the *Cambridge Chronicle*, his marriage to Estella Rector, which took place in Washington's Fifteenth Street Presbyterian Church in April, "was one of the fashionable events of the season in colored society." When the couple returned to Cambridge, the reception for "several hundreds of their friends" was held at his newly purchased house at 278 Harvard Street. A sign of his standing in the African American business community was the presence of Mrs. Booker T. Washington at the reception. The *Cambridge Chronicle* noted that Booker T. Washington himself had "originally intended to be there, but at the last moment his engagements in New York prevented his attendance," adding that "Mrs. Washington was the guest of Mr. and Mrs. Baldwin through all the past week as her husband is very well acquainted with Mr. Baldwin." The receiving line at the party included prominent local African Americans: Mrs. Samuel Courtney, Mrs. William Lewis, Mrs. Flora Ridley, and, despite whatever misgivings she might have had about Louis's friend Booker T. Washington, Miss Maria Baldwin.[70]

But in other spheres, things were not going well for Louis Baldwin. A year later, on April 23, 1904, the *Cambridge Chronicle* published a brief note in the section on real estate and building: "With liabilities amounting to $26,331.64 and assets of $6595, Baldwin & Dorsey, real estate brokers and builders, filed a voluntary petition of bankruptcy in the United States district court, Friday. The members of the firm are Louis F. Baldwin and Joseph A. Dorsey."[71] The lavish apartments in The Greenacre may not have been rented, or perhaps the expenses of building could not be covered in time. Whatever the cause of the failure of The Greenacre, its loss was a crushing blow. Elizabeth Pleck has noted that in the late nineteenth and early twentieth centuries, African Americans failed in business more often than any other group of American entrepreneurs. She sees lack of access to capital and systematic racism on the part of banks as key factors.[72] It is not clear what was involved in the bankruptcy of Baldwin & Dorsey, but it is quite evident that Louis Baldwin had no family connections or wider network to support him once he was in financial trouble.

Two months before the bankruptcy, in February 1904, doubtless hoping his affiliation as a Republican and his ties to Cambridge politicians could be called upon, Louis Baldwin sought a minor civil service position in Cambridge as assistant inspector of milk and vinegar with an annual salary of $400. The position involved a few hours' work in the early morning when milk was being delivered, and the salary, although low, would nonetheless have been significant to Louis Baldwin at this point. According to the *Cambridge Chronicle,* Baldwin was "said to be perfectly willing to accept the place."[73] The *Chronicle* reported that the civil service commissioners returned two applicants for the position — Matthew Hogan, a twenty-two-year-old conductor on the Boston Elevated Railway, and "Louis F. Baldwin, of the firm of Baldwin & Dorsey, the colored real estate dealer." Since Baldwin "was ahead of Mr. Hogan on the civil service returns" and had the backing of some influential individuals, he was expected to gain the position. But, the *Chronicle* reported, the inspector of milk, who made the final choice, "figured out that Mr. Hogan needed the job more and so gave it to him." That Matthew Hogan was white and Louis Baldwin black was not mentioned as influencing the decision.[74] Nevertheless, the racial connotations of the choice of the young Irish American streetcar conductor over the African American businessman and former councilman was not lost on everyone in Cambridge. In March 1904, the *Cambridge Sentinel* ran an article titled "Looks Like the Truth," which reported that a story was circulating that although Louis Baldwin had originally been chosen for the position, two aldermen had demanded that a white man be appointed instead. While the *Sentinel* article noted that political interests may also have been involved, the possibility that race was the true reason "is an awful condition of affairs if it is true."[75] It may have been an "awful" incident, but nothing further was done about it.

In May 1904, two months after Louis Baldwin failed to gain the position in city government, and three weeks after his bankruptcy, the *Cambridge Chronicle* reported that he had been appointed porter in the Boston post office at a salary of $500 per year.[76] By 1907, Louis Baldwin and his wife had disappeared from the Cambridge city directory. The 1910 census finds them living on Aspinwall Avenue in Brookline, Massachusetts, in a household with three other adult women, all listed as "mulatto," who were probably boarders. All of the other residents listed in neighboring properties on Aspinwall Avenue are categorized as white.

Louis Baldwin's position as a black man trying to succeed in the white-dominated business and political worlds in an era of overt and extreme racism was fraught. Through his father and his sister, he was acquainted with members of the old black Boston elite who were demanding full civil rights. But he also was a member of Booker T. Washington's National Negro Business League and seemed to accept Washington's cautious and accommodationist stance. Perhaps to further his own political ambitions, he defended a white mayor against accusations of racism. His presentation of his own racial identity was slippery, as shown in the information he presented to census takers in 1900 and 1910. Like his father, Peter, who sometimes gave his birthplace as Connecticut and other times claimed it was the West Indies, Louis Baldwin offered different versions of his origins. In Louis's case, the change was intended to suggest white ancestry. On the 1900 handwritten census record, he is categorized as black, but the original birthplace of his father as the West Indies has been crossed out and replaced by "Canada (white)." His mother's birthplace is still listed as Maryland. But on the 1910 handwritten census, Louis Baldwin is categorized as "mulatto," and the birthplace of both his parents is given as "Spanish West Indies."[77] Baldwin does not appear again in Massachusetts records. In the 1915 New York City census, a Louis F. Baldwin, fifty-two years old, occupation "real estate," was living alone in a room on 134th Street in Harlem; there is no mention of his wife. There is no further reference to Louis in any accounts of Maria Baldwin's life and no record that he ever returned to Boston.[78]

FRANKLIN SQUARE HOUSE

Louis Baldwin's financial collapse had a profound impact on his sister Maria. He had sold the house on Prospect Street to acquire capital for building The Greenacre. After Louis and Estella Baldwin's marriage and move to Harvard Street, Maria Baldwin continued to live as a renter at 196 Prospect Street. The nature of her financial dealings with her brother are not known, but any equity she had from the Prospect Street house must have vanished with Louis's bankruptcy. In 1905, Maria Baldwin moved from Cambridge to Boston. The circumstances surrounding this move are obscure, but she must have been forced to move, either because she could no longer afford the rent on the house on Prospect Street or because she was evicted by the new owners. Whatever the specific reasons, she left the large Cambridge house where she had lived for almost twenty years, and where she had brought together so many members of the African American community in literary groups and social gatherings, to live in the Franklin Square House, a residential hotel for single women in Boston in which she was often the only African American resident. In many ways this move captured the contradictions of Maria Baldwin's life. She was a school principal, a professional position of respect traditionally held by white men, but she was also a black woman living in an increasingly segregated and racist world. Her home needed to be a mark of her respectability, but she could not now afford to buy a house. Whether a white landlord would rent to an African American woman, no matter how distinguished, was uncertain at best, while the black community was increasingly being forced into more crowded, segregated areas in both Boston and Cambridge. Without the capital to buy a house in a "desirable" neighborhood, and without any family to support her or take her in, she turned to the Franklin Square House.

Established in 1902 by the Shawmut Avenue Universalist Church under the charismatic leadership of the Reverend George Perin, the Franklin Square House was intended to provide respectable lodging for single workingwomen. The population of single women workers was rapidly increasing in Boston, as it was in cities across the country. Women worked in department stores, the garment industry, and small factories; by 1900, nearly 20 percent of clerical workers were women and the numbers were increasing. Perin, who saw the goal of his ministry as reaching out to those in need in Boston, sought to establish a respectable and affordable residence for these women. In a *Boston Daily Globe* article, he described the project: "It is not to be a house of refuge, nor a charity nor a reform school. It will be for girls of small income, paying their own way and at the least possible charge which shall make it self-supporting and nothing more."[79] Perin campaigned for support among Boston philanthropists and reform groups for years before successfully establishing the Franklin Square House. On April 6, 1901, he addressed the Twentieth Century Club about his project. Maria Baldwin, who was a member of the club, may well have heard him speak. But even if she did not meet Perin, she would have known about the project, which was widely publicized.

The Franklin Square House was located in Boston's South End opposite Franklin Square Park. Although it was not the poorest area of Boston, the South End was a neighborhood in decline. A respectable bourgeois section of Boston in the mid-nineteenth century, the area began to be seen as less desirable with the establishment of the newly fashionable Back Bay neighborhood. By 1900 the South End was increasingly inhabited by recent migrants—young single white men and women from rural New England, New York, and Canada, immigrant families from

FIGURE 9. Postcard advertising the Franklin Square House. Courtesy of the South End Historical Society.

Europe, and African Americans from the South—all seeking work in the factories and small businesses of the city. The area contained both lodging houses and tenements.[80] The seven-story building that housed the Franklin Square House was a vestige of the South End's more fashionable past; it had been built as the St. James Hotel, then was remodeled and occupied by the New England Conservatory of Music. As a former hotel and conservatory, the Franklin Square House offered elaborate public spaces, including a library, reading room, and ornate lobby. There were also classrooms and free evening classes.

Conditions at the Franklin Square House were typical of a residential hotel. Each resident had a private room, some with a private bath, but there were no individual kitchens. Meals were served in the dining hall, and residents could invite guests to eat with them at twenty-five cents a meal. Rooms were cleaned and beds made by the staff. There was a laundry, and residents could pay to have their laundry done. Unlike at the YWCA and other women's residences run by charities, there was no curfew; residents were encouraged to meet friends, including male friends, in the downstairs public rooms. According to one account of the Franklin Square House, the early residents included "dressmakers, stenographers, factory girls, bookkeepers, teachers, milliners, and shop girls."[81] Maria Baldwin must have been by far the most distinguished resident. In 1904 the rates, including board, were between $1.25 and $7 per week, depending on the room and amenities. Maria Baldwin's annual salary was $1,000 or a little less than $20 weekly. Even if she took the largest room, ate most of her meals in the dining hall, and paid to have her laundry done, she could still easily have afforded to live there. In the early years, when she moved in, the Franklin Square House held from three hundred to four hundred women. In 1914 an additional building was added, increasing the number of residents to over eight hundred women. In a 1915 article, the New York Times called Franklin Square House "the largest residential hotel for women in the world."[82]

The Franklin Square House had many advantages, but its amenities must have been small consolation to Baldwin for the loss of her own home. Moving from Cambridge meant more than a change of address. It meant leaving the community in which she had lived her entire life, where she was a well-known figure who had the respect of both whites and African Americans. Now she lived in a single room in a large residential hotel, often the only African American among young white workingwomen. And Boston was becoming a more impersonal and hostile place for black people, despite its reputation for racial tolerance. As the African American writer Dorothy West wrote of Boston in these years in her novel The Living Is Easy: "Boston whites of the better classes were never upset nor dismayed by the sight of one or two Negroes exercising equal rights. They cheerfully stomached three or four when they carried themselves inconspicuously. To them the minor phenomenon of a colored face was a reminder of the proud role their forebears had played in the freeing of the human spirit for aspirations beyond the badge of house slave."[83] But the arrival of poor black southerners seeking to escape violence and poverty was another matter. By the turn of the twentieth century, increased numbers of African Americans, many of them poor, challenged the assumed tolerance of white Boston. And white southerners moving to New England brought their own more overt racism.

Despite the Reverend George Perin's humanitarian values, residents and staff of the Franklin Square House demonstrated the casual racism of the day. For example, they shared the common acceptance of minstrel shows, which featured white people made up in blackface as comic characters. At least during the first decade after its founding, annual minstrel shows were produced by the staff and residents to raise money for the house. The program for the 1904 minstrel show lists twenty numbers, including a "buck and wing" dance and the "cake walk."[84] The *Boston Daily Globe* described the 1908 minstrel show as having "all the prescribed features. There was a large circle, composed of girls seated in pretty white dresses and large red picture hats. On each end was a black-faced minstrel couple, one in man's costume with a full dress suit and tall hat, and his companion a dusky belle. The jokes went well and the solos and choruses were enthusiastically applauded."[85] The racism of the minstrel show was accepted almost everywhere in white society in these years, but the shows were deeply offensive to African Americans. Maria Baldwin must have observed the casual celebration of the minstrel shows in the Franklin Square House—her new home.

The minstrel shows were an example of unexamined and pervasive racism, but when Baldwin moved into the Franklin Square House, she experienced racism that was both more personal and more hostile. In *Following the Color Line*, his investigation into race relations in the South and North published in 1908, the white journalist Ray Stannard Baker cited an example of growing racism in Boston: "An attempt was even made a year or so ago by white women to force Miss Baldwin, the coloured school principal . . . who is almost one of the institutions of Boston, to leave Franklin House, where she was living. No one incident, perhaps, awakened Boston to the existence of race prejudice more sharply than this."[86] According to the account in the *Cambridge Chronicle*, when Baldwin moved into the Franklin Square House, "several southern girls" moved out rather than live in the same residence as an African American woman. The superintendent of the house, Miss Alice Grey, supported Baldwin, stating that it was "most deplorable that a good and accomplished woman should be debarred for this reason alone." Baldwin remained, but she received some criticism in the white press. Although the *Cambridge Chronicle* presented the actions of the southern women as unjust, it also equivocated that "while those who know her personally are aware of her culture and general superiority, it nevertheless seems a pity that Miss Baldwin should so place herself as to bring on such an attack."[87] The assumption, apparently, was that Baldwin should have found a place in the black community so the Franklin Square House could remain a segregated space for white women.

Baldwin's friend Archibald Grimké saw the incident in a different light. In his account in the black newspaper *The New York Age*, Grimké denounced what he called "colorphobia," which meant that "character, learning and womanhood" counted for nothing "if the person who possesses all these qualities happens to be colored." It was outrageous that Maria Baldwin's "fine character, accomplishments and distinction as a teacher and woman could not save her right here in Boston from the viperous hiss and sting of this American race hatred and contempt of colored people merely because they are colored." The result of the incident, Grimké concluded, was that "Miss Baldwin is still an honored, and now perhaps the most popular, guest at the Franklin House, while the four Southern fools have withdrawn from the house instead. Their withdrawal has hurt no one but themselves."[88]

Grimké celebrated Maria Baldwin but condemned the actions of another resident of Franklin Square House, a "colored teacher in one of the Southern universities of colored youth . . . who is white enough to pass easily, and who, as a matter of fact, was at the time actually passing for white." Even though this woman knew Baldwin and had visited her the year before in her home in Cambridge, she avoided meeting her in the Franklin Square House. Grimké roundly condemned her for cowardice, saying that she had a right to pass as white if white people saw her as such, but "when an incident occurs, as in the case of Miss Bald-win at the Franklin house, we expect, we have the right to expect, all such people to run up the red flag of their courage, of their devotion to the race. . . . They must speak then for the race, for the right, must place themselves on the weaker side of their race, be the consequences to them what they may."[89] Maria Baldwin must have appreciated Archibald Grimké's defense. She contin-ued to live at the Franklin Square House for the remainder of her life, apparently without incident. Encountering hostility and contempt as she tried to create a life in this new setting after the loss of her beloved home in Cambridge must have been a bitter reminder of the power and cruelty of racism. Although she con-tinued to speak for racial justice in many venues for the rest of her life, there is no evidence that she ever publicly mentioned the racist hatred she had herself experienced in the place where she now made her home.

CHAPTER FOUR

We Will Never Cease to Protest

By 1905, Maria Baldwin's long-held assumptions about her world were being tested. Her brother's financial collapse, the loss of her Cambridge home, the move to the Franklin Square House, and her direct encounter with racism there revealed the tenuousness of her vision of a tolerant and integrated society. For over twenty years she had worked closely with progressive whites in the Boston Society for Ethical Culture, the Free Religious Association, the Church of the Disciples, and the Twentieth Century Club. She was a member of the exclusive Cantabrigia Club, whose members included the most respectable white women of Cambridge. As principal of the Agassiz School, she was in a position of authority over white teachers and white children. But the incidents of the past few years—the prejudice of white clubwomen, the racist treatment of her brother Louis, her own encounter with the southern women at the Franklin Square House, and more broadly the continuing oppression of black people in the South and growing discrimination in the North— all challenged her belief in the possibility of racial harmony and the goodwill of white people.

The black intellectuals and reformers Baldwin knew and respected were increasingly militant in their demands for true equality and civil rights. Their differences with Booker T. Washington were growing sharper; William Monroe Trotter remained an implacable enemy, while W. E. B. Du Bois was becoming more public in his criticisms. Although there had been attempts to reconcile Du Bois and Washington in the months after the publication of *The Souls of Black Folk*, by 1905 the rift between the two was irreconcilable.[1] In October 1904, Du Bois had published a brief "Credo" in the progressive newspaper *The Independent*. Although he made gestures toward the values of piety and moral rectitude, the underlying message was an insistence on the equality of all races and the strength and pride of black people. Claiming the rights of citizenship for black Americans, Du Bois wrote, "I believe in Liberty for all men; the space to stretch their arms and souls; the right to create and the right to vote, the freedom to choose their friends, enjoy the sunshine and ride on the railroads, uncursed by color; thinking, dreaming, working as they will in a kingdom of God and love." According to the historian David Levering Lewis, the "Credo" was later published separately as a small poster and was widely displayed in African American homes.[2]

THE NIAGARA MOVEMENT

The disillusionment with Booker T. Washington was shared by a growing number of African Americans, particularly in the northern and border states. In July 1905, in response to an invitation from Du Bois, twenty-nine men, the majority college-educated northerners, met at Fort Eire, Ontario, on the Canadian side of Niagara Falls to discuss political strategy. William Monroe Trotter and Clement Morgan of the Boston Literary and Historical Association both attended. Despite her strong speech denouncing racism the year before as president of the association, Maria Baldwin, along with Ida B. Wells-Barnett and other black women leaders, was not there. No women were invited. At the end of the meeting, the men formed an organization they called the Niagara Movement and issued a "Declaration of Principles" that asserted African American claims to equality in all spheres.

The "Declaration of Principles" began by celebrating the progress that individual black Americans had made in the past decade but denounced the curtailment of black political and civil rights in that same period and the "denial of equal opportunities to us in economic life." It condemned the situation in the rural South, which amounted "to peonage and virtual slavery," but emphasized that "everywhere American prejudice, helped often by iniquitous laws, is making it more difficult for Negro-Americans to earn a decent living." It asserted the agency and ability of black men and denounced the view "that the Negro-American assents to inferiority, is submissive under oppression and apologetic before insults." It concluded that "persistent manly agitation is the way to liberty, and toward this goal the Niagara Movement has started and asks the co-operation of all men of all races."[3] The group was formally incorporated as the Niagara Movement in January 1906, and branches were soon established in a number of cities, including Boston. The leaders of the Boston branch were initially William Monroe Trotter and Clement Morgan. As a woman, of course, Maria Baldwin was not a party to their "manly agitation."

The Niagara Movement came to include most of the prominent opponents of Booker T. Washington and his ideas, but from the beginning there were tensions and differences among the members. Black politics in these years were complex, and Maria Baldwin soon found herself caught between shifting factions and allegiances. Although her brother Louis had been a member of Booker T. Washington's Negro Business League, Maria Baldwin was never associated with Washington. Her views were closer to those of W. E. B. Du Bois and friends like Clement and Gertrude Morgan and Flora Ridley, members of the Boston-Cambridge black elite, with its long-standing commitment to integration and participation in white churches and organizations. As a member of the executive board and later president of the Boston Literary and Historical Association, Baldwin had worked with the more militant William Monroe Trotter, who as a Harvard undergraduate had been a member of the group of students who met regularly at her house on Prospect Street. One of her oldest friends was Archibald Grimké, who had defended her over the Franklin Square incident and whom she had known since she was a member of Grimké's Banneker Club in the 1880s. Grimké's own political stance shifted over time. He had first been associated with Trotter's newspaper *The Guardian,* but in 1905 he began writing for the *New York Age*, a paper sympathetic to Booker T. Washington. To Trotter, and perhaps to Du Bois as well, this meant that Archibald Grimké was now a Bookerite. Grimké was not invited to the founding meeting of the Niagara Movement, although he later became a member. Sustaining friendships with these strong personalities would prove difficult for Baldwin as factions coalesced and split and individuals clashed over political strategy and power.

Baldwin became involved in the bitter quarrel between Grimké and Trotter soon after the founding of the Niagara Movement. The conflict erupted over the celebrations marking the birth of abolitionist William Lloyd Garrison, held in Boston in December 1905. Trotter revered Garrison and put all his energies and the resources of his Suffrage League into planning a major event. The three-day celebration included many of the leaders of black Boston as well as white supporters and descendants of the abolitionists. Julia Ward Howe spoke at one event, as did Pauline Hopkins. Soon after Trotter had announced his plans, supporters of Booker T. Washington announced that they would be holding competing events. At the celebrations on December 10, 1905, Baldwin's friend Clement Morgan spoke at two events organized by Trotter's Suffrage League—a ceremony held at the statue of Garrison on Commonwealth Avenue and a larger event held at Faneuil Hall—while her friend Archibald Grimké spoke at a competing celebration supported by the Bookerites, held at the Twelfth Baptist Church on Joy Street. Grimké's participation in the Bookerite event infuriated Trotter.

It is not clear whether Maria Baldwin was involved in either of these celebrations. She is not mentioned as a speaker at any of the events, although she is listed as serving on the resolutions committee of Trotter's Suffrage League celebration, along with almost one hundred others.[4] Being listed on these committees apparently did not necessarily imply active involvement. One of Booker T. Washington's local Boston supporters wrote Washington that "Mr. Trotter tried to include every Colored man woman and child in and about Boston. He has used *every* body's name as serving on some Committee, but the majority of the names

he is using without consent."[5] Although she was not on the program of the ceremonies on December 10 and 11, later that week
Baldwin presented a lecture on Garrison's life and work to the
congregation of Temple Adath Israel in Boston.[6] Whether her
lecture was connected to Trotter's group or to the Bookerites or
was independent of either is not known. Any connection with
the Bookerites would have infuriated Monroe Trotter, and even
maintaining a friendship with Archibald Grimké may have been
too much for him.

Despite its gender bias and internal conflicts, the Niagara
Movement attracted Maria Baldwin and other black women
leaders who shared its demands for full civil and political rights
for black people. Although no women had been invited to participate in the founding group in 1905, a few months later Du
Bois suggested the formation of a "woman's auxiliary" to be
associated with the Niagara Movement. To begin with, he suggested a small committee of women to make up the core of the
auxiliary, including Mrs. Charlotte Forten Grimké, Mrs. Clement Morgan, and Maria Baldwin.[7] Trotter disagreed. In his 1906
summary of the conflict in Boston, "A Brief Resume of the Massachusetts Trouble in the Niagara Movement," Du Bois noted,
"July 1906—Trotter opposed admission of women to the Niagara
Movement, and opposed Miss Baldwin and Mrs. Grimke in
particular."[8] At first glance, Trotter's opposition to Mrs. Grimké
seems understandable, given his anger at Archibald Grimké. But
the Mrs. Grimké referred to was not Archibald Grimké's wife,
who had died in 1898, but Charlotte Forten Grimké, the wife
of his brother, Washington, DC, minister Francis Grimké. But
perhaps to Trotter, all Grimkés were as one. His opposition to
Baldwin seems more surprising, for he had known her since he
was an undergraduate and had worked closely with her in the
Boston Literary and Historical Association. Baldwin's continuing friendship with Archibald Grimké, however, may well have
made her an enemy in his eyes.

Trotter succeeded in excluding Maria Baldwin from the committee to form a women's auxiliary. Nonetheless, she did join
the Niagara Movement. At the second annual meeting of the

movement, held at Harpers Ferry in August 1906, when women were finally allowed to join, Mrs. Clement Morgan was named the national secretary for women and Maria Baldwin was listed as a full member, although it is not clear whether she actually attended the event.[9] Baldwin did not take a leadership role in the movement, but she must have been well aware of its activities through her good friend Gertrude Morgan, who served as chair of the women's committee until the group disbanded. She must also have been familiar with the Niagara Movement's militant stance. In his final speech at the Harpers Ferry meeting, W. E. B. Du Bois pronounced, "Until we get these rights we will never cease to protest and to assail the ears of America."[10]

The militancy of Du Bois and the Niagara Movement reflected African Americans' growing sense of outrage at white racism. Just a few days before the Harpers Ferry meeting, a group of unknown men had rampaged through Brownsville, Texas. One white man was shot and killed, and military shells were found at the site of the shooting. Although there was no other evidence and no individuals were identified, local whites claimed that the violence was at the hands of black soldiers from the nearby army camp. In response, President Theodore Roosevelt dismissed the entire black regiment with dishonorable discharges. There was no trial and no chance for appeal. Black communities across the country were galvanized. September saw the Atlanta "race riot," in which white mobs attacked the black community. The number of black deaths was never known, but the official figure was twenty-five. Although events like these made clear the need for an organization actively opposed to racism, the Niagara Movement was short-lived. The group continued to be marked by internal dissension, particularly the conflict that developed in the Boston branch between Monroe Trotter and first Archibald Grimké and subsequently Clement Morgan. Trotter's dislike of Grimké seems understandable, since Grimké had left Trotter's paper, *The Guardian,* and begun to write for *The New York Age*. It is more difficult to untangle the reasons for the division between Trotter and Morgan, who in the beginning had shared leadership of the Boston branch of the Niagara Movement.

In 1907 a complete rift opened up between Trotter and Morgan. The immediate cause was a dispute over an event organized by Mrs. Ole Bull, a wealthy white supporter of the Niagara Movement. Mrs. Bull hosted a children's play, "Peter Peter's Pumpkin Patch," as a fund-raiser at her elegant home on Brattle Street in Cambridge. According to an account in the *Cambridge Tribune,* the play was performed by "200 negro children, representing the black-eyed susans, sunflowers, poppies, etc., in 'Mary Contrary's' garden, and the little pumpkins in Peter Peter's Pumpkin Patch." The play raised $65 for the Niagara Movement.[11] The Trotters refused to attend, apparently angry that Mrs. Trotter had not been invited to participate in planning the fund-raiser; they blamed the Morgans for her exclusion. Du Bois, who was caught in the middle, ultimately decided to support Morgan.[12] The Trotters then resigned from the Niagara Movement and did not participate in the group's third annual meeting, held in Boston in 1907.

Maria Baldwin remained a member of the Niagara Movement. Although she was not on the program as a speaker at the 1907 meeting, she was listed as one of the patrons of the conference. She remained friends with Du Bois, Archibald Grimké, and Clement and Gertrude Morgan, but her relationship with Monroe Trotter seems never to have recovered. As Trotter's biographer Stephen Fox writes of him: "The truth was as he defined it. Compromise was not flexibility, but cowardice. Other men were either manly or unmanly, with him or against him."[13] Du Bois somewhat more diplomatically described him to Mary Ovington as "a very difficult man to get along with whenever he differs from your own opinion."[14] A few months after he left the Niagara Movement, in April 1908, Trotter founded an alternative group, the Negro American Political League, later known as the National Equal Rights League. Maria Baldwin did not join.

THE FOUNDING OF THE NAACP

The Niagara Movement was a significant attempt to respond to the deteriorating civil and political rights of African Americans

FIGURE 10. Niagara Movement delegates, Boston, 1907. Department of Special Collections and University Archives, W. E. B. Du Bois Library, University of Massachusetts Amherst.

and to create an organization committed to achieving full citizenship and fighting racist practices, but it failed to attract a wide membership and lasted only four years. There were few white members; it faced unremitting hostility from Booker T. Washington and his followers; and, perhaps most important, it was split by internal conflicts. It had no more than four hundred members at its height. The 1908 Niagara conference in Oberlin was poorly attended, and after the last meeting in 1909 in Sea Isle City, New Jersey, the organization quietly dissolved. But there clearly remained a need for an organization to lead the fight for African American rights as the racial climate in the United States continued to worsen.

Some white progressives were also beginning to believe that a new organization for black civil rights was needed. Most white progressives had embraced Booker T. Washington in the years immediately following his 1895 Atlanta Exposition speech, but a decade later, there was increasing unease about his program of conciliation and hard work and his silence about racist violence and the erosion of civil rights for black people. In 1908, the muckraking white journalist Ray Stannard Baker published *Following the Color Line,* an investigation into race relations in the United States that offered white readers a firsthand account of black lives. Between 1906 and 1908, Baker visited cities and rural areas across the country, interviewing both blacks and whites and gathering material on race riots, lynchings, political splits within the black community, and social and economic life in a number of cities, including Boston.[15]

Baker visited Boston in 1906 or 1907. He noted that although there was no legal segregation of African Americans there, racist attitudes and practices were growing. While "a few years ago no hotel or restaurant in Boston refused Negro guests," he wrote, "now several hotels, restaurants and especially confectionery stores, will not serve Negroes, even the best of them." He described the increased prejudice among white landlords, who would no longer rent apartments or houses in white neighborhoods to black people. "The Negro in Boston, as in other cities," he wrote, "is building up 'quarters,' which he occupies to the increasing exclusion of other classes of people." At Harvard, where fifteen years earlier William Lewis, who was African American, had starred on the football team, now "a Negro baseball player was the cause of so much discussion and embarrassment to the athletic association that there will probably never be another colored boy on the university teams." African American medical students were no longer allowed to do residencies at the Boston Lying-In Hospital.[16] Baker saw only a few positive signs in greater Boston. "A colored woman, Miss Maria Baldwin," who was the principal of a school with more than six hundred white children and was "spoken of in the highest terms by the white people," was one of his rare examples of racial progress.[17]

A growing number of white progressives shared Baker's view of the worsening racial climate in the country. The year 1908, when Baker's *Following the Color Line* was published, was also the date of the Springfield, Illinois, race riot, in which a white mob inflamed by accusations that two black men had raped white women rampaged through the black community, burning houses and shops. At least seven people died, and the state was forced to call in the militia to restore order. That this violence occurred in the home of Abraham Lincoln shocked northern white liberals. In his article describing the riot, "The Race War in the North," the white reformer William Walling called for a revival of the spirit of the abolitionists and a new organization to support black rights. In February 1909, a small group of sympathetic whites including Walling, Mary White Ovington, and Oswald Garrison Villard, grandson of William Lloyd Garrison and editor of *The Nation,* issued a call for a conference "for the discussion of present evils, the voicing of protests, and the renewal of the struggle for civil and political liberty."[18] In May 1909, approximately three hundred people, roughly evenly divided between black and white, attended the two-day National Negro Conference in New York City. Speeches at the conference by well-known progressives, both black and white, denounced segregation and racist violence and demanded full citizenship for all. Among the speakers were W. E. B. Du Bois, John Dewey, and William Monroe Trotter. The only woman speaker was Ida B. Wells-Barnett, who spoke on "Lynching: Our National Crime." Booker T. Washington did not attend. At the conclusion of the conference, a Negro National Committee was established and was given the task of organizing a larger national conference to be held one year later and laying the groundwork for a nationwide organization.

It seems unlikely that Maria Baldwin was present at the National Negro Conference, since it was held in New York on a Monday and Tuesday—work days for her. Although she probably had not been present at the conference, she was chosen to serve on the Negro National Committee. She was a well-known figure, had been a supporter of the Niagara Movement, and was respected by Du Bois. She was also seen as a moderate who worked well with whites. In selecting the committee, the small group of organizers had to negotiate the tensions between Booker

T. Washington and his followers and the northern radicals deeply opposed to his ideas and tactics. Mary White Ovington, who was one of the organizers, later commented, "If Washington's name was omitted, the radicals agreed to have a few conservative names on the committee and not to include Washington's bitterest enemies."[19] In the end, the committee included well-known white progressives such as Jane Addams, Lillian Wald, and John Dewey, as well as Ovington, but only six African Americans.[20] Neither Booker T. Washington nor William Monroe Trotter was included. Instead more moderate figures were chosen, among them Archibald Grimké and Maria Baldwin.

The first meeting of the Negro National Committee took place on November 8, 1909, at the Liberal Club in New York. Du Bois was not present, and it is not known whether Baldwin attended. Oswald Villard, the white editor of *The Nation*, became chairman. At first the committee struggled. It failed to raise much money, its white members had other obligations, and there was tension between Du Bois and Villard. Still, the committee continued to meet and successfully organized the conference held May 12–14, 1910, at which the new organization was formally established and named the National Association for the Advancement of Colored People. The president of the new association was a white lawyer, Moorfield Storey. The only black member of the board of directors was W. E. B. Du Bois, who resigned from Atlanta University in the summer of 1910 to take on the editorship of *The Crisis*, the NAACP's monthly magazine.

The fact that all of the leaders except for Du Bois were white confirmed William Monroe Trotter's suspicions, but given the central role of white progressives in organizing the Negro Conference and the resources they had to contribute, it is not surprising that white figures dominated the new organization as well. As David Levering Lewis comments, "The widely held perception that what became the NAACP was started by African Americans is understandable but only symbolically true."[21] The presence of whites in the leadership of the early NAACP had some obvious advantages, most significantly economic. As Booker T. Washington's hold over white philanthropy became somewhat weaker, white resources moved to the new organization. But at the same time, the key role of Du Bois and *The Crisis* attracted northern African Americans. Although the NAACP did not formally replace the Niagara Movement, most of the former Niagara members, including Maria Baldwin, joined the new association.

In addition to the board of directors, a larger general committee was appointed to oversee the new organization, attract support, and raise funds. The committee included leading white progressives, among them John Dewey, Lillian Wald, Jane Addams, and Clarence Darrow, and black leaders such as John Hope Franklin, Charles Chesnutt, Archibald Grimké, Ida B. Wells-Barnett, Mary Church Terrell, and Maria Baldwin.[22] The work of the general committee seems to have been more symbolic than an active engagement with the day-to-day administration of the NAACP. Given her professional responsibilities and her commitment to other organizations in both Cambridge and Boston, this was doubtless fortunate for Maria Baldwin. Her appointment first to the Negro National Committee in 1909 and then to the general committee of the NAACP in 1910 probably reflects the respect in which she was held rather than an expectation that she would be centrally involved.

Baldwin was only one of a number of black women activists attracted to the NAACP. Clubwomen such as Mary Church Terrell and Josephine St. Pierre Ruffin were also early members, as was the activist Ida B. Wells-Barnett. The NAACP seemed to offer new scope for political action at a time when many black women's clubs were moving more toward an emphasis on class respectability and social work among the black poor. Although these women were more welcome in the NAACP than they had been in the earlier Niagara Movement, the new organization was still dominated by powerful men with traditional views of women. The leadership always seemed uneasy with the combative Wells-Barnett, for example, and she in turn had no patience with what she saw as their condescension. Historians have seen Maria Baldwin as more acceptable to the male leadership, despite the fact that she challenged gender norms as an unmarried woman holding a prestigious administrative position traditionally filled by a man. Paula Giddings describes Baldwin as "an unassuming, if accomplished, school principal" who was acceptable to both whites and black men.[23] Patricia Schechter agrees, arguing that for Du Bois and other leaders "committed to a manly response to racism," women like Mary Church Terrell and Maria Baldwin were far less threatening than radicals like Wells-Barnett.[24]

Baldwin's involvement with the NAACP was perhaps more symbolic than substantive, but she continued to be an advocate of the organization, both nationally and in Boston, which became home to one of the strongest local chapters. In 1909, encouraged by the Negro National Committee, a small group of activists had established the Boston Committee to Advance the Cause of the Negro. It was dominated by descendants of white abolitionists but also included well-known African American leaders such as Butler and Mary Wilson and Clement Morgan. In March 1911, the NAACP held its third national conference in Boston. Between eight hundred and one thousand people attended. Heartened by the growth of the NAACP, in February 1912, the Boston Committee to Advance the Cause of the Negro became the Boston branch of the NAACP. Its leaders were Butler Wilson and the white reformers Francis and George Garrison, the sons of William Lloyd Garrison. By the end of 1912, the branch had over 250 members.

Maria Baldwin was one of two African Americans appointed to the six-person executive committee of the Boston branch; the other was her old friend Clement Morgan.[25] Baldwin remained a member of the executive committee at least through 1915. The choice of Baldwin to serve on the committee was a natural one, given her involvement with the national NAACP, but it also must have reflected her connections to the white members of the Boston branch, many of whom were descendants of the earlier generation of abolitionists and reformers, as well as her long-standing friendships with both Clement Morgan and W. E. B. Du Bois. In contrast, although he had attended the 1909 New York meeting that led to the founding of the NAACP,

William Monroe Trotter never committed himself to the new organization.[26] According to Trotter's biographer Stephen Fox, "he stayed on the periphery, giving his support whenever the leaders of the group met his demanding principles."[27] Instead, he focused on his own National Equal Rights League and increasingly dominated the Boston Literary and Historical Association.[28] Baldwin, by contrast, was not a member of the league and seems to have withdrawn from active membership in the Boston Literary and Historical Association.

In the first decade of the NAACP's existence, the Boston branch was the nation's largest and strongest, and also the most integrated, with the greatest percentage of white members.[29] Perhaps because it was dominated by whites, in its early years the Boston branch took a moderate approach. As Frederick Jackson Garrison wrote to Oswald Garrison Villard in 1913, "Reasoning with, persuading, and appealing to the sense of justice is far more likely to cure evils than is a policy of attack."[30] In the beginning, the NAACP Boston branch focused on local racial issues, protesting individual cases of discrimination and segregation. In 1913 it was successful in ending the exclusion of African American boys from YMCA swimming pools and organized a rally against the Wilson administration's introduction of segregation in federal offices. In 1914 the branch successfully persuaded the Boston School Committee to withdraw a song book titled *Forty Best Songs* that included racist lyrics.[31] Maria Baldwin did not take a leading role in these activities, but as a member of the executive committee, she was made well aware of the daily evidence of the ongoing racism facing the Boston black community.

A DOUBLE LIFE

The first decade of the twentieth century saw the growth of a more militant consciousness and activism among African Americans. As a member of the Niagara Movement and the NAACP, Maria Baldwin shared this commitment to fighting racism, but she also continued to be deeply involved in her profession and dedicated to her work as principal of the Agassiz School. She led a kind of double life, well aware of racism and engaged in efforts to combat it, but at the same time participating in other reform movements and ruling over the small kingdom of her school. Admired and praised by whites and held up as an example of the tolerance and liberalism of Cambridge, she was respected in the black community as well, not only for her professional success but also for her integrity and strength. She was celebrated in the black community as an educator. Her participation in the summer school at Hampton Institute in 1899 is one example of her respected role in the world of black education. Another is the invitation she received in the summer of 1911 asking her to join the faculty of the Palmer Memorial Institute in Sedalia, North Carolina.

In 1911 the Palmer Institute was one of the most respected black schools in the South. It was a sign of Baldwin's stature as an educator that she was invited to join the faculty, but there was also a personal connection. Maria Baldwin was already well acquainted with Charlotte Hawkins Brown, the Palmer Institute's founder and head. Born Lottie Hawkins in North Carolina in 1883, Charlotte Hawkins Brown spent her childhood and youth in Cambridge. Like Maria Baldwin a graduate of Cambridge High School, young Lottie Hawkins seems to have viewed Maria Baldwin as a model and mentor. In an account of her youth, Brown wrote that in addition to the encouragement of her mother, she was inspired by the fact that "the position of Master of one of the select schools of the city of Cambridge was held by a beautiful brown skin woman, Maria Baldwin by name."[32] According to Brown's friend and biographer Ceci Jenkins, Baldwin knew Lottie Hawkins well. Jenkins wrote that "Miss Baldwin herself often gave the young woman much sound counsel. . . . She always advised her that it would be wise to do a large amount of reading—including current events and worthwhile books of various types. She said that she herself had had to follow such a course in order to cope satisfactorily with the mind of those children who came from homes where such matters were regularly discussed at the dinner table."[33]

Charlotte Hawkins Brown clearly shared Baldwin's intelligence and ability, but the details of her early years are difficult to sort out. Almost all accounts are based on her own tellings. As Glenda Gilmore notes, Brown's life is "so interwoven with myth—fiction that she fashioned to outmaneuver racism—that it is difficult to separate the reality of her experience from the result of her self-creation."³⁴ For example, Brown later claimed the friendship of Alice Freeman Palmer, the former president of Wellesley, and frequently told the story of how they met in the late 1890s in a Cambridge park, where the teenaged Hawkins was sitting on a bench reading Virgil. Later, although she had hoped to attend Radcliffe College, she decided to enter normal school to prepare to be a teacher instead. She then contacted Alice Freeman Palmer, asking for her help. Impressed by the articulate and scholarly teenager, Palmer agreed to help support her at the Salem Normal School. But Palmer wrote first to Maria Baldwin, who testified to Hawkins's ability and character.³⁵ It is not clear, however, how much further contact Hawkins actually had with Palmer. After only one year in normal school, Hawkins, who had changed her given name to the more formal Charlotte Eugenia, was recruited by the American Missionary Association to go south to teach in a school in the small poor black community of Sedalia, North Carolina. Almost immediately after Hawkins arrived, the school closed. Although she was barely twenty, Hawkins managed to raise enough money to establish a small school of her own. Alice Freeman Palmer died soon after the new school was established, and Hawkins then changed its name to the Palmer Memorial Institute in her honor. She always referred to the school by its full name when soliciting funds from the old New England elite, although she called it "the Sedalia school" when approaching southern whites and in her interactions with Maria Baldwin.³⁶

By 1911, the year she wrote to Baldwin offering her a position at the institute, Brown had become one of the best-known black educators in the South and the Palmer Institute a nationally recognized elementary and secondary school.³⁷ Baldwin's response to the invitation was somewhat ambiguous. After apologizing for her delay in responding, Baldwin confessed to being "sorry to have to write that I cannot go to Sedalia, as much as my heart desires it." She cited the changes made by the new Cambridge superintendent, who had imposed many more responsibilities on principals. Under the circumstances, Baldwin wrote, she felt she could not leave her post. She concluded: "There is no other school which I would like as much as yours. Your cheering account of progress gives me great satisfaction. I have great faith in you, a faith which you have never disappointed."[38] Baldwin well understood the need to support schools in black communities in the apartheid South, and it is possible that her heart did call her to work in Sedalia, but there were strong reasons for her to remain in Cambridge.

Baldwin's brief experience as a young woman working in a segregated school in Maryland had shown her something of the realities of teaching in the South, and her interaction with Georgia clubwomen over the support of a black kindergarten when she was a member of the Woman's Era Club had made clear the strain and difficulty of working with southern whites. Her professional success and her identity as a black New Englander with a commitment to complete integration and full civil rights for black people must have made the idea of teaching in a segregated southern school hard to accept. And it would have been difficult for Baldwin, who enjoyed universal respect and authority in her professional life in Cambridge, to move to the rural South to work under Brown, a woman she had mentored who was almost thirty years her junior. There is no reason to doubt that she was pleased by Brown's accomplishments as a black woman, and she certainly understood the need for well-run schools for black children in the South. But whether Baldwin really desired to leave behind the place where she had lived her entire life, her many friends, her position as principal, and the esteem in which she was held by both African Americans and whites is doubtful. In her gracious letter to Brown, Baldwin expressed regret that she could not accept the offer to teach at the Palmer Institute, but surely she was relieved to remain in Cambridge, where she could maintain her multifaceted life as a school principal, lecturer, and activist.

Baldwin's life in Boston and Cambridge was full. In addition to her professional obligations as principal of the Agassiz School and her participation on the executive committee of the Boston branch of the NAACP, she continued to participate in both white and black clubs and organizations. She frequently spoke on racial issues to white audiences. In February 1911, Baldwin and W. E. B. Du Bois spoke at a program sponsored by the Twentieth Century Association in Boston. Baldwin had been a member of the association since 1898, but this was her first public lecture there. In the years before the First World War, the Twentieth Century Association had become the leading venue for progressive reformers in Boston, sponsoring lectures on education, municipal reform, immigrants, miners, unions, women's suffrage, and foreign affairs. Speakers included such well-known figures as Harvard president Charles Eliot, Rabbi Steven Wise, and the psychologist G. Stanley Hall.[39] In his address, Du Bois spoke on "The Individual Negro and Society," urging Bostonians to strongly support equality in rights as an example to the whole nation. Baldwin followed with what the *Boston Globe* called "an eloquent address, in which she said that the doors of opportunity were not open to colored boys and girls as they were to white children and gave several examples from her own observations."[40]

In June 1911, Baldwin participated in a memorial service for the white abolitionist Colonel Thomas Wentworth Higginson. At the event, which the *Cambridge Tribune* described as "attended mostly by Negroes," leaders of Boston's black community celebrated Higginson's activities on behalf of African Americans. In her remarks Baldwin described Higginson's life as "one of beautiful integrity, the simplicity of which blessed the community in which he lived."[41] In January 1912, she addressed the Woman's Alliance of the Roslindale Unitarian Church on "The Negro Problem," a talk the *Cambridge Tribune* described as a kind of Bookerite celebration of hard work and determination: "There were no lamentations over the present situation, but a presentation of facts showing deprivations of opportunity, and instances of rebuffs and discouragements which try the spirit of those who have the desire for self help."[42] Another article in that issue of the *Tribune* noted that "Miss Baldwin possesses to an unusual degree the optimism of her race; but is not disposed to ignore the complex conditions under which she finds the race laboring." Her lectures were called "a treat both for white and colored auditors." The reporter celebrated her "rich, sympathetic voice, her rare choice of English and her flowing and eloquent speech."[43]

Baldwin frequently lectured on poetry, one of her great passions. Her former students from the Agassiz School remembered how she had them memorize poetry, and the African American Harvard students who met at her Prospect Street house recalled her love of Tennyson. In 1909, she lectured on Tennyson's *Idylls of the King* to the exclusive Cantabrigia women's club, where she was one of the few black members. By the early twentieth century, Baldwin had begun to celebrate the work of the well-known African American poet Paul Laurence Dunbar. When Dunbar died in 1906, she spoke at a local commemoration of his life and work.[44] In the next few years, she gave several lectures on Dunbar and recitations of his poetry, including two presentations to the Cantabrigia Club in 1907 and 1913. A *Cambridge Chronicle* article described the 1913 talk as "most inspiring," noting "her warm appreciation of the poet, expressed in the most exquisite English."[45]

Like many middle-class white women reformers of her generation, Baldwin participated in the broader progressive movement for social reform, including the settlement house movement, which emerged around the turn of the twentieth century. Settlement houses in the United States, modeled on British settlements such as Toynbee Hall in London, were first established in the late 1880s in response to the influx of immigrants to the country. They tended to be founded and run by middle-class reformers, offering services and education to the urban poor, but shaped by the reformers' own cultural values. The focus of most of these settlements was on acculturation, citizenship, and Americanization programs. In the cities of the Northeast in particular, immigrants from eastern and southern Europe had begun to replace the Irish and Germans who had previously made up the majority of immigrants. By 1900, 66 percent of the Massachusetts population were either immigrants or first-generation Americans, most of them speaking languages other than English and members of religious groups that were not Protestant—the majority Catholic and a minority Jewish or Eastern Orthodox Christian. The newcomers lived in crowded tenements, and their poverty, foreignness, and very visible presence led to a surge of nativism, a belief in an imagined past of linguistic and religious purity based on the claim of Anglo-Saxon superiority. In the United States, founded on a belief in racial hierarchy, newcomers with obvious cultural, religious, and linguistic difference were perceived as inferior. Nativism, which built upon the underlying edifice of white racism, in turn was intertwined with ideas of social Darwinism and the eugenics movement. But while the founders of the early settlement houses shared the nativist belief in the natural superiority of native-born, English-speaking Protestant whites like themselves, they also believed that with proper education and training, the newcomers could be assimilated into the dominant culture. The settlement houses thus came to provide valuable services to urban communities.

Although the great majority of settlement houses were intended for white European immigrants, there were also a smaller number focused on the needs of African Americans. These did not provide English language instruction or preparation for naturalization but were similar to other settlements in offering support for mothers, children's programs, cultural activities, and social groups. There was a long tradition of black women helping those in need in the black community through churches and informal groups, but at the turn of the century, black Boston women reformers, like their white counterparts, began to organize more formally to offer services to those in need.[46] In 1904 the Harriet Tubman Crusaders, a group of black women members of the Women's Christian Temperance Union (WCTU), opened the Harriet Tubman House as a residence for single black women who were discriminated against in the increasingly segregated Boston housing market. At first they rented a South End brownstone, but in 1909 Julia Henson, a member of the Crusaders, offered her own South End townhouse as the permanent home of the Harriet Tubman House.[47]

Baldwin's most extensive engagement with the settlement house movement was with the Robert Gould Shaw House, a more traditional settlement house in the South End which opened in 1908, four years after the Harriet Tubman House. The Robert Gould Shaw House was founded by Robert A. Woods, a well-known white Protestant social reformer who had helped establish the nearby South End House. According to an article in *The Crisis*, when black people came to the South End House for help, they were often isolated and met with "offensive remarks." Rather than address and challenge racism at the South End House, Woods and other white social workers decided to found a separate settlement house "in which the colored people should have first claim, though none would be excluded."[48] Supported in large part by white philanthropy, the Robert Gould Shaw House was located on Hammond Street in the South End in a four-story brick building with nine classrooms, a large auditorium, and a big yard in the back.

In a 1909 *Alexander's Magazine* article on the Robert Gould Shaw House, the superintendent, Miss Augusta Eaton, related the circumstances of its founding. Hammond Street was the center of a neighborhood that increasingly housed African Americans who were concentrated there, according to Eaton, because "the influx of Jews to the neighborhood scattered the Negroes and they moved further up into the South End." Eaton claimed that by the time the Robert Gould Shaw House was established, there were "between six and seven thousand Negroes" in and around Hammond Street.[49] The house offered a wide range of activities and services, including a kindergarten, sewing club, cooking club, boys' club, girls' club, mothers' club, singing club, orchestra, and young men's Bible class. In the summer, the house opened a playroom for children and organized picnics and outings to the country and the seashore. Although it accepted members of all races, the Robert Gould Shaw House was essentially a black space. When it first opened, it was viewed with some suspicion by William Monroe Trotter, who objected that in creating an institution directed at black people, the house was in effect perpetuating segregation.[50] There may have been some support for Trotter's views in the black community, but the services the house provided and the space it offered free of the racism often

found in white-dominated Boston seems to have led to its acceptance.[51] According to Augusta Eaton, the Robert Gould Shaw
House reached out to the local community, including the members of the Sojourner Truth Club, black women who, she said,
had "banded together for the purpose of a social and missionary
work and many cases of destitution were relieved and many sick
people made comfortable through their efforts."[52]

The women of the Sojourner Truth Club may have been
embraced by the workers of the Robert Gould Shaw House, but
the director, Robert Woods, also turned to African Americans
better known in the white community for advice and guidance.
In addition to hiring a black resident worker, he invited both
Maria Baldwin and Flora Ridley to serve on the council that gov-
erned the house.[53] Both women were members of the progressive Twentieth Century Club and were well known to white
reformers and philanthropists in Boston. Their involvement
surely must have added to the house's status in the eyes of these
reformers. Baldwin maintained her involvement with the Robert Gould Shaw House, which was located within walking dis-
tance of the Franklin Square House where she now lived. In 1913
she taught a class on English literature there. Although it is not
clear whether she continued to teach classes, for the rest of her
life she supported the Robert Gould Shaw House as a member of
its council and by fund-raising.[54]

Baldwin was also involved with a settlement house in Cambridge. By the 1890s Cambridge had become a major manufac-
turing center, providing working-class jobs for native-born rural
whites, immigrants from southern and eastern Europe and the
West Indies, and African Americans escaping rural poverty in
the South. In the last decades of the nineteenth century, the black
population of Cambridge began to increase, reaching 3,500 in
1910.[55] In June 1914, Baldwin was elected one of the directors of
the Cambridge Neighborhood House, located in an area of Cambridge populated by immigrants, Irish Americans, and African
Americans.[56] The Neighborhood House, which was more racially
mixed than the Robert Gould Shaw House, provided programs
typical of urban settlement houses of this period: a mothers'

class, a kindergarten, a playground, and classes for children and teenagers in cooking, music, art, mechanics, and drama. It was also home to a Lithuanian chorus.[57]

In addition to her work with the two settlement houses, Baldwin continued to be an active supporter of women's suffrage. In these years, the movement for the vote was gaining strength nationwide. Baldwin, like other influential African American women leaders such as Josephine St. Pierre Ruffin and Flora Ridley, had been committed to the cause since the 1880s.[58] In 1915 Baldwin was made an honorary vice president of the Cambridge Political Equality Association, a white-dominated group of leading Cambridge professionals and progressives who supported the campaign.[59] That year *The Crisis* published a special issue on women's suffrage that included pieces by twenty-six prominent African American men and women. Among the contributors were Alice Dunbar Nelson, Josephine St. Pierre Ruffin, Mary Church Terrell, and Maria Baldwin. In her piece, Ruffin argued that "equality of the sexes" meant "more progress toward equality of the races" and that exercising the right to suffrage would reveal African American women's high moral qualities. Dunbar Nelson, the widow of poet Paul Laurence Dunbar and colleague of Maria Baldwin's sister Alice at Howard High School in Delaware, took a somewhat different stance, claiming that voting was the expression of true citizenship and would allow women to move into the wider world outside the domestic sphere of the home. Dunbar Nelson argued that "no person living a mentally starved existence can do enduring work in any field, and woman without all the possibilities of life is starved, pinched, poverty stricken."[60]

In her contribution "Votes for Teachers," Maria Baldwin did not mention race. Instead, she focused on the contributions of women teachers, arguing that they had already shown that they exercised their vote wisely in school board elections, in which women participated in many parts of the country. "Women teachers," Baldwin wrote, "have found out that even so meager a share of voting power has given them a definite influence." Baldwin argued that candidates in school board elections had to take the views of women teachers more seriously once they had the vote. The extension of suffrage would only increase the power of women teachers. Furthermore, teachers had a "rich inheritance of idealism; to teach well," she claimed, "one must be devoted and unselfish. . . . Probably no other work is done less in the commercial spirit." With women's suffrage, teachers would need to "transfer to their use of the ballot this habit of fidelity to ideals."[61] Baldwin's piece is interesting both in what it celebrated and in what it failed to address. In focusing solely on teaching, she avoided the issues of discrimination, violence, and poverty faced by the majority of African American women. And in speaking of the generic "teacher," she not only ignored the specific barriers faced by women teachers but also was silent about the racism faced by all African American teachers, men as well as women.

THE BIRTH OF A NATION

The second decade of the twentieth century saw an even stronger grip of Jim Crow in the South but also increasing militancy among African Americans. In Boston, Monroe Trotter continued his defense of black civil rights through his National Equal Rights League and his newspaper, *The Guardian*, which was widely read in the Boston black community. But the national organization that spoke most directly against racism and for the rights of African Americans was the newly established NAACP. By 1915 the NAACP and its journal *The Crisis*, edited by Du Bois, were emerging as leading voices in the struggle for civil rights. Although the NAACP had been founded through the initial impetus of a small group of white progressives, its membership was soon overwhelmingly black. The new organization was immediately tested by a series of events that strengthened segregation and spread racist views throughout the nation. Nationally, African Americans across the country were shocked by the actions of the new administration of President Woodrow Wilson. African Americans had supported Wilson's 1912 presidential campaign, but they were soon disillusioned. Wilson, the former president of Princeton, was a southerner, and once he took office, his assumptions of white superiority and acceptance of racial segregation became clear. Under his administration, African American federal workers were segregated from whites for the first time since federal agencies were integrated after the Civil War. Federal agencies had remained one of the few fully integrated settings in the age of Jim Crow. After Wilson's change of policy, not just workplaces but restrooms and cafeterias in government offices were divided by race.

The NAACP mounted widespread protests against the introduction of segregation in federal offices, including public demonstrations and resolutions sent to both the president and members of Congress.[62] In Boston, William Monroe Trotter wrote powerful denunciations of the actions of the Wilson administration. A year after the decision to introduce segregation, and after numerous protests from the black community, Trotter was granted a meeting with President Wilson in the White House. According to Trotter's own account published in *The Crisis*, he told Wilson that segregation was "a public humiliation and degradation, and entirely unmerited and far-reaching in its injurious effects, a gratuitous blow against ever loyal citizens and against those, many of whom have aided and supported your elevation to the Presidency of our common country." Wilson responded that segregation was in the interests of black people because it reduced "friction." When Trotter replied that Wilson's view was "untenable" and that black and white civil servants had been working together without any tension for fifty years, Wilson was outraged and told Trotter that his manner was offensive. Although Trotter defended himself, the meeting was soon ended.[63] Wilson refused to cancel the segregation order.

The introduction of segregation at the federal level was a blow, but the most damaging expression of racism came in the spring of 1915 on the cultural front, with the opening of D. W. Griffith's epic film *The Birth of a Nation*. The film was based on Thomas Dixon's novel (and later play) *The Clansman*, a racist work consciously intended both to counter the narrative of *Uncle Tom's Cabin* and to justify the practice of lynching by portraying black men as animalistic rapists and the Ku Klux Klan as a group of noble white men defending the virtue of helpless white women. It was the racist nature of *The Birth of a Nation* that made it the focus of African American protest, but it was the quality of the production—its cinematography, its length, and the power of its melodrama—that made the film both so effective and so dangerous. Met with critical acclaim by white reviewers, the film was enormously popular with white audiences.

The Birth of a Nation revolutionized the place of film in US culture. Previously, most films had lasted only fifteen minutes or so, were cheaply produced, and were directed at working-class audiences. But *The Birth of a Nation* ran over three hours and told an elaborate and complex story. By far the most expensive film ever made, and the most profitable up to that time, it was the first to charge admission prices similar to those for live theater. It was shown at the White House, the Supreme Court, and Congress. *The Birth of a Nation* would have been notable in the history of film simply for its scope and innovation. But it also was a deeply political film, which presented a narrative of American history in which whites—and especially white women—were endangered by predatory and dangerous black men. The plot concerned the Civil War and Reconstruction, but the message was contemporary. As the director D. W. Griffith boasted, the goal "was to create a feeling of abhorrence in white people, especially white women, against colored men."[64] NAACP branches across the nation protested the showing of *The Birth of a Nation* and called for the National Board of Censorship to shut down the film. The organization filed criminal charges against the producer, arguing that the film was false, offended common decency, and would incite racial violence.[65] There was no response from the National Board of Censorship.

Racism in the late nineteenth century was pervasive, but it could be viewed as a stubborn remnant of slavery times. In the light of the rapid technological and cultural changes of the early twentieth century, there was a sense of endless possibility and a more equitable future. But *The Birth of a Nation* employed the most modern technology to convey the most vicious racism. Cinema, along with other new inventions such as the automobile and telephone, seemed a sign of progress. Racism, however, was not merely as strong as ever but was made even stronger and more acceptable when expressed in such a dazzling modern form. All across the nation, African Americans denounced the film for its racist portrayal of black men and its glorification of white violence. It was particularly shocking to black Bostonians, who saw themselves as the inheritors of the abolitionist tradition with full civil and political rights. The historian Evelyn Brooks Higginbotham described the conflict over *The Birth of a Nation* as "the most ominous racial incident in Boston in anyone's memory, probably the most ominous since the Civil War era."[66] All the leading black organizations and churches condemned the film, but Monroe Trotter and his National Equal Rights League and the Boston chapter of the NAACP led the fight to have the film banned. The Boston protests were the largest in the nation.

The Birth of a Nation was scheduled to open in Boston on April 10, 1915. In the days before the opening, black organizations mobilized against the film. The Boston NAACP and Monroe Trotter called for a hearing, which was held before Mayor James Curley on April 7. In addition to Trotter, Butler Wilson, head of the Boston NAACP, and Mary Ovington from the NAACP's New York office spoke against showing the film, while a number of figures, including the director, D. W. Griffith, spoke in its defense. Curley vacillated, and in the end, the film opened in Boston on April 10 with only a few of the more inflammatory racist scenes cut.

On April 17 a mass demonstration organized by Trotter and the NAACP was held to protest the film. At 7:30 that evening, over five hundred black protesters gathered outside the Tremont Theater, where the film was being shown. They were met by one hundred policemen with another hundred in reserve. When the black protesters attempted to buy tickets to the film, they were refused, although a white man was allowed to enter. Monroe Trotter was refused a ticket and then, along with a number of other protesters, was arrested for disturbing the peace. The few members of his group who were admitted to the theater threw eggs at the screen. Fights between blacks and whites broke out afterward, while across the street on Boston Common, speakers denounced the film and the treatment of the black protesters.[67] The next day, on April 18, a mass protest meeting was held in Faneuil Hall. Over two thousand African Americans and approximately three hundred whites gathered to protest the showing of *The Birth of a Nation*. The meeting was followed by a mass rally on the Boston Common.[68] On April 19, protesters marched to the State House to demand that the governor act to ban the film. Although promises were made, in the end the film continued to be shown. Protests also continued.

On April 25, 1915, eight hundred black women gathered in the Twelfth Baptist Church in Roxbury to protest the film in what was claimed to be the largest gathering of black women in Boston's history.[69] The meeting was organized by a new generation of Boston black women, led not by the old New England elite but by women who had recently moved to the city and who were more sympathetic to the militant stance of William Monroe Trotter than to the measured approach of the older generation. The main force behind the meeting was Olivia Ward Bush-Banks. A published poet, Bush-Banks had moved to Boston from her home in Providence a few years earlier. She taught theater classes at the Robert Gould Shaw House, where she may well have met

FIGURE 11. *Birth of a Nation* protest, Boston, 1915. The Crisis Publishing Co., Inc.

Maria Baldwin. Although she was identified as the organizer of the protest meeting, Bush-Banks was not present on April 25. Instead the meeting was led by Minnie T. Wright, a respected community leader and member of a black parents' group in Boston. Trotter also attended. Among the speakers at the meeting was the militant Dr. Alice McKane, one of the few black women doctors in the country. She and her husband, Dr. Cornelius McKane, had moved to Boston in 1909 after a long career in Savannah. In Boston, Alice McKane joined both the NAACP and Trotter's National Equal Rights League. She was shocked by the blatant racism of *The Birth of a Nation.* According to an account in the *Boston Globe:* "The malignant errors in the picture affected her so that she never wished to look again upon white people. She said she wept for a whole day after seeing the picture."[70] In her speech at the April 25 meeting, Dr. McKane urged: "Shall we fight for existence, or shall we not exist because we are black? I say fight, fight to the bitter end; fight until the last drop of blood is gone."[71] At the end of the meeting a new organization of black Boston women was proposed. Olivia Ward Bush-Banks was elected president and Dr. Alice McKane vice president.[72]

A meeting of eight hundred black women to protest the racism of *The Birth of a Nation* was a significant event, but Josephine St. Pierre Ruffin, Flora Ridley, and Maria Baldwin did not participate. Baldwin was involved with another meeting that took place on April 25, a protest against *The Birth of a Nation* held at the First Parish Church in Cambridge. According to an account in the *Boston Daily Globe,* "The church was crowded, the majority of the congregation being colored people." The speakers were also black, among them Baldwin herself, who read Paul Laurence Dunbar's poem on Frederick Douglass. Baldwin may have made a commitment to participate in the Cambridge meeting, but her absence, along with that of Ruffin and Ridley, from the large black women's meeting in Boston also suggests the gap between the older generation and a new group of women representing the changing population of Boston.

Although Maria Baldwin did not participate in the protest meeting of black women in Boston, she was deeply upset by *The*

Birth of a Nation. In addition to the April 25 meeting, she participated in an interracial event condemning the film a week later
on May 1, also held at the First Parish Church in Cambridge.
White speakers included the church's minister, Samuel Crothers; Charles Eliot, president of Harvard; and Oswald Villard,
head of the national NAACP. African American speakers were
Cambridge lawyer William Lewis and Maria Baldwin. Crothers
began the meeting by recalling the New England abolitionists,
who "stood by the side of any man who was insulted and made
his cause their own." He asked his audience, "Are we of the same
high spirit?" *The Birth of a Nation*, he argued, was not a work of
art or a spectacle; it was "an affront" that "taught that the negro
is a brute who must be kept down by sheer terrorism." Protest
"should not be made by negroes alone, but by all who care for
American idealism and for the rights of man." William Lewis
spoke of the outrage that Boston, "which Abraham Lincoln said
had done more than any other city in the union to bring on the
war of emancipation," should be insulted by the showing of *The
Birth of a Nation*. And the film was more than just insulting. Lewis
argued that it was propaganda, with the goal of "stirring up the
people of the east and the west and the north that they would
consent to allowing the southern program of disfranchisement,
segregation and lynching of the negro, and finally to the repeal of
the fourteenth and fifteenth amendments to the constitution."[73]
Maria Baldwin contributed her reading of Paul Laurence Dunbar's poem "Frederick Douglass," which she had also presented
at the April 25 meeting. The poem includes this stanza:

> And he was no soft-tongued apologist;
> He spoke straight-forward, fearlessly uncowed;
> The sunlight of his truth dispelled the mist
> And set in bold relief each dark-hued cloud;
> To sin and crime he gave their proper hue,
> And hurled at evil what was evil's due.

The choice of this poem, with its insistence on standing up to
evil, was quite unlike Maria Baldwin's usual offerings to white
audiences.

For Maria Baldwin, who had gained success in the white
world and maintained friendly relationships with white people,
The Birth of a Nation was a direct challenge. The film itself denied
the humanity of African Americans in the most stereotyped
and brutal way, and the uncritical celebration of the film and its
popularity with white audiences exposed the extent of white racism. A sense of her despair is revealed in a story about Baldwin
recounted by a white acquaintance:

> I never heard her say anything harsh, but once she did say some-
> thing which revealed her deep feeling, her sensitiveness to the
> wrong done to those to whom she belonged and loved. It was
> during the time of the presentation in Boston of the "Birth of a
> Nation," and she felt an insult had been offered to the race itself.
> I asked some of the colored race to meet with me one afternoon
> just for an expression of good-will and so I said to Miss Baldwin
> when I asked her to read from Paul Dunbar's poems, that we will
> just sing at the end "My country, 'tis of thee." She said, "Please
> do not sing that for it would break my heart when I know of the
> feeling of so many in Boston and throughout the country, who do
> not recognize truly the fact that this is our country. I might sing it
> another time, but not now."[74]

The Birth of a Nation brought home the extent of white racism
to Maria Baldwin and other black Bostonians. Pressured by
protests, the Massachusetts legislature finally passed legislation
forbidding performances that would incite racial or religious
prejudice. Nonetheless, in July 1915, the Boston Board of Censorship decided that the film could continue to be shown. Nationwide, *The Birth of a Nation* was banned in a few places, but by the
end of 1916 it was available almost everywhere. Yet although the
Boston protesters may not have been able to remove *The Birth of
a Nation* from theaters, they mobilized the black community in
ways not seen since the abolitionist movement.[75] This battle was
lost, but in the process both William Monroe Trotter's National
Equal Rights League and the Boston NAACP gained stature as
leaders of the African American community, and a new, more
militant generation was mobilized. The Boston black community

itself was growing rapidly as African Americans moved to northern cities seeking escape from the apartheid world of the South. Racist practices in Boston housing created more strongly black areas of the city, which in turn encouraged new forms of cultural identity and brought forth new leaders. Maria Baldwin's place in this new world was not yet clear.

Keen of Wit, a Brilliant Mind

The Birth of a Nation was a blow to Maria Baldwin's long-held hope that a more equitable and just society could emerge in the United States. In many ways the world was being transformed, yet racism was as pervasive as ever. Her own life was changing as well. She was sixty in 1916 and her health was beginning to fail. She was still the head of the Agassiz School, but she was becoming less active politically, making fewer public appearances, and was no longer a central figure in black political organizations. The world of African American politics itself was in flux. Booker T. Washington had died in late 1915, and the NAACP, which led protests against *The Birth of a Nation* in cities across the United States, was gaining strength. August 1916, more than a year after the protests over the film, saw the convening of the Amenia conference, a three-day meeting of black leaders called by the NAACP with the goal of reconciling the different factions among black activists. Two hundred invitations were sent out. In the end, some fifty people attended, including leaders from both the South and the North, supporters of both Booker T. Washington and the NAACP. Most of the participants were men, but a few women attended, among them the southern school leader Lucy Laney and clubwoman Mary Church Terrell. But Maria Baldwin was not present. It is not known if Baldwin was invited but declined or if she was simply overlooked, but her absence at this historic meeting seems symbolic of her declining role in the wider black struggle for civil rights.

After 1916 Baldwin retreated further from the activities of the Boston chapter of the NAACP, which were increasingly shaped by the president of the branch, Butler Wilson, and his wife, Mary. Mary Evans Wilson had grown up in Oberlin and was a graduate of Oberlin College. She was the daughter of a politically active family; her father had been an abolitionist, and both an uncle and a cousin had died as members of the Harpers Ferry raiders led by John Brown. After graduating from Oberlin, Mary Evans taught in Washington, DC. In 1894 she married Butler Wilson, then a young Boston attorney. The couple moved to a townhouse in Rutland Square in the South End, where, between 1895 and 1906, Mary Evans Wilson gave birth to six children. She was understandably not much involved in public life in these years. She was not active in the Niagara Movement, for example, although her mother, Henrietta, gave a speech celebrating John Brown at the meeting of the Niagara Movement at Harpers Ferry in 1906.[1] As her children grew up, Wilson turned her considerable talent and energy to building the new Boston branch of the NAACP. Francis Garrison later called Butler Wilson "the real life" of the Boston branch, but Mary Evans Wilson was equally central. In 1915 alone, she held almost 150 parlor meetings seeking to build support among African American women.[2] Maria Baldwin was not involved.

From 1905 until her death, Baldwin lived in the Franklin Square House in Boston's South End, commuting to Cambridge each day on the electric trolley along Massachusetts Avenue. Although in these years the South End was a racially mixed area with an increasingly black population, in the Franklin Square House itself, except for Baldwin, virtually all the residents were single white women. There is no evidence of further racist incidents like that created by the southern women who moved out in 1905 rather than share the same residence with her. Instead, by all accounts, Baldwin was greatly respected. After her death, a Franklin House publication described her as "unassuming, generous, full of wit and unusually intelligent . . . a source of great joy to all who knew her best."[3] But the Franklin Square House was a residential hotel, not her own home. She remained a single woman living in a single room, an African American professional living among younger white workingwomen. She had no close family nearby; her brother, Louis, had left Cambridge and Boston after his financial collapse, and her sister, Alice, was absorbed in her life in Delaware. She left no evidence that she was lonely, but surely at some level she must have felt isolated, given the contradictions of her life.

Unlike many of her contemporaries, Maria Baldwin never married. Other black women leaders of her generation married after they became established in their careers: Flora Ruffin Ridley at twenty-seven, Mary Church Terrell at twenty-eight, Ida Wells-Barnett at thirty-two. Baldwin's choice to remain single may well have been influenced by the prohibition against married woman teachers, which was widely enforced in white and integrated schools. Boston public schools, for example, refused to hire married women (or to retain women teachers once they married) until the bar was finally struck down in 1953. Segregated black schools seem to have been much less affected by the ban; there are many examples of black women who continued to teach in segregated school systems after they married. But for the most part, particularly in urban schools, the practice was widespread. It is not clear whether or not Cambridge had an official policy against married teachers, but it was certainly customary in Cambridge for women teachers to resign once they wed.

As is true of many other aspects of Maria Baldwin's personal life, the reasons she remained single are not known. Her sister Alice also never married. Like Maria, Alice was a teacher, but she worked in a segregated school where she had the support of a close-knit group of other activist black women teachers. She was one of a group of eight black women who founded the Delaware NAACP in 1914. Others in the group included teachers Edwina Kruse, Alice Broadnax, and Alice Dunbar Nelson. For the rest of her life Alice Baldwin lived in all-female households in Wilmington with other black women teachers, including Broadnax and Kruse.[4] Perhaps Maria and Alice Baldwin valued their professional lives over marriage, or they may merely have preferred to remain single. That we have no evidence of Maria's or Alice's romantic relationships with either men or women does not mean they had no relationships. It means that this part of their history, like so much of the inner life of black women of this generation, is simply unknown.

While virtually nothing is known about Maria Baldwin's intimate relationships or her feelings about living in the Franklin Square House, it is clear that she was deeply engaged with events at the Agassiz School. In April 1915 the old building was torn down in preparation for the construction of a new school. Classes for the rest of the spring were held in the auditorium of the nearby Peabody School in half-day sessions, with the lower grades attending in the morning and the upper grades in the afternoon. Baldwin not only was responsible for the logistics of holding classes in a new space and on a new timetable but also was involved with the planning of the new school building. One member of the Cambridge Common Council recalled that in the discussions about the construction of the new school, he "discovered the great executive qualities of which Miss Baldwin was possessed. In many ways the building was a tribute to Miss Baldwin, there was a distinctive atmosphere in the Agassiz school due to her personality."[5]

The new Agassiz School was a larger and more impressive place, and in August 1916 the School Committee voted to give Baldwin, as head of the school, the prestigious title of master rather than principal. The *Cambridge Tribune* noted that Baldwin was "the second woman teacher to enjoy the distinction in Cambridge."[6] It seems clear that Baldwin's promotion to master was not simply the result of the increased size of the Agassiz School. As principal, Baldwin had gained the respect of teachers, children, and their parents; she was well known as a strong and innovative educational leader. She welcomed outside experts to her school, including Harvard professor Ralph Beatley, who introduced new methods of teaching mathematics in the elementary grades, and a faculty member from the Museum School, who suggested new methods of art instruction. Under her leadership the Agassiz School held the first open-air classroom in

Cambridge, hosted the first parent-teacher group in Cambridge, and employed the first school nurse.[7]

In September 1916, just before the Agassiz School began the school year in its new building, the *Cambridge Chronicle* published a long interview with Baldwin that captures her professional commitment, her understanding of children, and her leadership. The public persona she put forward shows both the personal modesty and the professional ability remarked upon by both black and white observers. Typically, Baldwin was reluctant to discuss her own contributions: "'We hope to make the new school realize its possibilities, that is about all there is to say at present,' she said. 'You see,' she continued, 'I'd much rather not talk about things now. Everything is so unsettled. We don't know yet how many children there will be, and though my mind is just seething with schemes it's too early to formulate any definite plans. Besides, I'd much rather do something first and talk about it afterward.'"[8] Instead, Baldwin talked about the year of transition between the old school and the new.

Not surprisingly, the new Agassiz School was not completed on time, and classes were held at a lecture hall at Harvard for the 1915–16 school year. Despite concerns that the school could become "a neighborhood nuisance," things went well. At first, Baldwin told the *Chronicle,* she was worried that the children would be tempted by the many "lovely gardens" nearby: "Every time a child brought a bunch of flowers for some teacher we had to inquire very closely into where they came from, though it did seem rather ungrateful." But there were no incidents, and the children were well behaved. She was disappointed that the new school did not have a large playground but described the other advantages the building offered for modern education. It had "splendid, long corridors" for indoor games, and an assembly hall where a stereoscope could be used to show pictures—in geography lessons, for example. She noted that one of the parents was contributing photographs from *National Geographic* magazine. Baldwin praised the parents: "I can't tell you how much the members of the Agassiz School Parents' Association have helped not only with time but with money. It makes our work so much easier to have the cooperation of the parents." Baldwin concluded: "I want so much to succeed with the work and am looking forward eagerly to the opening of School. Perhaps there will be more to say then, but, really . . . I'm not the apostle of any new theory, and all I can do is to work as hard as I can for the success of the school."[9]

Maria Baldwin's characterization of herself was typical of her public demeanor as a dedicated and hardworking educator. Descriptions of Baldwin as a school leader all emphasize her authority and the respect and affection she inspired. But accounts of the Agassiz School itself differ between white and black observers. In the early twentieth century, residents of Cambridge inhabited a formally integrated city but in fact lived in very different neighborhoods and social worlds and consequently saw and understood the world through different lenses. Black observers' accounts of Maria Baldwin and the Agassiz School, for example, emphasize that the students and the staff of the school were white. On the one hand, in his 1917 article on Baldwin in *The Crisis*, W. E. B. Du Bois characterized the school as "one of the best in the city . . . attended by children of Harvard professors and many of the old Cambridge families. The teachers under Miss Baldwin, numbering twelve, and the 410 pupils, are all white."[10] Harvard president Charles Eliot, on the other hand, described Baldwin as "head of the best grammar school in the city system, serving the children of all races."[11] In her recollection of the Agassiz School under Baldwin's leadership, Isabel Whiting, who was white, described the school as made up of about four hundred pupils "of the varied American types of race, color, and creed, a fellowship unselfconscious."[12] For African Americans in the early twentieth century, the very fact that a black woman could be in a position of authority over white children and teachers was something to emphasize and celebrate. In white accounts, it is almost as though Maria Baldwin's presence alone made the school a multiracial institution. In fact, there may have been an occasional black student at the Agassiz School, but since elementary schools in Cambridge were based on neighborhoods, and neighborhoods were informally but strongly segregated by race and class, it is unlikely that there were very many.

If the student body at the Agassiz School sometimes included children of color, the school's staff was white, as almost certainly were the members of the Agassiz School Parents' Association. All accounts of Baldwin as principal and master of the Agassiz School describe her as having cordial relationships with both her staff and the members of the Parents' Association. Baldwin was a member of a number of white-dominated groups and corresponded with prominent white reformers. Less is known of her personal relationships with white people. One white woman of her acquaintance was Cornelia James Cannon, an active member of the Parents' Association whose five children all attended the Agassiz School. The Cannons' eldest child, Bradford, was born in 1907 and must have entered the first grade at the Agassiz in 1912 or 1913. The others soon followed. According to Cannon's daughter Marion Cannon Schlesinger, her mother and Baldwin "were great friends and she came often to our house for dinner."[13]

Cornelia Cannon was a strong supporter of public education. Progressive private schools were being founded across the country in these years. In Cambridge, a small progressive school was begun in 1915 on Shady Hill, near the Cannon home and close to the Agassiz School. Many professional and academic families sent their children to the new Shady Hill School, but the Cannon children continued to attend the Agassiz public school under the leadership of Maria Baldwin. Marion claimed that many of her mother's "more conventional and timid academic friends were shocked at her sending us to public school as though she were committing us to some sort of custodial institution."[14] In a 1917 article Cannon defended the public schools, arguing, following Dewey, that public schools were essential to democracy. They were common schools for the common good.[15]

Like many other white women activists, Cannon was involved with a number of social reform causes in the years before the First World War. She participated in the "friendly visitor" movement, which entailed visiting immigrant families to instruct them in proper cultural mores, campaigned for a public library, attended Cambridge City Council meetings, and wrote countless letters to newspapers on local and national issues. She denounced lynching and the Ku Klux Klan, supported the NAACP, and defended African American students at Harvard. But Cornelia Cannon does not seem to have been aware of the way race shaped her own life, let alone the lives of black people. As was true of other women of her class, Cannon's involvement in reform was made possible because she employed a servant. Cannon's daughter remembered a "long-suffering family of colored girls" who emerged daily "from some vague remote hinterland."[16] Eventually a black woman, referred to by Schlesinger in her memoir only by her first name, Hortense, stayed on as the family's maid and cook. Marion Schlesinger remembered the relationship between Cannon and Hortense "as of two equals: both were ladies."[17] This claim of equality between the white mistress and the black servant reflects a blindness to the realities of race and class that seems to have been typical of the prewar white progressives of Cambridge and casts doubt on Schlesinger's claim that her mother and Maria Baldwin were "great friends."

THE SOLDIERS' COMFORT UNIT

Maria Baldwin's world, with its delicate balance between her accomplishments as a respected educator in white progressive Cambridge and the challenge of being a black woman in a racist society, was shaken by the entry of the United States into the First World War in April 1917. As the nation prepared for war, racial tensions increased across the country. White resentment of black southerners seeking work in northern industrial cities led to white-on-black violence, most famously in the attacks in East St. Louis in the summer of 1917, which the NAACP later called "a massacre." In the segregated US Army, black units were given the most menial tasks, but the very presence of armed and uniformed black soldiers raised racial fears among whites. A few weeks after the East St. Louis massacre, in August 1917 a small group of armed African American troops stationed near Houston reacted to a series of racist incidents by marching into the city in protest. A confrontation with whites turned violent and resulted in the deaths of sixteen whites and four African Americans. In response, the entire African American Twenty-fourth Infantry was removed from Houston under armed guard. There followed a series of military trials of the accused African American soldiers. At the first trial, thirteen soldiers were condemned to death and immediately hanged. African Americans across the country were well aware of the stark contrast between these executions and the failure of white officials to respond to lynchings in the South or riots like the one in East St. Louis, where whites had attacked and killed blacks with impunity.

Despite white violence, the segregated army, and the racist and contemptuous treatment black soldiers received from white officers and enlisted men, most African American organizations, including the NAACP, supported the war. In The Crisis, W. E. B. Du Bois argued that black men should join the fight as a defense of democracy. Many others saw military service as a way to demonstrate black patriotism and bravery as part of the battle to gain full citizenship. There was tremendous pressure on the black community to be seen as patriotic Americans, whatever their experience of racism or the complexity of their private beliefs. As was true for other African Americans, Maria Baldwin was faced by competing loyalties—between allegiance to her country and the defense of her race, which was in so many ways being betrayed by that same country. Baldwin, like many other African American women, responded to this dilemma by seeking to help African Americans involved in the war effort, both soldiers and workers. She turned to a model of activism familiar to her from her participation in the Woman's Era Club twenty-five years earlier. Baldwin had not been active in a black women's club since, but in these years the black women's club movement had continued to expand. By 1916, the National Association of Colored Women comprised over 1,500 clubs. Although the political influence of the women's clubs would begin to decline in the more militant climate of the 1920s, when the First World War began, the clubs were still a powerful force within black communities.[18] The National Association of Colored Women's Clubs, for example, raised $5 million for the Third Liberty Loan drive and

$300,000 for the Red Cross.[19] Across the country, African American women's clubs were establishing social centers for black soldiers, helping black women working in war industries, and providing food and support for African American soldiers in their segregated units.

In her history of African American women's contributions to the war effort, Alice Dunbar Nelson claimed that the women threw themselves joyfully into war work and "remembered no grudges, solicited no favors, pleaded for no privileges." Instead, they were imbued "with the flaming desire to do their part in the struggle of their native land," putting "great-heartedness and pure patriotism above the ancient creed of racial antagonism."[20] But when Dunbar Nelson described the actual experiences of African American women in war work, the picture was different. For example, black women were excluded from local branches of the Red Cross or segregated into Red Cross units supervised by white women. They were not allowed to be nurses until June 1918, when they were stationed in hospitals serving black troops; the armistice came before any black nurses would be sent to the European battlefields. Dunbar Nelson described a gradual loss of enthusiasm for the war in black communities, doubtless, she said, the result of "the old, old stories of prejudice and growing bitterness in the labor situation; rumors of increased lynching activities—from all these a lukewarmness toward the conduct of the war had grown up in various cities."[21]

Maria Baldwin may have shared these misgivings, but she also clearly felt the need to support black soldiers. In the spring of 1918, Baldwin and her old allies Flora Ridley and Josephine St. Pierre Ruffin were part of a small group of African American women who gathered at the Franklin Square House to form a new women's club they called the Soldiers' Comfort Unit. Baldwin and Ridley were dominant figures in the new organization. Baldwin was elected chair of the executive committee and was one of the two "official speakers" chosen to represent the unit in public meetings, while Ridley's comments and suggestions are frequently included in the minutes of the early meetings.[22] Josephine St. Pierre Ruffin, now seventy-six, was also a member, although she did not take a leadership role. According to the club's minutes, the goal of the Soldiers' Comfort Unit was to extend hospitality and comfort to soldiers and sailors. That the group was an organization of black women and that the servicemen they sought to support were African American men in segregated units was implicit but not stated. A second black women's organization, led by Mary Evans Wilson, was formed at about the same time. This group began as a knitting circle, first making scarves and sweaters for the troops and then working with the Soldiers' Comfort Unit to organize entertainments and other services. Alice Dunbar Nelson, who had known Maria Baldwin since the days of the Woman's Era Club, singled out the achievements of the Soldiers' Comfort Unit in her history of black women's clubs and the war, calling it an example "of the hundreds of similar organizations made up of women who instinctively got together to work for the great cause."[23]

Only a few months after the founding of the Soldiers' Comfort Unit, Baldwin stepped down from her position as chair, perhaps because of ill health. She was increasingly showing the signs of heart disease. In June 1918, Mrs. Lucie Lewis was elected to replace her. But Baldwin must have recovered; in October, Lewis resigned and Baldwin was "unanimously named in her place."[24] In the last months of the war the unit focused on providing food and clothing to the troops at Fort Devens and worked with Mary Wilson's group to maintain a center on Columbus Avenue where black soldiers could come for hospitality and in the broadest sense "comfort" in what must have been an unfamiliar and possibly hostile city, particularly for those who came from rural communities in the South. Among its other activities, the center offered dances for the soldiers on leave in the city. The Boston civil rights activist Melnea Cass remembered volunteering as a hostess and dancing with the soldiers there when she was a young woman.[25]

To support these activities, the Soldiers' Comfort Unit organized fund-raising events of different kinds. In October 1918, the unit organized a month-long exhibition of sculpture and other artistic work by one of their members, Meta Warrick Fuller. Born into a middle-class family in Philadelphia, Meta Warrick had shown artistic talent at a young age. After completing art school in the United States, she studied sculpture in Paris, becoming a protégé of Auguste Rodin. She was a well-known and prolific sculptor when she married Dr. Samuel Fuller in 1907. The couple settled west of Boston in Framingham, where Fuller gave birth to three sons and for a time was absorbed in domestic responsibilities. She soon returned to sculpture. In 1913 she created a plaster cast of *Emancipation*, in honor of the fiftieth anniversary of the Emancipation Proclamation, now cast in bronze and situated in Harriet Tubman Park in Boston. During her years in Framingham she must have made connections with the Boston black community. In 1918 she was a member of the Soldiers' Comfort Unit. Her work was showcased in the unit's fall sculpture exhibition. It was for sale, and Fuller offered half of any sales to the organization.[26]

In addition to supporting a hospitality center in the South End and holding fund-raising events, the Comfort Unit brought food and other goods to the African American soldiers stationed at Fort Devens. In August 1918, Mrs. Walter Stevens reported on a trip to Fort Devens by twenty-five members of the unit, who "carried individually pies, cakes, and candies." Mrs. Stevens herself brought twelve packets of cigarettes, and others bought $10 worth of chocolates to bring. Mrs. Steven reported that "all of these donations were most gratefully received by the boys who in appreciation for this kindness served the ladies with lemonade and fruit. The ladies particularly enjoyed the lemonade as they drank from the army tin coffee cups."[27] The image of the respectable women of the Soldiers' Comfort Unit handing out slices of pie and cake and drinking lemonade from tin cups is an appealing one. But life at Fort Devens was not a series of friendly social get-togethers for the black soldiers stationed there.

When the war ended in November 1918, the black troops remained at Fort Devens. The first indication of racial tension came in complaints from African American soldiers of the segregated Thirteenth Battalion, 151st Depot Brigade, who were awaiting demobilization. According to letters they wrote to both the War Department and the national NAACP, the soldiers were subjected to racist comments, physical abuse, and humiliation from white southern officers. The War Department sent an investigator, who claimed the problem was solved. But in January 1919, a group of women from the Soldiers' Comfort Unit visited the camp again and distributed fruit and tobacco "to both colored and white." At the January 23 meeting of the Soldiers' Comfort Unit, several members asked about the condition of the men. According to the minutes of the meeting, the women who had visited found the soldiers "at first rather despondent . . . having dull, monotonous times." Lucie Lewis "asked for information as to why the colored men were detained in camp against their will." Maria Baldwin cautiously advised "a thorough investigation of conditions" at Fort Devens before the organization took any action.[28]

In the spring of 1919, African American soldiers wrote again to the NAACP, reporting that the racist incidents persisted and were becoming worse. Butler Wilson of the NAACP's Boston branch went to Fort Devens to investigate and concluded that the allegations were true. Nonetheless, the War Department brought no formal charges against the white officers, and eventually the black soldiers were discharged.[29] The conditions experienced by these black soldiers at Fort Devens were only one example of the racism that faced African Americans across the country. Lynching and other forms of violence against African Americans continued unabated in the South. In 1919, which one historian has called "the year of racial violence," seventy-eight African Americans were lynched, and race riots broke out in twenty-eight cities.[30] There was also new militancy in the black community, particularly among returning soldiers.

The minutes of the March 13, 1919, meeting of the Soldiers' Comfort Unit describe the visit of two returning soldiers who had been members of the "famous Buffaloes," a reference to the US Army's Ninety-second Infantry Division, an all-black division that fought with distinction in France in 1918. According to the minutes, Maria Baldwin asked the soldiers, "Has the experience in the war made the men any harder?" The answer was yes:

"Srgt. Johnson said that as most of the boys were from the South and they at the beginning of the war being ignorant of the use of war weapons, had now become most proficient, and upon their return to the Southland should reasons demand they would scientifically aim at the bull's eye and never fail." The sergeant also "felt that this war had done more for the Negro than any similar crisis."[31] This comment captures the militancy called for by W. E. B. Du Bois in his widely quoted 1919 column in *The Crisis* in which he argued that it was right for black soldiers to have fought in the war, but "we are cowards and jackasses if now that the war is over, we do not marshal every ounce of our brain and brawn to fight a sterner, longer, more unending battle against the forces of hell in our own land. We *return*. We *return from fighting*. We *return fighting*."[32]

THE LEAGUE OF WOMEN FOR COMMUNITY SERVICE

In May 1919, the women of the Soldiers' Comfort Unit debated the future of the organization, now that the war was over and the black soldiers were leaving Fort Devens. As Alice Dunbar Nelson commented: "After a year of work the Soldiers' Comfort Unit found itself facing a still larger field, the returning soldiers coming from scenes of horror and devastation with problems and needs. Like all of the war organizations of the women of the race, they found their work had only just begun."[33] The women decided to continue to meet. For them, as for other women, meeting together provided friendship and support, as well as a way to continue to serve the black community.[34] Now that the war was over, Maria Baldwin, as president of the organization, suggested that their goal should shift from supporting black soldiers to "an effort to better the condition among young girls."[35] The members agreed and voted to change the name of the organization to the League of Women for Community Service.

The League of Women for Community Service was not the only black women's group to emerge in postwar Boston. Another grew out of the service group led by Mary Evans Wilson. During the war, the two groups had worked together, but in 1919, after the war had ended, they formally established two separate women's clubs. It may seem somewhat strange that there were two such clubs, led by politically active women who had known each other for years. The sociologist Adelaide Cromwell, who knew black Boston society well, saw tension between Josephine St. Pierre Ruffin and Mary Evans Wilson as the source of the founding of these two separate but very similar organizations. Both women were not just politically active but socially prominent, being the wives of well-known lawyers; George Ruffin had been the first black judge in Boston, while Butler Wilson was the head of the Boston branch of the NAACP. There may well have been competition between these two strong-willed women, and perhaps past grievances too. The Soldiers' Comfort Unit incorporated an existing, long-standing black women's bridge club, which, Cromwell notes, "significantly, Mrs. Wilson had never been asked to join."[36] In December 1919, the group of women led by Wilson established a formal organization of their own. This became the Women's Service Club, which soon acquired a three-story townhouse at 464 Massachusetts Avenue in the declining neighborhood of the South End of Boston as its headquarters.

With the growth of membership, the League of Women for Community Service also needed a permanent home. Two settlement houses—the Harriet Tubman House and the Robert Gould Shaw House—were suggested, but in 1920 the club found a place of its own, the Farwell Mansion, an elegant South End town house at 558 Massachusetts Avenue, just a block away from the new Women's Service Club at 464 Massachusetts Avenue.[37] According to Adelaide Cromwell, the mansion was "famous for its carvings, rare wood and marble, silver door hinges and locks, gold-leaf chandeliers, and hand-carved mahogany woodwork."[38] The league was able to purchase the property with the financial help of Maria Baldwin, who must have been able to save a considerable sum while living in the Franklin Square House. Baldwin first took title of the property and then deeded it over to the league. The members of the league showed their appreciation at their April 8 meeting by giving Baldwin a chair in thanks. According to the minutes, at the end of the meeting, "the Secretary was prevailed upon to kidnap the President from the room so that formal action could be taken for presenting Miss Baldwin with the chair she had so admired."[39]

The League of Women for Community Service met weekly from September through June. It focused on service work in the black community, emphasizing support for girls, but also sponsored a soup kitchen, gave food and clothing to needy families, and held bazaars and other fund-raisers for St. Monica's Home, Charlotte Hawkins Brown's school in Sedalia, and other recipients. As Lorraine Roses documents, the league was also central in the black community of Boston in supporting cultural events and black artists.[40] These forms of community support were typical of black women's clubs across the county. While these groups have been criticized for providing charity rather than working for deeper political change, Geoff Ward has argued that, given entrenched racism, charity sometimes was the only possible course of action to address the pressing needs of the black community, and the clubs' activities prepared the way for the later civil rights movement.[41] In the case of the League of Women for Community Service, the club not only supported social improvement projects similar to those undertaken by white women's clubs but also, like the NAACP and other black organizations, was centrally concerned with questions of race and ways to combat racism.

FIGURE 12. Mobilizing the next generation against racism: *The Crisis*, 1918. The Crisis Publishing Co., Inc.

In the meetings of the League of Women for Community Service, Maria Baldwin often acted as a teacher, raising issues and
suggesting readings to the members of the club. In early 1919 she
recommended that members read an article called "Reconstruction and the Colored Woman" in the trade union journal *Life
and Labor*. The article, written by Forrester Washington, a black
social worker who had graduated from Tufts in 1909 and probably was personally known to Baldwin, documented the racist
discrimination faced by black women workers at the end of the
war. Black women, Washington wrote, "have been universally
the last to be employed. They have been given, with exceptions,
the most undesirable and lowest paid work and now that the war
is over they are the first to be released." He called on employers
to meet "the democratic ideal" of fairness.[42] There is no record of
the women's discussion of this article, but Washington's account
of the treatment of black women workers is an example of the
kinds of topics discussed by the women of the league, who were
well aware of both racism and growing protest in the black
community. At the April 1920 meeting of the league, the women
discussed racial discrimination in the Massachusetts National
Guard. A committee was appointed to draft a petition to the governor "protesting against the effort to drop col'd from the Militia."[43] Later that month, Baldwin urged all the members to read
W. E. B. Du Bois's recently published *Darkwater*, a compilation of
his autobiographical pieces, poems, and social criticism.[44]

In *Darkwater*, Du Bois touches on a wide range of topics: the
underlying colonial rivalries that led to the First World War, the
cultural achievements of Africa, the connections between capi-
talism and racism, the contributions of black women, women's
right to the vote, and his own experiences of racism. In many
ways, *Darkwater* continues the themes of *The Souls of Black Folk*,
published seventeen years earlier, but the pieces in *Darkwater*
are sharper in their critique of racism and more clearly directed
to a black audience. In the chapter "The Souls of White Folk,"
for example, Du Bois points out that the concept of whiteness,
"a very modern thing," is grounded in the "assumption that of
all the hues of God whiteness alone is inherently and obviously

better than brownness or tan."[45] Du Bois then traces the murderous expressions of racism—the lynchings, the white race riots,
the insults and humiliations that African Americans in both
North and South understood and experienced. He also challenges the meaning of white charity:

> So long . . . as humble black folk, voluble with thanks, receive bar-
> rels of old clothes from lordly and generous whites, there is much
> mental peace and moral satisfaction. But when the black man
> begins to dispute the white man's title to certain alleged bequests
> of the Fathers in wage and position, authority and training, and
> when his attitude toward charity is sullen anger rather than hum-
> ble jollity . . . then the spell is suddenly broken, and the philanthro-
> pist is ready to believe that Negroes are impudent, that the South
> is right.[46]

In the chapter "Of Work and Wealth," Du Bois reveals his own
ambivalence about relationships with whites. When young black
students asked him, "Do you trust white people?" Du Bois felt he
had to lie and say yes, but in fact, he said to himself, "You do not
and you know that you do not, much as you want to."[47]

Maria Baldwin was clearly moved by *Darkwater*. Du Bois's
analysis of whiteness and the almost universal assumption of
superiority held by white people must have touched her deeply
and perhaps crystallized her own uneasiness about the unspoken
beliefs of white people about race, particularly as the eugenics
movement and ideas of scientific racism gained strength across
the country and in the white Cambridge academic community
she knew so well. In addition to suggesting that the members
of the League of Women for Community Service read *Darkwater*, she discussed it with her friends and acquaintances, among
them Cornelia James Cannon. Later, Cannon told her daughter
Marion Schlesinger that Baldwin was "big and tolerant about
the whole subject."[48]

Like many other white Cambridge progressives, Cornelia
James Cannon admired Maria Baldwin. After Baldwin's death,
Cannon wrote effusive appreciations of Baldwin as a school
principal and as a person. She spoke of Baldwin's "combination

of tenderness and firmness" that "made her beloved and revered by the children under her care and enabled her to achieve a school atmosphere combining to an unusual degree, freedom and control."[49] But Cannon held contradictory ideas about race. Easily swept up in political and cultural crusades, she embraced the eugenics movement. Harvard was one of the centers of academic eugenics. Harvard faculty members were influential advocates, founding pro-eugenics groups, publishing articles in scholarly journals, and actively supporting laws prescribing the sterilization of "defective" individuals. Eugenics was deeply intertwined with ideas of racial hierarchy that placed those of northern European descent (so-called true whites) at the top and other groups in descending order beneath them, from Italians to "Asiatics" to Africans. Both Harvard president Charles Eliot and his successor, Lawrence Lowell, were enthusiastic advocates of eugenics. Eliot, a believer in racial purity, included Irish Catholics among the lower orders, while Lowell supported Harvard's quota on Jewish students.[50] Cannon eagerly adopted these views, confident of white racial superiority and fearful of the taint of immigrants and black people. Although she praised Maria Baldwin, she seems to have placed her in a separate mental category from African Americans in general. In 1920, the same year Baldwin was discussing *Darkwater* with her, Cannon wrote to her mother, "I wish we could have an Anglo-Saxon civilization." Cannon's biographer Maria Dietrich believes that underlying Cannon's eugenicist views was "an all-pervasive, bottomless dread of racial displacement."[51]

In the early 1920s, Cannon began to publish articles defending eugenics. In her 1922 article "American Misgivings," she cited the results of the intelligence tests developed for the US Army in World War I by her friend Robert Yerkes, a Harvard professor who had served a term as president of the American Psychological Association. The tests, which at the time were seen as scientific proof of an innate racial hierarchy and black inferiority, are now viewed as deeply racist and a prime example of the destructive impact of weak and poorly constructed psychological methods.[52] They claimed to show that 89 percent of "Negro" recruits were under the mental age of thirteen, as opposed to 47 percent of white recruits. The results were sobering in general, but to Cannon they showed conclusively that, as she wrote, "in the education of the negro race, we are confronted by an educational problem of a very special kind."[53] For Cannon, the answer was segregation and vocational education. Cannon must have been preparing this article in the final months of Baldwin's life, a time when Cannon's daughter Marion Schlesinger remembered them as "the best of friends."[54] Perhaps Maria Baldwin had some sense of Cannon's views. When she suggested that Cannon read Du Bois's *Darkwater*, was she thinking of Du Bois's critique of whiteness and his own distrust of white people?

It may have been the growth of scientific racism and the eugenics movement, or the widespread popularity and acceptance of *The Birth of a Nation* among whites, or the continuing white-on-black violence and increasing black militancy in the aftermath of the First World War, but Maria Baldwin more and more moved away from involvement in white-dominated organizations and looked instead to the League of Women for Community Service as a home for her activism. Baldwin had long been a supporter of women's suffrage, and like progressive women across the country, after the passage of the Nineteenth Amendment in August 1920, she turned her attention to mobilizing the women's vote. Once the amendment became law, the league invited white representatives of both the Republican women's committee and the League of Women Voters to come and speak about getting out the women's vote.[55] But despite reaching out to create an alliance with white reformers, the group's members focused their own energies on black women.

Baldwin and the League of Women for Community Service continued to support other projects and institutions in the black community, among them the Palmer Memorial Institute, Charlotte Hawkins Brown's school in Sedalia, North Carolina. In January 1921, Baldwin participated in a benefit program held at Harvard for the Palmer Institute, which an article in the *Cambridge Tribune* described as a "School Conducted by Former Cambridge Girl." The program included a presentation of the accomplishments and needs of the school and music by "talented colored men and women." Baldwin read from the poems of Paul Lawrence Dunbar.[56] In a February 1921 letter to Brown, Baldwin noted that a number of members of the league had attended the Harvard program, some had already bought tickets to an upcoming Boston benefit concert, and members had made various kinds of handwork (including twenty-five hats) to be sold at a benefit fair for Sedalia.[57]

The members of the League of Women for Community Service clearly appreciated Baldwin. February 1921 was the first anniversary of the league's purchase of 558 Massachusetts Avenue. According to the minutes of the league's February meeting, Flora Ridley "made a few graphic and felicitous references to the occasion in her weekly report—and the entire membership felt highly honored in learning that we still have the 'Cambridge monument' in the President's chair."[58] At the annual election of officers held later that month, Baldwin was easily reelected president. But in June 1921, she once again stepped down from leadership of the league, perhaps another indication of her weakened physical condition as a result of heart disease. But when the league reconvened after its summer break in September, Baldwin was back. The minutes noted, "We all rejoiced to welcome the return of our Pres. who presided with her usual grace and charm and who in her introductory remarks emphasized the importance of carrying on all work and activities that have been outlined for the coming season."[59]

The league continued to be concerned about racial issues both in the North and in the South, where rural black people lived under a system of sharecropping, a form of tenant farming very close to servitude. At a meeting in the spring of 1921 on the issue, Flora Ridley read "an editorial from the *New York Age* touching on the peonage cases in Georgia." The group decided to send a letter of protest to the Georgia congressmen.[60] Then, at the September 15 meeting that year, regular business was suspended while the league heard a stark firsthand account of racist violence from an African American couple who were "refugees from Tulsa, Oklahoma," a reference to the recent Tulsa race massacre.

When a group of armed black men in Tulsa had gathered to protect a black man from a possible lynching, enraged white mobs
supported by white National Guard units burned and destroyed
homes, churches, and businesses in the black section of Tulsa;
estimates of deaths ranged from 35 to 150, and hundreds were
left homeless.[61] The Tulsa man at the league meeting "gave a very
graphic description of the horrors of the riot in that city. . . . Very
pathetic also was the story of how he and his family escaped
with only their lives." The league presented the family with $27
and sent clothing to other victims.[62]

SHE DIED A TEACHER

The account of the Tulsa riot brought the realities of murderous
white racism vividly home to the Massachusetts members of the
League of Women for Community Service and surely confirmed
their dedication to supporting the black community. But Maria
Baldwin would not be a part of any future struggles. On January 9, 1922, she collapsed at the Copley Plaza Hotel in Boston
while speaking at a fund-raising event for the Robert Gould
Shaw House. She was rushed to the hospital but died before she
arrived. Flora Ridley, who was attending the meeting with her,
accompanied her in the ambulance.[63] The cause of her death was
given as "heart trouble." She was sixty-six years old. Cornelia
James Cannon later described the immediate impact of her death
on the Agassiz School: "I went up the next day and spent the
morning at the school—the weeping heartbroken teachers could
hardly control themselves enough to carry on the school and the
children were full of awe and sadness."[64]

Baldwin's funeral was held at the historic Arlington Street
Church in Boston. The large Unitarian church was filled. According to one obituary, among the mourners were "the entire Agassiz Grammar school of Cambridge, the Cambridge school
committee, with most of the officials of that city."[65] For two days
before the funeral, her body had lain in the parlor of the League
of Women for Community Service at 558 Massachusetts Avenue,
surrounded by floral arrangements, several from the parents,

teachers, and students of the Agassiz School. Seven ministers, black and white, participated in the funeral service. Both black and white men were pallbearers. The white pallbearers included one of the founders of the Ethical Society of Boston and several other supporters of African American causes. Black pallbearers included Clement Morgan and Flora Ridley's husband, Ulysses Ridley.[66]

Maria Baldwin's death elicited numerous statements of condolence and tributes to her as a person and as an educator. For many whites, Baldwin was a loving maternal figure who had dedicated her life to the children of the Agassiz School. Cornelia Cannon wrote in the *Cambridge Chronicle* that "generations of children look back with loving gratitude to the training she gave them in truth telling, uprightness, consideration for others and devotion to duty."[67] Another parent marveled "at the wisdom and gentleness with which she dealt with each problem. . . . She had a remarkable power of enlisting the child's cooperation in any disciplinary problems. She never felt, and she never failed to tell the child so, that it was any victory to impose her will upon him. The child must make the decision and take the action himself."[68] On January 30, 1922, a meeting of the Cambridge School Committee entered a statement about her career into its minutes. It referred to her life of service, her "influence for good," her "high courage in overcoming obstacles," and her "devotion to her chosen work." In its resolution on the occasion of her death, the Cambridge City Council touched on the same themes, concluding, "Her life was gentle, and the element of goodness was strongly entrenched in a nature that felt deeply the religion that spells service."[69] A tribute to Baldwin was published in the Franklin Square House journal *Girls* a week after her death. The tribute praised her graciousness but also her wit and intelligence. It concluded with a poem containing these lines:

> She has gone and we will miss her
> There will be one vacant chair,
> But our thoughts are rich with memories,
> Of her spirit, splendid — rare!
> Kind and fair in all her judgments,

Keen of wit—a brilliant mind,
'Mongst friends here, and over yonder,
Ne're a truer will we find!

The tribute concluded that "the Franklin Square House feels it has been honored to have her as a guest."[70]

In most tributes to her by whites, Maria Baldwin was presented as an admirable figure, but there was no acknowledgment of her role in the black communities of Cambridge and Boston or her political involvement in the fight for racial justice. Instead, whites tended to celebrate her dedication to the children of Cambridge and to downplay the fact of Baldwin's race. In her memoir of growing up in Cambridge, Marian Schlesinger recalled how Baldwin "made an impression on me as a small child in the first grade: her ample figure as she came to visit 'our room,' the low quiet timbre of her voice, and her seemingly effortless control. I cannot remember that we thought anything of her being black."[71] One former school committeeman later said: "From the first day I saw her I realized that she was a rare character. Her poise and dignity, her calmness and beautiful voice struck me at once and I felt that her mere presence must be a valuable lesson to all the children. Several parents told me their children realized this and always spoke of her in admiration and affection, but never spoke of her color."[72]

A month after her death, on February 17, 1922, a memorial service was held at the Agassiz School to celebrate Maria Baldwin and establish a college scholarship fund for a graduate of the school in her name. The obituary in the *A.M.E. Church Review* commented that "this service together with that held by the children of her school earlier in the day and that on the day of the funeral, was probably the most remarkable tribute ever paid by white people to the worth of a colored person."[73] Baldwin's sister Alice spoke briefly at the Agassiz service, describing Maria's love of the school in maternal terms: "She gave to the school the love that women give to their own children: a great maternal care that filled her life and made her supremely happy."[74] Most of the white speakers at the memorial service also saw Baldwin as a living example of selflessness and dedication, but one white speaker did mention race. He acknowledged that Baldwin was aware "of the difficulties that were around her and around the people of her own race. . . . Many a time I have talked with her in regard to those deep and tragic problems of all of us." But he saw her as idealistic and tolerant: "I never found her to flinch in her idealism, in her thoughts of what ought to be. Never, on the other hand, did I find in her any bitterness, but just biding her time for the great changes, which must take place in this and every community."[75] For this speaker, Baldwin was a noble figure who was waiting patiently for changes that would inevitably come.

In the black community Maria Baldwin was celebrated as an example of black ability and accomplishment, but she was also remembered as a leader in the wider struggle for racial justice and civil rights. In a column in *The Crisis*, W. E. B. Du Bois, who had known her all of his adult life, offered a tribute that acknowledged what Baldwin had faced and overcome and also what she symbolized to both the black and white worlds: "She fought domestic troubles and bitter never-ending insults of race difference. But she emerged always the quiet, well-bred lady, the fine and lovely Woman." It was typical of Du Bois that he described her in the gendered imagery of the day, yet he also presented her as a complex and capable person who had suffered personal tragedy and continued to work for racial justice until the end of her life. Du Bois, who knew well her activism over the years—in the Woman's Era Club, the Boston Literary and Historical Association, the Niagara Movement, the NAACP, and so many other areas of struggle—saw how the lens of racism had distorted her accomplishments in the memory of whites. His tribute concluded: "She died a teacher, teaching men, women and children; and how strange a mockery of our democracy it is that most Americans are chiefly interested to know that her pupils, her thousands of public-school pupils, were white Massachusetts school children."[76]

Three months after Maria Baldwin's death, the League of Women for Community Service organized a meeting at the Twentieth Century Club to discuss the establishment of a memorial history room in her honor.[77] William Lewis, the former US assistant attorney general, Charles Eliot, former president of Harvard, and Baldwin's old friend Flora Ridley all spoke. Lewis, who had known Baldwin since attending the reading group at her Prospect Avenue home, spoke of her "glorious personality, her gentle inspiration, and the uplift of her great soul" and noted that she loved "Boston . . . and especially the abolitionists." President Eliot, true to character, said he had always admired Maria Baldwin and was especially impressed that "she attained to the respect and good-will of the school committee and this despite the fact there were many Irish Catholics on the committee."

In her remarks, however, Flora Ridley struck a very different tone. She traced the changes in Boston from her youth, when she and Baldwin had read Whittier and Longfellow and revered the abolitionists, to the present day, when black youth saw their "greatest hope and largest future in the development of what is being termed race consciousness." In a statement that surely drew upon her own and Maria Baldwin's experiences, she outlined the changes that had taken place over the past forty years, from their hopes for a truly equal and integrated society to a belief in the need for black self-reliance and pride in black identity and ability. In the years following the Civil War, Ridley said, "the negro thought it his duty to put his past behind him and merge himself into the life of the community and to strive only to become a good American citizen" But "the negro has not been received." Instead, "thrown back upon himself, race pride is coming to his support; race pride, race achievement is becoming the slogan of our student group, that great and growing body on whom our hopes depend." The best memorial to Maria Baldwin, their "lost leader," Ridley concluded, would be to establish a room "which will be a record of the achievements of negro patriots, of negro citizens, and which will symbolize also the fight for freedom."[78] In preparation for the history room, an exhibition on African American accomplishments was organized as a way of celebrating her life. This "Exhibition of Negro Achievement" was held at the Boston Public Library in October 1922. Much of the material from this exhibit formed the basis for the permanent Baldwin Memorial Library at the League of Women for Community Service at 558 Massachusetts Avenue.

The dedication of the library took place on December 20, 1923. Flora Ridley as chair and Josephine St. Pierre Ruffin as a member of the organizing committee helped prepare this memorial to Baldwin. In her statement in the souvenir program for the dedication, Ridley noted that the library's collection was now small but welcomed any contributions: anything written by African Americans, materials bearing on antislavery agitation or agitators, any pamphlets, circulars, pictures, or photographs. Several people had already contributed materials or provided support. She mentioned club member Meta Warwick Fuller, who had lent materials and also "contributed a distinguished series of lectures in connection with the exhibition." Others who made loans included the writer Alice Dunbar Nelson. Ridley discussed the genesis of the idea of establishing a library of black life. The desire to "spread knowledge concerning the Negro—to focus attention more directly upon his contribution to American life and history, which might otherwise be lost or overlooked, and, not the least of the desires, an impulse to inspire to literary and artistic activity" had been discussed by the League of Women for Community Service for some time. With "the tragic death of its leader Miss Baldwin," the league had decided to establish the room as "a fitting testimony to her memory." It was a tribute that would connect the past—a recognition of the black history of which Maria Baldwin had been a part—with hopes for the future, so young people could learn about the accomplishments of an earlier generation as inspiration. The idea of a library, a place of knowledge and reflection, also seemed an appropriate memorial to Maria Baldwin as a person. "A part of the room has been equipped for quiet study," Flora Ridley wrote, "in an atmosphere which may suggest something of the calm, the intellectuality, the sweet dignity of her for whom the room is named."[79]

～ AFTERWORD ～
Maria Baldwin and Historical Memory

Although Maria Baldwin is now honored in Cambridge, she is less recognized in the broader context of African American history. There are a number of reasons why Baldwin's contributions have been forgotten. Although in her lifetime she was celebrated by both black and white communities, by the time of her death the political and cultural world she had known was being transformed. By the turn of the twentieth century, African Americans from the South were beginning to move to the North and West in greater and greater numbers, bringing experiences and culture very different from those of the small African American elite of which Baldwin was a member. There was a wide divide between these new black Bostonians, who soon created their own forms of resistance to racism and celebrations of black urban culture, and the older black elite. The years of Jim Crow in the South and the ascendancy of scientific racism and increase of de facto segregation in the North called into question the possibility of the multiracial democracy envisioned by Baldwin and her generation. After the First World War there was a new sense of defiance in black communities across the nation. In response to white-on-black violence in the years following the war, black men and women fought back in increasing numbers.[1] But Maria Baldwin, with her measured public persona and participation in the white world, seemed out of touch with this new militancy. And of course as a woman, Baldwin saw her accomplishments diminished even in her lifetime as she was perceived through a gendered lens. When W. E. B. Du Bois, one of her closest allies and strongest supporters, described her in his eulogy in *The Crisis* as "the quiet, well-bred lady, the fine and lovely Woman," his words belied her struggles and accomplishments, calling forth instead the image of the respectable middle-class clubwoman, hardly the militant defender of the race.[2]

In her lifetime, Baldwin was a living example to African Americans of black capability and full citizenship. An outstanding orator in a world where lectures and speeches were a primary means of communication, Baldwin appeared in public as a highly cultured, dignified person, worthy of respect. Pauline Hopkins seems to have spoken for the entire black community when she described Baldwin's address to the Brooklyn Academy in 1897 as fulfilling "our fondest hopes, covering herself and us with new honors."[3] For Hopkins as for other black contemporaries, Baldwin's successes in the white world were a triumph not just for Baldwin but for the race as well.[4] There is no evidence that Maria Baldwin believed that her own success would counter the racism that permeated her world, but she did serve as a powerful symbol of black ability. When she spoke before white audiences, frequently the only African American on the podium, she was the embodiment of black achievement. But these speeches and presentations seem always to have been restrained, and to have avoided the issue of race altogether. At the Agassiz School, in her dealings with her white staff, students, and their families—many of them well educated and privileged—she conducted herself as if race was not an issue. She does not seem to have spoken of her identity or experiences as a black woman, but always appeared as the composed and caring head of her school. Because she did not raise the question of race in her dealings with white children and parents or in her presentations to white audiences, whites might imagine that race was insignificant and that racism didn't exist, even though Baldwin herself was well aware of the racism that permeated all aspects of life in the United States and was engaged in struggles to combat it.

Baldwin's close relationships with whites and what could be seen as her appropriation of white cultural values—her love of classic British literature, her participation in white religious and

social organizations, and perhaps most significantly her dedication to the education of white rather than black children—also
opened her to criticism from a generation celebrating black identity. Baldwin's 1922 obituary in the *A.M.E. Church Review*, for
example, noted that "until very recent years her life was passed
so completely among whites that only her face itself served to
show her not one of them."[5] In *The Living Is Easy*, which sati-
rized the pretensions of the black Boston Brahmins of the early
twentieth century, the African American novelist Dorothy West
was sharply critical of one of her characters, a black teacher who
teaches white children. West, born in 1907 into an aspiring black
Boston family, certainly knew of Baldwin, by then a celebrated
figure in the local black community. In her novel West describes
the teacher as being "too contented with her white pupils to
yearn to mother a colored child."[6] Although there were a few
other African American women teachers in and around Boston
at this time, Maria Baldwin was by far the best known and most
successful—and she was the only black teacher whose pupils
were predominantly white. West's character was fictional, but
the critical comment clearly could be applied to Baldwin.

Maria Baldwin died in January 1922, in the aftermath of the
First World War and on the cusp of the Harlem Renaissance.
Three years after her death, Alain Locke published *The New
Negro*, a compilation of work from leading African American
writers, including a number of younger and less well-known figures. To this new generation, shaped by the growing militancy
of the postwar world and the broad movement of modernism,
Maria Baldwin must have seemed a figure from the distant past.
In comparison to the openness to questions of sexuality and the
celebration of southern black life in the writing of authors like
Jean Toomer and Zora Neale Hurston, the values of a woman
so deeply immersed in nineteenth-century New England culture
would have appeared antiquated. And in the context of subsequent black political struggle in the United States, particularly
during and after the civil rights and Black Power movements,
Maria Baldwin hardly fit the image of the militant fighter for
racial justice, often imagined as a young black man. In recent

years the contributions of black women to the civil rights movement have been increasingly recognized, but the thoughtful and cultured public persona of Maria Baldwin, whose professional life was spent among whites and who taught white children, could never compare to figures like Ella Baker or Septima Clark.[7]

As W. E. B. Du Bois noted, Baldwin was fundamentally a teacher, but her accomplishments as an educator have not been mentioned in most histories of education in the United States. A number of excellent studies of black women teachers have appeared, arguing for their significance and political contributions, including works on black women educators of Baldwin's generation and the generation that immediately followed.[8] In her influential article "We Specialize in the Wholly Impossible" and her broader study *A Forgotten Sisterhood*, Audrey McClusky examines the lives and work of the influential school leaders Lucy Craft Laney, Mary McLeod Bethune, Nannie Helen Burroughs, and Charlotte Hawkins Brown, all of whom founded schools for black children in the segregated South.[9] There have been several studies of Anna Julia Cooper, teacher and principal of the prestigious M Street High School in Washington, DC, and the leading black woman intellectual of her generation.[10] In *Uplifting the Women and the Race,* Karen Johnson, who has explored the history of black women teachers in a number of works, compares the lives and educational philosophies of Cooper and Nannie Helen Burroughs.[11] Like Maria Baldwin, all of these women participated in organizations to benefit the black community — the woman's club movement, settlement houses, and national political organizations. But they also without exception worked in black communities and schools and dedicated themselves to black children and youth, seeing education as an essential part of the broader struggle for civil rights and racial justice.[12]

Maria Baldwin was not part of this tradition of black women teachers who were embedded in black communities and committed to the education of black children. Her decision to become a teacher was shaped by the conventions and circumstances of the world she entered as a young adult. As was true for most other educated women of her generation, both black and white, there were few other employment choices available to her. Her career as a teacher of white children was also a matter of circumstance. She taught white children because she lived in a largely white city and needed to work in order to care for her family after the death of her father. She began teaching in the Cambridge public schools through the intervention of black community leaders, who argued that she was highly qualified and that her race should not be a barrier. It was her innate talent, energy, and hard work that led to her success and made her a symbol of black achievement for both the black and white worlds. Baldwin also was an educator of the black community, although her educational work for the race took place outside the public schools in informal settings and black organizations. She founded a reading group for young black Harvard students, taught classes at the Robert Gould Shaw Settlement House, hosted the Omar Circle in her home on Prospect Street, and guided the reading of the members of the League of Women for Community Service. Her achievements and her activism themselves provided a lesson for black young people like Charlotte Hawkins Brown that black excellence could be recognized and that they too could succeed. She achieved a great deal, but her public persona as the black teacher and principal of a white school simply does not fit the narrative of the other outstanding black women educators of her time.

There is also the question of historical memory, of what is remembered and what forgotten. Influenced by the black women's activism of the woman's era of the late nineteenth century and the growing militancy of the first two decades of the twentieth century, Maria Baldwin became more and more engaged with the black freedom struggle as a member of organizations opposing racism and working for civil rights and full citizenship. But this commitment to black resistance has been largely lost. Knowledge of Baldwin as a significant public figure has rested on short biographical sketches by early African American popular historians who published summaries of the accomplishments of outstanding black citizens. Both Hallie Q. Brown in her 1926 *Homespun Heroines and Other Women of Distinction* and Benjamin

Brawley in his 1937 *Negro Builders and Heroes* included sketches of Baldwin. The African American librarian and historian Dorothy Porter built upon their work, publishing short biographical pieces on Baldwin in the *Journal of Negro Education* and later *Notable American Women*.[13] The work of these authors was significant in documenting individual black accomplishment in a society that discounted the value of black lives and denied the abilities and even the humanity of black people. But in Baldwin's case, their portrayals depended heavily on recollections by whites in the memorial events held after her death. None of these commemorations mentioned her participation in and contribution to black organizations or anti-racist work. Although Porter describes Baldwin as "a strong advocate for equal justice to all men" and "a fervent opponent of American class segregation and prejudice," Porter, like Brown and Brawley, is silent about Baldwin's involvement in the Woman's Era Club, the Boston Literary and Historical Association, the Niagara Movement, or the NAACP.[14]

Then there is the question of class and how it is perceived. Baldwin is remembered as one of the New England educated black elite, which, like other black middle class groups, has been subject to criticism for adopting white cultural values and accommodating to a fundamentally unjust racist society. Central to black middle-class and elite identity was the claim of respectability, but respectability itself has been criticized as a strategy for countering racism. A number of scholars have argued that material success, respectability, or educational progress alone will not lead to true equality; racism itself must be directly named and dismantled. Critics have maintained that there is an innate contradiction in the desire to achieve respectability in the face of deeply embedded racism and that a more effective strategy is open opposition to racist beliefs and practices. While black achievement and respectability have symbolic power, they are inadequate by themselves to dismantle a racist status quo and in some cases intensify class tensions within black communities. Black respectability can even confirm racist stereotypes; as some black people achieve success and respectability in the white world, those who do not meet white expectations of success can confirm racist stereotypes of black inferiority. In this view, it is a mistake on the part of middle-class African Americans to imagine that meeting white conceptions of respectability or personal success will erode racism. Instead, this strategy can obscure the underlying power of racism by offering the false hope that material prosperity or cultural expressions of proper behavior will challenge a society structured by white privilege and power.[15]

These are powerful and persuasive arguments, but historical studies of both middle-class and working-class black communities during the years of the nadir complicate this analysis, raising questions about the nature of both resistance and respectability in terms of class, culture, and historical moment. Histories of the lives of poor and working people have contributed to a more complex understanding of how African Americans responded to and resisted a deeply racist society at all levels.[16] Scholars also have recognized the quiet activism of the black middle class, noting the variety of ways in which courageous and articulate black men and women, both in the North and in the oppressive apartheid society of the South, provided leadership and worked against racist practices and institutions in a world that was increasingly hostile and dangerous for black people. As Kevin Gaines comments, "Collective memory recognizes the service of countless parents, teachers, ministers, musicians, and librarians as community builders."[17]

Middle-class black women and the concept of respectability has also been a significant issue for feminist historians and theorists. A number of historians have explored middle-class black women's responses and resistance during the years of the nadir.[18] Black women reformers and clubwomen in particular have been criticized by some scholars for their uncritical appropriation of white middle-class conceptions of respectability.[19] But others have argued that respectability should be viewed in the context of struggles over representation. Explaining the significance of images of black women, they have argued that racist tropes portraying black women as immoral, hypersexualized, and criminal place them outside the boundaries of citizenship and justify symbolic and physical violence. Thus cultural work countering these representations can also be a form of resistance. Victoria Wolcott, whose study of black women reformers in Detroit provides a nuanced analysis of the way the idea of respectability was mobilized in the black freedom struggle, argues that respectability is "particularly open to competing definitions, inflections, and meanings."[20] Although it can reflect and heighten class divisions within black communities, it also can be employed in a wider sense to demonstrate black equality and the right to full citizenship. Both Evelyn Higginbotham and Michele Mitchell agree. In her seminal study of women reformers in the black Baptist Church, Higginbotham claims that although the educated black elite she studied "reproduced and disseminated the reigning values of middle-class Protestant America," they also "expressed a race consciousness that united black men and women in a struggle for racial dignity and self-determination."[21] Mitchell, who has examined the strategies African Americans employed to create identities asserting their worth and supporting "their collective well-being" in the vicious racist climate of the nadir, argues that among these strategies were the defense of black character and the embrace of modes of living similar to those advocated by middle-class white progressives. Respectability became "subversive in contexts where Afro-Americans consciously decided not to allow stereotypes and insults to affect their own measure of self-worth."[22]

Elizabeth McHenry has called for "a greater understanding of the common forms of oppression faced by black Americans, as well as a more complex vision of what constitutes resistance."[23] In the light of this more complex vision of resistance, it is important to distinguish between what Maria Baldwin came to symbolize—how her public presentation of self was read—and her own experiences and political commitments. It is understandable that without a full knowledge of Baldwin's life and activism, she could be seen as accommodating to the white world and enacting white conceptions of respectability. If she was seen exclusively as a respectable black woman successfully negotiating the white world, then her pride in her own black identity, her participation in the black struggle for civil rights, and what Du Bois called her "quiet courage" could be overlooked. But her life was much more varied than her public persona at the Agassiz School or her performance as a proper and respectable black woman would suggest. Although located in the black middle class and certainly embracing white Anglo-American high culture, Maria Baldwin, like the other members of the Boston black elite of these years, also articulated and stood for racial equality and full citizenship for black people.

It is difficult to examine the life of any historical figure without making judgments from the perspective of our own time. Historical figures, of course, are not above criticism, but I believe we should try to understand lives empathetically while retaining our own ethical and political values. Like many other educated African Americans of her time, Maria Baldwin embraced her identity as both black and American. She lived the struggle described by Evelyn Higginbotham to find a "common ground on which to live as Americans with Americans of other racial and ethnic backgrounds." As Higginbotham points out, "This search for common ground—to be both black and American—occurred as the nation worked assiduously to deny this possibility by isolating the 'Negro's place' within physical and symbolic spaces of inferiority."[24] Baldwin's experience growing up black in both black and white settings, embracing what she saw as the moral values of New England, celebrating the abolitionist tradition, and succeeding in a white-dominated world but well aware of the power and growth of racism, led to a kind of hybrid identity. As Thomas Holt argues, rather than imagining human beings as isolated individuals acting out of a unique set of emotions and aspirations, we should view individuals as located within a particular historical context "grounded in social processes and framed by historical moments," and seek to understand the discursive and material constraints within which they make sense of the world and act.[25] While we cannot fully know how Maria Baldwin made sense of the world, we can try to see her historically as a person whose identity was deeply shaped by the representations and specific historical moments through which she lived, who, despite living in a society that denied the possibility of reconciling Du Bois's two-ness of being both black and also American, took a stand on the side of full equality and rights for black people as Americans. Baldwin's life raises questions about the meaning of teaching as work for black women, conceptions of race and varieties of racism, and the forms of accommodation and resistance that are possible in different historical moments. Her accomplishments are significant and alone are reason why she should be included in our understanding of the black experience in the United States, while the issues raised by her life—the ongoing power of racism and resistance to it, the complexity of identity, and the choices we are faced with in worlds not of our own making—continue to confront us today.

NOTES

INTRODUCTION

1. Nathaniel Vogel, "The Mismeasure of Maria Baldwin," *Peacework* (April 2002): 1.
2. Rayford Logan, *The Negro in American Life and Thought: The Nadir, 1877–1901* (New York: Dial Press, 1954).
3. e. e. cummings, *Six Nonlectures* (Cambridge: Harvard University Press, 1962), 30.
4. Adelaide Cromwell, *The Other Brahmins: Boston's Black Upper Class, 1750–1950* (Fayetteville: University of Arkansas Press, 1994), 54.
5. W. E. B. Du Bois, "Man of the Month," *The Crisis* 13, no. 6 (April 1917): 281.
6. Hopkins used the phrase "daughter of the revolution" in a speech she presented at the William Lloyd Garrison Centennial Celebration in Boston on December 16, 1905. Cited in Lois Brown, *Pauline Hopkins: Black Daughter of the Revolution* (Chapel Hill: University of North Carolina Press, 2008), 9.
7. John Cumbler, *From Abolition to Rights for All: The Making of a Reform Community in the Nineteenth Century* (Philadelphia: University of Pennsylvania Press, 2007).
8. Evelyn Brooks Higginbotham, *Righteous Discontent: The Women's Movement in the Black Baptist Church, 1880–1920* (Cambridge: Harvard University Press, 1993), 4.
9. W. E. B. Du Bois, *The Souls of Black Folk* (New York: Penguin, 1989), 5.
10. Cromwell, *The Other Brahmins.*
11. See Dorothy Porter, "Maria Louise Baldwin, 1865–1922," *Journal of Negro Education* 21 (Winter 1952): 94–96; Dorothy Porter, "Maria Baldwin," in *Notable American Women*, ed. Edward James (Cambridge: Harvard University Press, 1971), 86–88; "Maria Louise Baldwin," in Hallie Q. Brown, *Homespun Heroines and Other Women of Distinction* (1926; Freeport, NY: Books for Libraries Press, 1971), 182–93; Benjamin Brawley, *Negro Builders and Heroes* (1937; Chapel Hill: University of North Carolina Press, 1965), 170–71.
12. See Caroline Gebhard, Katherine Adams, and Sandra Zagarell, "Reflections on the Archive: Alice Ruth Moore Dunbar-Nelson," *Legacy: A Journal of American Women Writers* 33, no. 2 (2016): 384–91.
13. Darlene Clark Hine, "Rape and the Inner Lives of Black Women in the Middle West," *Signs* 14, no. 1 (1989): 912. See also Deborah Gray White, *Too Heavy a*

Load: Black Women in Defense of Themselves, 1894–1994 (New York: W. W. Norton, 1999). The diary of the author and educator Alice Dunbar Nelson, a colleague of Maria Baldwin's sister Alice, is unique as an account of the inner life of an African American woman of this period. Alice Dunbar Nelson, *Give Us Each Day* (New York: W. W. Norton, 1984).

14. "Obituary—Maria L. Baldwin," *A.M E. Church Review* 38, no. 4 (April 1922): 218.

CHAPTER ONE: A NEW ENGLAND GIRLHOOD

1. Maria Baldwin" (born September 13, 1856), Massachusetts Birth Records, 1840–1915, available at Ancestry.com.
2. Barbara Fields, *Slavery and Freedom on the Middle Ground* (New Haven: Yale University Press, 1985).
3. George Levesque, *Black Boston: African American Life in Urban America, 1750–1860* (New York: Garland Publishing, 1994), 250–53.
4. Jeffrey Bolster, *Black Jacks: African American Seamen in the Age of Sail* (Cambridge: Harvard University Press, 1997), 6.
5. Bolster, *Black Jacks*, 214.
6. Bolster, *Black Jacks*, 220.
7. Bolster, *Black Jacks*, 230.
8. Jeffrey Bolster, "'To Feel Like a Man': Black Seamen in the Northern States, 1800–1860," *Journal of American History* 76, no. 4 (March 1990): 1184
9. For a discussion of black ownership of property in this period, see Elizabeth Pleck, *Black Migration and Poverty* (New York: Academic Press, 1979).
10. Pleck, *Black Migration and Poverty*, 209.
11. Adelaide Cromwell, *The Other Brahmins: Boston's Black Upper Class, 1750–1950* (Fayetteville: University of Arkansas Press, 1994), 39.
12. Stephen Kantrowitz, *More Than Freedom: Fighting for Black Citizenship in a White Republic, 1829–1889* (New York: Penguin, 2012), 52.
13. Pleck, *Black Migration and Poverty*, 13.
14. Levesque, *Black Boston*, 9.
15. The Second Evangelical Congregational Church of Cambridge, known as "the abolitionist church," was an integrated church. Kit Rawlins, personal communication, January 10, 2019.
16. This information comes from several sources. The anonymous author of her obituary in the *A.M.E. Church News*, who seems to have known her well, wrote shortly after her death, "In the life of Mollie Louise Baldwin the colored race reached its finest example of accomplished womanhood and the nation, its best hope for racial adjustment." "Maria L. Baldwin Obituary," *A.M.E. Church Review* 38, no. 4 (April 1922): 217.
17. William Schouler, *A History of Massachusetts in the Civil War* (Boston: E. P. Dutton and Co., 1868), 480.
18. Maria L. Baldwin, "A Night Watch," *The Woman's Era* 1, no. 6 (September 1894): 2.
19. Kantrowitz, *More Than Freedom*, 7.
20. Kantrowitz, *More Than Freedom*, 312.

21. Pleck, *Black Migration and Poverty*, 104.

22. "Speech of Dr. John Rock," *The Liberator* 30, no. 11 (March 16, 1860): 42.

23. Kantrowitz, *More Than Freedom*, 315.

24. Philip Rubio, *There's Always Work at the Post Office* (Chapel Hill: University of North Carolina Press, 2010), 21.

25. Rubio, *There's Always Work at the Post Office*, 20.

26. Cromwell, *The Other Brahmins*, 49.

27. See Robert Smith, "William Cooper Nell, Crusading Black Abolitionist," *Journal of Negro History* 55, no. 3 (July 1970): 182–99.

28. Conference on Research in Income and Wealth, *Trends in the American Economy in the Nineteenth Century* (Princeton: Princeton University Press, 1960), 457.

29. Kantrowitz, *More Than Freedom*, 133.

30. Robert H. Nylander, "Maria Baldwin" file, Cambridge Historical Commission; "Maria Louise Baldwin 1856–1922" file, Cambridge History Room, Cambridge Public Library; Pauline Hopkins, "Famous Women of the Negro Race VII: Educators," *Colored American Magazine* 5, no. 2 (June 1902): 127.

31. Marriages Registered in Boston, 1836, Massachusetts, Town and Vital Records, 1620–1988, s.v. John St. Pierre and Eliza Mahinnick, available at Ancestry.com.

32. The most complete contemporary narrative of the life of Josephine St. Pierre Ruffin is found in the biographical collection *Representative Women of New England*, edited by Julia Ward Howe and published in 1904, in Ruffin's lifetime. Ruffin and Howe were colleagues in the American Women Suffrage Association and other reform movements, and it seems most likely that Ruffin saw the narrative before it was published. Of course this assumes only that Ruffin approved of the narrative, not that it was completely accurate. *Representative Women of New England* identifies Josephine St. Pierre's parents as John St. Pierre and Eliza Menhenick. John St. Pierre's father was Jean Jacques St. Pierre, who was born in Martinique and moved to Taunton, Massachusetts, "probably early in the nineteenth century." Jean Jacques St. Pierre married Betsey Hill, who claimed to be the granddaughter of an African prince who escaped slavery and married an Indian woman. Eliza Menhenick is described as a Cornishwoman born in Bodmin, Cornwall. "Josephine St. Pierre Ruffin," in *Representative Women of New England*, ed. Julia Ward Howe (Boston: New England Historical Publishing Co., 1904), 335–39. An account of the St. Pierre family can also be found in an unpublished manuscript by Josephine St. Pierre Ruffin's daughter Flora Ridley, "Other Bostonians," 1942, Heslip-Ruffin Family Papers, box 1, folder 8, Amistad Research Center, Tulane University.

33. "Josephine St. Pierre Ruffin," 336.

34. Dolita Cathcart, "White Gloves, Black Rebels: The Decline of Elite Black National Political Leadership in Boston, 1920–1929" (PhD diss., Boston College, 2004), 94.

35. Kantrowitz, *More Than Freedom*, 427.

36. Pleck, *Black Migration and Poverty*, 98.

37. Teresa Blue Holden, "Earnest Women Can Do Anything: The Public Career of Josephine St. Pierre Ruffin, 1842–1904" (PhD diss., Saint Louis University, 2005), 20.

38. Holden, "Earnest Women Can Do Anything," 98.
39. Hallie Q. Brown, *Homespun Heroines and Other Women of Distinction* (1926; Freeport, NY: Books for Libraries Press, 1971), 151–52.
40. Josephine St. Pierre Ruffin, "Trust the Women!" *The Crisis* (August 1, 1915): 188.
41. "A Baldwin Memorial Room," *Boston Transcript*, March 18, 1922.
42. Hopkins, "Famous Women of the Negro Race VII: Educators," 127.
43. The term "mulatto" was commonly used by both whites and blacks in this period to describe people of biracial descent.
44. Frank A. Hill, "The Public Schools of Cambridge," in *The Cambridge of Eighteen Hundred and Ninety-Six*, ed. Arthur Gilman (Cambridge: Riverside Press, 1896), 195.
45. William Bradbury, *The Cambridge High School History and Catalogue* (Cambridge: Moses King, 1882).
46. Normal schools were established throughout the United States in the mid-nineteenth century in conjunction with the spread of the common school movement. They provided one- or two-year courses of study to prepare young people (overwhelmingly young women) to work in the newly established public elementary schools. The English name "normal school" is taken from the French term *école normale*.
47. According to Anthony Neal, a second African American Boston teacher attended the Boston Normal School in the 1880s. This was Harriet Smith, who graduated in 1886. In 1891 there were only two African Americans teaching in Boston. Anthony Neal, "Pioneering Black Teachers Led the Way in the 1800s," *Bay State Banner*, March 1, 2018.
48. City of Cambridge, Report of the School Committee, 1870, 11, Cambridge Room, Cambridge Public Library. The training school was abolished in 1882. "Training School," *Cambridge Chronicle*, July 1, 1882, 5.
49. City of Cambridge, Report of the School Committee, 1870, 10–11, Cambridge Room, Cambridge Public Library.
50. Michael B. Katz, "The 'New Departure' in Quincy, 1873–1881: The Nature of Nineteenth-Century Educational Reform," *New England Quarterly* 40, no. 1 (March 1967): 20.
51. City of Cambridge, Report of the School Committee, 1880, 14, Cambridge Room, Cambridge Public Library.
52. "Training School," *Cambridge Chronicle*, June 26, 1875.
53. *Cambridge Chronicle*, May 1, 1878.
54. Anthony Neal, "Maria Louise Baldwin: An Eminent Educator, Civic Leader, Speaker," *Bay State Banner*, May 23, 2013.
55. Linn Boyd Porter, "Color Line Not Drawn and Merit Recognized," *Cambridge Chronicle*, August 29, 1903.
56. Massachusetts, Death Records, 1841–1915, s.v. Peter Baldwin (d. 1880), available at Ancestry.com.
57. "Men of the Month," *The Crisis* 13, no. 6 (April 1917): 281.
58. Benjamin Brawley, *Negro Builders and Heroes* (Chapel Hill: University of North Carolina Press, 1937), 277; Dorothy Porter, "Maria Louise Baldwin," in *Notable American Women* (Cambridge: Belknap Press of Harvard University Press, 1971), 87.

59. William Hazel, "Colored Teachers in Our Public Schools," *Cambridge Chronicle*, December 4, 1880.
60. "Report of the Superintendent of Schools," in *The Mayor's Address and the Annual Reports of the City Council of the City of Cambridge* (Cambridge: Tribune Publishing Company, 1881), 285–86.
61. Porter, "Color Line Not Drawn and Merit Recognized."
62. Hopkins, "Famous Women of the Negro Race VII: Educators," 127.
63. Reports of the School Committee and the Reports of the Superintendent of Schools, 1882–1922, Cambridge Room, Cambridge Public Library.
64. Hopkins, "Famous Women of the Negro Race VII: Educators," 128.
65. Brown, *Homespun Heroines and Other Women of Distinction*, 185.
66. Hopkins, "Famous Women of the Negro Race VII: Educators," 128.
67. Cathcart, "White Gloves, Black Rebels," 139.
68. Porter, "Color Line Not Drawn and Merit Recognized."
69. Porter, "Color Line Not Drawn and Merit Recognized."
70. Baldwin was doubtless quite comfortable with the literature curriculum adopted by the Cambridge schools in 1899, which emphasized classic British and American works such as *Robinson Crusoe, Swiss Family Robinson, A Man Without a Country, Silas Marner,* and *Ivanhoe.* Students also memorized poetry by Whittier, Longfellow, Tennyson, and Emerson. Charles Wadelington and Richard Knapp, *Charlotte Hawkins Brown and Palmer Memorial Institute* (Chapel Hill: University of North Carolina Press, 1999), 51.
71. Horace Scudder later argued for the teaching of classic American literature in the public schools, or as they were then called common schools, as a way of creating loyal American citizens. In his 1888 lecture "The Place of Literature in Common School Education," Scudder called for teaching the classic literature of New England as a way of countering the danger of what he called the "cry of Labor in Poverty," a reference to growing labor unrest. He also proclaimed the value of British literature as a way of defining American identity as English-speaking and Protestant to the new generation of immigrant children now entering the public schools. Horace Scudder, *Literature in School: An Address and Two Lectures* (Boston: Houghton Mifflin, 1888), 5–33. For a discussion of Scudder's views, see Nina Baym, "Early Histories of American Literature: A Chapter in the Institution of New England," *American Literary History* 1, no. 3 (Autumn 1989): 459–88.
72. "Not Apostle of Any New Theory," *Cambridge Chronicle*, September 16, 1916.
73. Richard Kennedy, *Dreams in the Mirror: A Biography of E. E. Cummings* (New York: Liveright, 1980), 29.
74. Elizabeth Thaxter Hubbard, "Life Was Lovely," *Harvard Magazine* (November–December 1988): 63.
75. "Former Pupil of Miss Maria Baldwin Recalls Happy Days in Her Class," *Cambridge Chronicle-Sun*, undated clipping, Maria Baldwin file, Cambridge Historical Commission.
76. "The Agassiz" 3, no. 3 (March 1922): 4, Maria Baldwin file, Cambridge Historical Commission.
77. "The Agassiz" 3, no. 3 (March 1922): 6, Maria Baldwin file, Cambridge Historical Commission.

CHAPTER TWO: THE WOMAN'S ERA

1. Deborah Gray White, *Too Heavy a Load: Black Women in Defense of Themselves, 1894–1994* (New York: W. W. Norton, 1999), 25.

2. Elizabeth McHenry makes a similar point: "The emergence of a powerful and empowering woman's era in the midst of the disempowering barrage of discriminatory laws and racial violence of the 1890s points to a central irony: these years of debilitating racial conflict and exclusion were the very years that found black women banding together to demand that they, in the words of Fannie Barrier Williams, 'be known and recognized for what we are worth.'" Elizabeth McHenry, *Forgotten Readers: Recovering the Lost History of African American Literary Societies* (Durham: Duke University Press, 2002), 201. See also Anne Firor Scott, "Most Invisible of All: Black Women's Voluntary Associations," *Journal of Southern History* 56, no. 1 (February 1990): 10.

3. Many scholars have given 1859 as Hopkins's birth date, but Mitchell Verner and Cynthia Davis show that both Hopkins's high school records and the 1870 census list her birth date as 1856. Mitchell Verner and Cynthia Davis, *Literary Sisters* (New Brunswick: Rutgers University Press, 2011), 54.

4. Hazel Carby, *Reconstructing Womanhood: The Emergence of the Afro-American Woman Novelist* (New York: Oxford University Press, 1987), 7.

5. Martha S. Jones, *All Bound Up Together* (Chapel Hill: University of North Carolina Press, 2007), 175.

6. Mark Schneider claims that Baldwin "was probably better connected to white society than any other Boston African American of her time." Mark Schneider, *Boston Confronts Jim Crow* (Boston: Northeastern University Press, 1997), 103.

7. Hallie Q. Brown, *Homespun Heroines and Other Women of Distinction* (1926; Freeport, NY: Books for Libraries Press, 1971), 183.

8. Brown, *Homespun Heroines*, 190–91. In the 1880s, Higginson came into conflict with black Republicans when he unsuccessfully ran for Congress on the Democratic ticket. Nonetheless he seems to have continued to see himself as a friend and ally of African Americans.

9. White, *Too Heavy a Load*, 70.

10. Adelaide Cromwell, *The Other Brahmins: Boston's Black Upper Class, 1750–1950* (Fayetteville: University of Arkansas Press, 1994). Willard Gatewood argues that it is important to recognize the existence of social class divisions among African Americans: "Failure to consider class divisions in the black community would contribute to what Bayard Rustin once termed the 'sentimental notion of black solidarity' and to the perpetuation of the myth that black society is a homogeneous mass without significant and illuminating distinctions in prestige, attitudes, behavior, culture, power, and wealth." Willard Gatewood, "Aristocrats of Color North and South: The Black Elite, 1880–1920," *Journal of Southern History* 54, no. 1 (February 1988): 3.

11. "Sets in Colored Society," *Boston Globe*, July 22, 1894.

12. Gatewood, "Aristocrats of Color North and South," 7.

13. Gatewood, "Aristocrats of Color North and South," 5. See also chap. 6, "The Color Factor," in Willard Gatewood, *Aristocrats of Color: The Black Elite, 1880–1920* (Bloomington: Indiana University Press, 1990), 149–81.

14. Deborah Gray White, for example, argues that "owing to their economic and blood ties to white America, the mulatto upper and middle classes were more familiar and more at ease with white cultural norms, and consequently are at once envied and distrusted by the black masses." White, *Too Heavy a Load*, 79.

15. Christine Lee to Mary Church Terrell, February 25, 1896, cited in Elizabeth Pleck, *Black Migration and Poverty in Boston, 1865–1900* (New York: Academic Press, 1979), 113.

16. Gatewood, "Aristocrats of Color North and South," 20.

17. Pauline Hopkins, "Famous Women of the Negro Race VII: Educators," *Colored American Magazine* 5, no. 2 (June 1902): 128–29; Linn Boyd Porter, "Color Line Not Drawn and Merit Recognized," *Cambridge Chronicle*, August 29, 1903.

18. White, *Too Heavy a Load*, 98.

19. Millington Bergeson-Lockwood, *Race Over Party* (Chapel Hill: University of North Carolina Press, 2018), 65.

20. Bergeson-Lockwood, *Race Over Party*, 136.

21. Dorothy Porter, "Maria Baldwin," in *Dictionary of American Negro Biography* (New York: W. W. Norton, 1982), 21.

22. David Levering Lewis, *W. E. B. Du Bois: Biography of a Race* (New York: Henry Holt and Co., 1993), 100–101.

23. "Pay Tribute to Negro Teacher," *Boston Herald*, March 18, 1922.

24. John Daniels, *In Freedom's Birthplace* (New York: Arno Press, 1969), 274.

25. W. E. B. Du Bois, "Maria Baldwin," *The Crisis* (April 1922): 248–49.

26. Joy James argues that "Du Bois' writings . . . show a reverence for his mother, familial women as well as personal friends and acquaintances, profeminist politics, and a censorious revisionism in obscuring the pioneering works of [Anna Julia] Cooper and [Ida B.] Wells-Barnett. The divers and conflictual nature of these relationships point to a 'double consciousness' muddled with the contradictions of his gender politics." Joy James, *Transcending the Talented Tenth: Black Leaders and American Intellectuals* (New York: Routledge, 1997), 41.

27. See Brittney C. Cooper, *Beyond Respectability: The Intellectual Thought of Race Women* (Urbana: University of Illinois Press, 2017).

28. Shaun Alexander, *An Army of Lions: The Civil Rights Struggle before the NAACP* (Philadelphia: University of Pennsylvania Press, 2012), 51.

29. "Colored Men Gather," *Boston Daily Globe*, June 1, 1892.

30. Paula Giddings, *When and Where I Enter: The Impact of Black Women on Race and Sex in America* (New York: Bantam Books, 1985), 30.

31. At the World Columbian Exposition later that year, the veteran activist Frances Harper proclaimed that this was "the threshold of woman's era." Hazel Carby, "'On the Threshold of Woman's Era': Lynching, Empire, and Sexuality in Black Feminist Theory," *Critical Inquiry* 12 (Autumn 1985): 264.

32. Gatewood, *Aristocrats of Color*, 215.

33. *The Woman's Era* 1, no. 1 (1894). There is some contradictory evidence suggesting that the Woman's Era Club existed earlier than this. The entry on Josephine St. Pierre Ruffin in Elizabeth Lindsay Davis, *Lifting as They Climb* (1933; New York: G. K. Hall and Co., 1996), says the club was founded in 1890. Rodger Streitmatter refers to two letters written by Ruffin in 1890 with the letterhead "The

Woman's Era." He also mentions a passage in one of the letters that refers to "the May *Era*." Since the first issue of *The Woman's Era* was dated 1894, this must have been a mistake in transcription. Rodger Streitmatter, *Raising Her Voice: African-American Women Journalists Who Changed History* (Lexington: University Press of Kentucky, 1994), 173. In an article in the *Colored American Magazine,* the journalist Pauline Hopkins cites the date of the founding of the Woman's Era Club as 1873, but this was clearly a misprint. Pauline Hopkins, "Famous Women of the Negro Race IX: Club Life among Colored Women," *Colored American Magazine* 5, no. 4 (August 1, 1902): 34.

34. Florida Ruffin Ridley, "Josephine St. Pierre Ruffin's Daughter Makes a Brilliant Speech before Clubwomen in Toledo, Ohio," *Chicago Defender,* May 22, 1937.

35. Hopkins, "Famous Women of the Negro Race IX," 34.

36. Elsa Barkley Brown, "Negotiating and Transforming the Public Sphere," *Public Culture* 7, no. 1 (Fall 1994): 107–46. Stephanie Shaw emphasizes that it is important to recognize the tradition of voluntary associations among black women before the 1890s, but she also acknowledges that the founding of black women's clubs at the turn of the twentieth century created a structure that allowed black women "to speak more profoundly about problems specific to them as black women and problems that affected them as they affected the race." Stephanie Shaw, "Black Clubwomen and the Creation of the National Association of Colored Women," *Journal of Women's History* 3, no. 2 (Fall 1991): 20.

37. Gail Bederman, *Manliness and Civilization* (Chicago: University of Chicago Press, 1995).

38. Bergeson-Lockwood, *Race Over Party,* 137.

39. Cited in Dolita Cathcart, "White Gloves, Black Rebels: The Decline of Elite Black National Political Leadership in Boston, 1870–1929" (PhD diss., Boston College, 2004), 140.

40. Scholars disagree about the nature of the black women's clubs. Gerda Lerner argues that while black women's clubs, like white clubs, were led by educated middle-class women, the black clubs were not simply social clubs. Lerner writes that black clubwomen "frequently successfully bridged the class barrier and concerned themselves with issues of importance to poor women, working mothers, tenant farm wives. They were concerned with education, self and community improvement, but they always strongly emphasized race pride and race advancement." By contrast, Deborah Gray White highlights the class composition of the clubs, arguing that "seldom did African-American women organize across class lines. Poor, working-class, and middle-class women all organized nationally but mostly within their own groups." Gerda Lerner, "Early Community Work of Black Clubwomen," *Journal of Negro History* 59, no. 2 (April 1974): 167; White, *Too Heavy a Load,* 17.

41. McHenry, *Forgotten Readers,* 204.

42. Fannie Barrier Williams, "The Club Movement among Colored Women of America," cited in Cooper, *Beyond Respectability,* 17.

43. Crystal Feimster, *Southern Horrors: Women and the Politics of Rape and Lynching* (Cambridge: Harvard University Press, 2009), 112.

44. Ann Massa, "Black Women in the 'White City,'" *American Studies* 8, no. 3 (December 1974): 319–37.

45. Quoted in Teresa Holden, "Earnest Women Can Do Anything: The Public Career of Josephine St. Pierre Ruffin, 1842–1904" (PhD diss., St. Louis University, 2005), 132.

46. "Club News: Boston, the Woman's Era Club," *The Woman's Era* 1, no. 1 (1894).

47. Martha S. Jones, *All Bound Up Together* (Chapel Hill: University of North Carolina Press, 2007).

48. "Club News: Boston, the Woman's Era Club,"*The Woman's Era* 1, no. 1.

49. "Club News: Boston, the Woman's Era Club," *The Woman's Era* 1, no. 1.

50. Cromwell, *The Other Brahmins,* 78; McHenry, *Forgotten Readers,* 242.

51. Pauline Hopkins, "Whittier, the Friend of the Negro," in *Daughter of the Revolution: The Major Nonfiction Works of Pauline E. Hopkins,* ed. Ira Dworkin (New Brunswick: Rutgers University Press, 2007), 253.

52. See the discussion in Carby, "On the Threshold of the Woman's Era."

53. Carby, *Reconstructing Womanhood,* 93.

54. White, *Too Heavy a Load,* 49.

55. Beverly Guy-Sheftall, *Daughters of Sorrow: Attitudes toward Black Women, 1880–1920* (Brooklyn: Carlson Publishing, 1990), 107.

56. Flora Ridley, "Greeting," *The Woman's Era,* 1, no. 1 (1894).

57. McHenry, *Forgotten Readers,* 206.

58. "Cantabrigia Club," *Cambridge Chronicle,* October 7, 1893.

59. "Cambridge Clubwoman," *The Woman's Era* 1, no. 2 (1894).

60. The Tanners were the parents of the well-known painter Henry Ossawa Tanner.

61. Sarah Tanner, "Reading," *The Woman's Era* 2, no. 3 (1895).

62. Cited in McHenry, *Forgotten Readers,* 235.

63. "Difficulties of Colonization," *The Woman's Era* 1, no. 1 (1894).

64. "Editorial," *The Woman's Era* 2, no. 1 (1895).

65. "An open letter to Laura Ormiston Chant," *The Woman's Era* 1, no. 3 (1894). Also reprinted in Ida B. Wells-Barnett, *Crusade for Justice: The Autobiography of Ida B. Wells* (Chicago: University of Chicago Press, 1970), 198.

66. Wells-Barnett, *Crusade for Justice,* 199.

67. "The Silence of Mrs. Chant," *The Woman's Era* 1, no. 5 (1894).

68. Maria Baldwin, "On the Question of Whether There Should Be a National Convention of Black Women's Clubs," *The Woman's Era* 1, no. 2 (1894).

69. Davis, *Lifting as They Climb,* 16.

70. Maude Jenkins, "The History of the Black Clubwomen's Movement in America" (PhD diss., Teachers College, Columbia University, 1984), 61.

71. "Let Us Confer Together," *The Woman's Era* 2, no. 3 (1895).

72. Fannie Barrier Williams, "The Club Movement among Colored Women of America," in *The New Negro for a New Century,* ed. J. E. McGrady (Chicago: American Publishing House, 1900), 397.

73. "Conference Notes," *The Woman's Era* 2, no. 4 (1895).

74. Edwina Kruse, a well-known black woman educator and principal of the high school in Wilmington, Delaware, where Alice Baldwin was teaching, was also in Boston that July and most probably attended the conference. "Social Notes," *The Woman's Era* 2, no. 5 (1895).

75. "Three Sessions: Convention of Colored Women Opened," *Boston Globe,* July 30, 1895.

76. Josephine St. Pierre Ruffin, "Address of Josephine St. P. Ruffin, President of Conference," in Davis, *Lifting as They Climb*, 17–19.
77. Matthews died from tuberculosis at the age of forty-six in 1907. See Cheryl Hicks, *Talk to You Like a Woman* (Chapel Hill: University of North Carolina Press, 2010), 91–122; Steve Kramer, "'Uplifting our 'downtrodden sisterhood': Victoria Earle Matthews and New York City's White Rose Mission, 1897–1907," *Journal of African American History* 91, no. 3 (2006): 243–66.
78. Fred Miller Robinson and Victoria Earle Matthews, "The Value of Race Literature: An Address," *Massachusetts Review* 27, no. 2 (Summer 1986): 169–91.
79. Jenkins, *History of the Black Clubwomen's Movement*, 67.
80. "From the Woman's Era Club to the Women of This Country," *The Woman's Era* 2, no. 4 (1895).
81. "The Negro Exhibit at Atlanta," *The Woman's Era* 2, no. 9 (1895).
82. "Booker T. Washington Delivers the 1895 Atlanta Compromise Speech," http://historymatters.gmu.edu/d/39.
83. "Statement of Goals," *The Woman's Era* 2, no. 7 (1895).
84. "Editorial," *The Woman's Era* 3, no. 4 (1896).
85. Williams, "The Club Movement among Colored Women of America," 384.
86. Williams, "The Club Movement among Colored Women of America," 404.
87. Josephine St. Pierre Ruffin to Ednah Cheney, May 19, 1896, MS A10.1, 68, Rare Books and Manuscripts, Boston Public Library.
88. Josephine St. Pierre Ruffin to Ednah Dow Cheney, March 24, 1896, MS A10.1, 87, Rare Books and Manuscripts, Boston Public Library.
89. Josephine St. Pierre Ruffin to Ednah Dow Cheney, March 24, 1896, MS A10.1, 87, Rare Books and Manuscripts, Boston Public Library.
90. Josephine St. Pierre Ruffin to Ednah Dow Cheney, May 22, 1896, MS A10.1, 69, Rare Books and Manuscripts, Boston Public Library.
91. Josephine St. Pierre Ruffin, "Statement," November 17, 1897, the Woman's Era Club, Rare Books and Manuscripts, Boston Public Library.
92. "African Americans in Brookline: Seeking the First Homeowner," http://brooklinehistory.blogspot.com/2012/05/african-americans-in-brookline-seeking.html.
93. Josephine St. Pierre Ruffin to Ednah Dow Cheney, March 25, 1897, MS A10.1, 97, Rare Books and Manuscripts, Boston Public Library.
94. "Report of the Woman's Era Club for 1899," The Woman's Era Club, Rare Books and Manuscripts, Boston Public Library.
95. White, *Too Heavy a Load*, 65. The political and personal differences among the clubwomen exploded over the reelection of Terrell as president of the NACW in 1899. The bylaws of the association limited the presidency to two terms for any individual. When Terrell was reelected that year to a third term, a number of club members were outraged. The Woman's Era Club denounced the election; Ruffin, along with Anna Julia Cooper and Ida B. Wells-Barnett, refused to attend national meetings of the NACW for many years.
96. "Obituary—Maria L. Baldwin," *A.M.E. Church Review* 38, no. 4 (April 1922): 218. The group was doubtless influenced by the Omar Khayyam clubs formed to celebrate the poem *The Rubaiyat of Omar Khayyam*, which had been translated into English by Edward Fitzgerald in 1859 and had become widely admired in

educated and artistic circles in late nineteenth-century England and the United States. The first club was established in London in the 1890s. The Boston club first met in 1900. All the members of these two clubs were men, and the focus of their meetings seems to have been the life and work of the Persian poet Omar Khayyam himself or various "oriental" subjects. Another focus of the Boston meetings apparently was the excellent lunches that were served. "Omar Khayyam Club of America, Some Doings of the Omar Khayyam Club of America" (Boston: Privately printed, 1922).

97. Almira Park, "Recollections of the Omar Circle," cited in Cromwell, *The Other Brahmins*, 84.

98. *The Woman's Era* 3, no. 3 (August 1896).

99. "What to Read," *The Crisis* (August 1, 1911): 168. Baldwin had several months to prepare her lecture. The first full-length biography of Stowe, published in 1889, would have been available to her, but she could not have read Charles Stowe's 1897 biography of his mother, which was not published until after Baldwin's lecture.

100. The African American novelist Frances Harper spoke at the Brooklyn Institute in 1892 on "Enlightened Motherhood," but this was not a Washington's Birthday address.

101. Baldwin, the article claimed, "spoke substantially as follows." "Washington's Birthday Address," *Brooklyn Eagle*, February 23, 1897.

102. "Washington's Birthday Address."

103. *Cambridge Tribune*, August 21, 1897.

104. "A Deserved Honor," *Cambridge Tribune*, April 17, 1897.

105. "Massachusetts Teachers Meet," *Cambridge Chronicle*, November 26, 1898.

106. Membership lists, carton 6, Twentieth Century Association Records, Massachusetts Historical Society, Boston.

107. The 1906 membership list identifying members' occupations includes thirty-eight principals of schools, thirty-three college professors, many ministers, and a couple of rabbis. The occupation of 144 members is given as "charity and philanthropist." Fifty-five lawyers are listed but only eighteen merchants. *Bulletin of the Twentieth Century Club* 1, no. 1 (October 1901), carton 27, Twentieth Century Association Records, Massachusetts Historical Society.

108. Pauline Hopkins, "Famous Women of the Negro Race VII: Educators," *Colored American Magazine* 5, no. 2 (June 1902): 128–29.

109. Hopkins, "Famous Women of the Negro Race VII: Educators," 128.

110. Anne-Elizabeth Murdy, *Teach the Nation: Public School, Racial Uplift, and Women's Writing in the 1890s* (New York: Routledge, 2003), 15.

111. See the essays in Karin Stanford, ed., *If We Must Die: African American Voices on War and Peace* (Lanham, MD: Rowman and Littlefield, 2008), for examples of these differing views.

112. *The Woman's Era*, for example, had condemned the annexation of Hawaii. Francesca Morgan, *Women and Patriotism in Jim Crow America* (Chapel Hill: University of North Carolina Press, 2005), 73.

113. "Anti-Lynchers in Boston," *New York Times*, May 21, 1899.

114. "Meeting of Anti-Imperialists," *Cambridge Chronicle*, May 20, 1899.

115. Statement read by Archibald M. Grimké at Charles Street Church, Boston. First

printed in I. D. Barnett et al., "Open Letter to President McKinley by Colored People of Massachusetts" (n.p., n.d.), 2–4, 10–12.

116. "The Summer School of Methods," *The Southern Workman* 38, no. 8 (August 1899): 283–85.

117. Maria Baldwin, "The Changing Ideal of Progress," *The Southern Workman* 29, no. 1 (January 1900): 15–16.

118. Baldwin, "The Changing Ideal of Progress," 15–16.

119. Jane Smith, "The Fight to Protect Race and Regional Identity within the General Federation of Women's Clubs, 1895–1902," *Georgia Historical Quarterly* 94, no. 4 (Winter 2010): 495.

120. Smith, "The Fight to Protect Race and Regional Identity," 497.

121. See the analysis of the life and work of white southerner Rebecca Latimer Felton, who called for the lynching of a thousand black men a week if that was needed to protect white women, in Feimster, *Southern Horrors.*

122. Mrs. Frank P. Gale, letter to the editor, *Boston Daily Globe*, May 30, 1899.

123. "For Education of the Negro," *Boston Daily Globe*, June 16, 1899.

124. Josephine St. Pierre Ruffin, "An Open Letter to the Educational League of Georgia," in *Masterpieces of Negro Eloquence*, ed. Alice Dunbar-Nelson (New York: Bookery Publishing Company, 1914), 173–76. It is not clear where Ruffin's letter was first published, but it seems to have been written in 1899.

125. "To Uplift Negro Children," *Boston Daily Globe*, November 15, 1899.

126. "Josephine St. Pierre Ruffin," in *Representative Women of New England*, ed. Julia Ward Howe (Boston: New England Historical Publishing Company, 1904), 337.

127. Smith, "The Fight to Protect Race and Regional Identity," 504.

128. Smith, "The Fight to Protect Race and Regional Identity," 503.

129. Maria Baldwin to Ednah Dow Cheney, January 11, 1901, MS A10.1, 118, Rare Books and Manuscripts, Boston Public Library.

130. Maria Baldwin to Ednah Dow Cheney, February 10, 1901, MS A10.1, 122, Rare Books and Manuscripts, Boston Public Library.

131. "Josephine St. Pierre Ruffin," 338.

132. The club was described as still meeting regularly by John Daniels in his 1914 study of black Boston, *In Freedom's Birthplace*, but there seems to be no other reference to the club after 1904.

CHAPTER THREE: CONTENDING FORCES

1. "Prospectus of the New Romance of Colored Life," *Colored American Magazine* 1, no. 4 (September 1900): 196.

2. Lois Brown, *Pauline Elizabeth Hopkins: Black Daughter of the Revolution* (Chapel Hill: University of North Carolina Press, 2008), 6.

3. The *Colored American Magazine* began publication in Boston in 1900. For four years, Hopkins was deeply involved with the journal, publishing fiction and serving as literary editor. She published three serialized novels and numerous pieces on contemporary black life, including her series "Famous Women of the Negro Race." In 1904, when the magazine was sold to a group in New York closely associated with Booker T. Washington, Hopkins lost her position as editor. In November 1904, a notice appeared informing readers that Hopkins had

NOTES TO PAGES 89-92

severed her relations with the magazine and returned to Boston. In 1916, Hopkins and Walter Wallace founded a magazine called *The New Era*, but it lasted for only two issues. After the failure of *The New Era*, Hopkins did not return to journalism or fiction but continued to work as a stenographer at MIT until her death from an accidental fire in her home in 1930. Richard Yarborough, introduction to Pauline Hopkins, *Contending Forces* (New York: Oxford University Press, 1988).

4. Hazel Carby sees all of Pauline Hopkins's writings as profoundly political, arguing that Hopkins created fictions "which could explain the present and which had a pedagogic function for both her characters and her audience." Hazel Carby, *Reconstructing Womanhood: The Emergence of the Afro-American Woman Novelist* (New York: Oxford University Press, 1987), 123.

5. Hopkins's depiction of Mrs. Willis is somewhat ambivalent. In financial need after the death of her husband, a successful politician and public figure, the fictional Mrs. Willis sets herself up as a lecturer on "the woman question" and the advancement of African American women. To that end, she supports the idea of women's clubs. Hopkins wrote, "She succeeded well in her plans: conceived in selfishness, they yet bore glorious fruit in the formation of clubs of colored women banded together for charity, for study, for every reason under God's glorious heavens that can better the conditions of mankind." Hopkins, *Contending Forces*, 147.

6. Hopkins, *Contending Forces*, 150–51.

7. Hopkins, *Contending Forces*, 256.

8. In his classic work *Negro Thought in America, 1880–1915*, August Meier argues that the clustering of black opinion into two opposing positions "is far from a complete description of the situation." Meier writes that "there were inconsistencies, the twistings and turnings, the attempts to hold to both clusters of ideologies—or to parts of both—or to shift from one to the other that were characteristics of probably the majority of the articulate." August Meier, *Negro Thought in America, 1880–1915* (Ann Arbor: University of Michigan Press, 1963), 169.

9. Cyrus Adams, "The Afro-American Council," *Colored American Magazine* 3, no. 6 (March 1903): 337. For a detailed analysis of the Afro-American League and the Afro-American Council, see Shaun Alexander, *An Army of Lions: The Civil Rights Struggle Before the NAACP* (Philadelphia: University of Pennsylvania Press, 2012).

10. Meier, *Negro Thought in America, 1880–1915*, 50.

11. Mark Schneider, "*The Colored American* and *Alexander's*: Boston's Pro–Civil Rights Bookerites," *Journal of Negro History* 80, no. 4 (Autumn 1995): 157–69.

12. Willard Gatewood, "Aristocrats of Color North and South: The Black Elite, 1880–1920," *Journal of Southern History* 54, no. 1 (February 1988): 3–20.

13. Stephen Fox, *The Guardian of Boston: William Monroe Trotter* (New York: Athenaeum, 1971), 26.

14. Hopkins, *Contending Forces*, 50.

15. Hopkins, *Contending Forces*, 277.

16. Even in Boston, individuals and organizations were conflicted about Washington. In a 1900 editorial, for example, *The Colored American Magazine* defended

Washington against accusations "that he caters too much to the opposite race at the expense of his own." The editorial argued that this was an unwarranted charge against a "benefactor" who "does not deserve censure, criticism and calumny." At the same time, the editors strongly condemned lynching and disfranchisement in the South. Schneider, "*The Colored American* and *Alexander's*," 160.

17. Linn Boyd Porter, "Color Line Not Drawn and Merit Recognized," *Cambridge Chronicle*, August 29, 1903.
18. *Cambridge Chronicle*, October 25, 1902; *Cambridge Tribune*, February 14 and December 5, 1903; "Harriet Beecher Stowe," *Cambridge Tribune*, February 7, 1903.
19. "Local Mention," *Cambridge Chronicle*, May 25, 1901; "Representative Cambridge Women at Springfield." *Cambridge Chronicle*, November 2, 1901.
20. Evelyn Brooks Higginbotham, *Righteous Discontent: The Women's Movement in the Black Baptist Church, 1880–1920* (Cambridge: Harvard University Press, 1993), 5.
21. Elizabeth Pleck, *Black Migration and Poverty: Boston, 1865–1900* (New York: Academic Press, 1979), 110.
22. John Daniels, *In Freedom's Birthplace* (1914; New York: Arno Press, 1969), 226.
23. Dorothy Emerson, June Edwards, and Eilene Knox, *Standing Before Us: Unitarian Universalist Women and Social Reform, 1776–1936* (Boston: Skinner House Books, 2000), 402–3.
24. *Cambridge Tribune*, June 16, 1894. St. Monica's Home was supported by the Episcopal Sisters of St. Margaret, whose convent was in Louisburg Square in Boston. St. Monica's moved from Beacon Hill to Rockledge, former home of William Lloyd Garrison, in Roxbury in 1904. The home closed in 1989.
25. See Sidney Warren, *American Freethought, 1860–1914* (New York: Columbia University Press, 1943).
26. The Boston Society for Ethical Culture, *Addresses by the Speakers William Babcock and Clara Bisbee* (Dorchester, MA, 1902).
27. Benjamin Brawley, *Negro Builders and Heroes* (Chapel Hill: University of North Carolina Press, 1937), 278; Dorothy Porter, "Maria Louise Baldwin, 1856–1922," *Journal of Negro Education* 21, no. 1 (Winter 1952): 94.
28. Editorial, *The Index* 11, no. 523 (January 1, 1880): 1.
29. "Free Religious Association," *Cambridge Chronicle*, June 9, 1900.
30. Free Religious Association, *Proceedings at the Thirty-fifth Annual Meeting* (Boston: Free Religious Association, 1902), 3.
31. Free Religious Association, *Proceedings at the Thirty-fifth Annual Meeting*, 7.
32. *Cambridge Tribune*, May 28, 1904.
33. "Recent Deaths," *Boston Transcript*, January 10, 1922. For a history of Boston Unitarianism, see Peter Richardson, *The Boston Religion: Unitarianism in Its Capital City* (Rockland, ME: Red Barn Publishing, 2003).
34. National Center for Educational Statistics, *120 Years of American Education: A Statistical Portrait* (Washington, DC: US Department of Education, 1993), 55.
35. *Cambridge Chronicle*, July 19, 1884.
36. *Cambridge Press*, November 30, 1889.
37. *Cambridge Chronicle*, May 31, 1890.
38. Louis Baldwin's exact role with these two papers is unclear. In his 1914 study of

black Boston, *In Freedom's Birthplace*, John Daniels states that Louis Baldwin was co-editor of *The Courant* and *The Republican*. The Cambridge city directory for 1891–1894, however, lists his occupation as "business manager, newspaper."

39. *Cambridge Chronicle*, August 17, 1889.

40. Eben Miller, *Born Along the Color Line: The 1933 Amenia Conference and the Rise of a National Civil Rights Movement* (New York: Oxford University Press, 2012), 40.

41. "Notes and Comments," *The Woman's Era* 3, no. 3 (August 1896). Although men made up the majority of cyclists in the 1890s, women also cycled. And in the Boston area there were several African American cycling clubs and one well-known black woman cyclist, Kitty Knox, who wore bloomers and competed successfully with men in races until she was forced out by the imposition of a color bar by white cycling organizations. See Lorenz Finison, *Boston's Cycling Craze, 1880–1900* (Amherst: University of Massachusetts Press, 2014).

42. Gloria Hull, *Color, Sex, and Poetry: Three Women Writers of the Harlem Renaissance* (Bloomington: Indiana University Press, 1987), 42. In 1894 Alice Moore, then a young woman living in New Orleans, contributed reports on the women's clubs of Louisiana to *The Woman's Era*.

43. "House at 196 Prospect Street: Information as Recorded in the Middlesex Registry of Deeds," Maria Baldwin folder, Cambridge Historical Commission.

44. *Cambridge Chronicle*, August 5, 1893.

45. By 1902 Joseph Dorsey was the vice president and executive officer of the Middlesex Real Estate Association and treasurer of the Cambridge Home Association. "Joseph Dorsey, Candidate for Common Council Nomination, Ward Four," *Cambridge Tribune*, November 8, 1902.

46. *Cambridge Chronicle*, September 19, 1896.

47. "Indignation Meeting," *Cambridge Chronicle*, October 10, 1896.

48. "Indignation Meeting."

49. "Local Election Results," *Cambridge Chronicle*, December 9, 1899.

50. "Local Church Dedication," *Cambridge Chronicle*, March 17, 1900.

51. "The Right of the Negro to a University Education," *Cambridge Chronicle*, February 3, 1900; "Meeting on Behalf of Atlanta University," *Cambridge Chronicle*, March 24, 1900.

52. "Atlanta University," *Cambridge Tribune*, June 27, 1903.

53. Schneider, "*The Colored American* and *Alexander's*," 158.

54. Booker T. Washington, "The National Negro Business League," in *Progress of a Race*, ed. John Gibson (Naperville, IL: J. L. Nichols and Co., 1902), 237–38.

55. "National Negro Business Men's Convention," *Colored American Magazine*, 1, no. 4 (September 1, 1900): 257.

56. "House at 196 Prospect Street: Information as Recorded in the Middlesex Registry of Deeds," Maria Baldwin Folder, Cambridge Historical Commission.

57. "The Greenacre," *Cambridge Tribune*, October 19, 1901.

58. "Received at The Greenacre," *Cambridge Tribune*, June 14, 1902.

59. Adelaide Cromwell, *The Other Brahmins: Boston's Black Upper Class, 1750–1950* (Fayetteville: University of Arkansas Press, 1994), 62.

60. "Historical Sketch of the Boston Literary and Historical Association," box 11, The Guardian Collection, Howard Gotlieb Archival Research Center, Boston University.

61. Elizabeth McHenry, *Forgotten Readers: Recovering the Lost History of African American Literary Societies* (Durham: Duke University Press, 2002), 3.

62. McHenry, *Forgotten Readers*, 142.

63. Elsa Barkley Brown, "Negotiating and Transforming the Public Sphere," *Public Culture* 7, no. 1 (Fall 1994): 107–46.

64. Minutes of the Boston Literary and Historical Association, January 27 1902, box 11, The Guardian Collection, Howard Gotlieb Archival Research Center, Boston University.

65. Minutes of the Boston Literary and Historical Association, May 13, 1902, box 11, The Guardian Collection, Howard Gotlieb Archival Research Center, Boston University.

66. McHenry, *Forgotten Readers*, 166.

67. Minutes of the Boston Literary and Historical Association, April 21, 1902, box 11, The Guardian Collection, Howard Gotlieb Archival Research Center, Boston University.

68. Minutes of the Boston Literary and Historical Association, March 7, 1904, box 6, The Guardian Collection, Howard Gotlieb Archival Research Center, Boston University. The minutes of the Boston Literary and Historical Association from 1905 to 1913 are missing, so it is not possible to follow Baldwin's involvement with the club in these years. After 1913, the topics of the meetings continued to be focused on race issues, but Baldwin is not listed as an officer of the association.

69. Minutes of the Boston Literary and Historical Association, March 7, 1904, box 6, The Guardian Collection, Howard Gotlieb Archival Research Center, Boston University.

70. "Mr. Baldwin's Reception." *Cambridge Chronicle*, April 25, 1903.

71. "Real Estate and Building," *Cambridge Chronicle*, April 23, 1904.

72. Pleck, *Black Migration and Poverty*, 153.

73. *Cambridge Chronicle*, February 13, 1904.

74. "Hogan Appointed," *Cambridge Chronicle*, February 20, 1904.

75. "Looks Like the Truth," *Cambridge Sentinel*, March 5, 1904.

76. "Boston News," *Cambridge Chronicle*, May 14, 1904.

77. Information about birthplace and race was elicited by census takers from each respondent. Although census information is not always accurate, it seems unlikely that census takers would have made up this information.

78. I have found no further mention of Louis Baldwin. He did not participate in Maria Baldwin's funeral in 1922, although Alice Baldwin spoke at the ceremony.

79. "Residence for Women," *Boston Daily Globe*, April 7, 1901.

80. Edward Shapiro, "Robert A. Woods and the Settlement House Impulse," *Social Service Review* 52, no. 2 (June 1978): 217.

81. Beth Hinchcliffe and Bonnie Hurd Smith, *The House That Love Built* (Privately printed, n.d.), 35, carton 1, 1882–1909, Franklin Square House, 2012-M-132, Schlesinger Library, Radcliffe Institute, Harvard University.

82. Hinchcliffe and Smith, *The House That Love Built*, 60.

83. Dorothy West, *The Living Is Easy* (1948; New York: Feminist Press, 1982), 40.

84. Hinchcliffe and Smith, *The House That Love Built*, 82.

85. "Franklin Square House Minstrel Show," *Boston Daily Globe*, February 5, 1908.

86. Ray Stannard Baker, *Following the Color Line* (1908; New York: Harper Torch-books, 1964), 121.

87. Editorial, *Cambridge Chronicle,* September 16, 1905.

88. Archibald Grimké, "Carrying Prejudice to Boston," *New York Age,* December 21, 1905.

89. Grimké, "Carrying Prejudice to Boston."

CHAPTER FOUR: WE WILL NEVER CEASE TO PROTEST

1. The Committee of Twelve, founded in 1904, was an attempt to bridge the differences between black leaders and create a common front to fight racism. Members included Archibald Grimké, T. Thomas Fortune, Charles Chestnutt, Booker T. Washington, and Du Bois. The conflicts within the group proved irreconcilable and Du Bois soon resigned. Shawn Alexander, *An Army of Lions* (Philadelphia: University of Pennsylvania Press, 2012), 222–24.

2. David Levering Lewis, *W. E. B. Du Bois: Biography of a Race, 1868–1919* (New York: Henry Holt and Co., 1993), 312.

3. "Niagara Declaration of Principles, 1905," Massachusetts Digital Common-wealth, https://www.digitalcommonwealth.org/search/commonwealth-oai:org 69469k.

4. The Garrison Centenary Committee of the Suffrage League of Boston and Vicin-ity, *The Celebration of the One Hundredth Anniversary of the Birth of William Lloyd Garrison* (Boston, 1906), 66.

5. Stephen Fox, *The Guardian of Boston: William Monroe Trotter* (New York: Athe-neum, 1970), 99.

6. "Cambridge Heights Items," *Cambridge Tribune,* December 16, 1905.

7. Angela Jones, *African American Civil Rights: Early Activism and the Niagara Move-ment* (New York: Praeger, 2011), 190.

8. W. E. B. Du Bois, "A Brief Resume of the Massachusetts Trouble in the Niagara Movement, Cleveland, Ohio, 1907 December," 1, http://credo.library.umass .edu/view/full/mums312-b004-i182.

9. Niagara Movement, Massachusetts Branch, official ballot of the Niagara Move-ment, 1907, http://credo.library.umass.edu/view/full/mums312-b004-i143.

10. Cited in Lewis, *W. E. B. Du Bois,* 330.

11. "Negro Children," *Cambridge Tribune,* June 15, 1907.

12. Lewis, *W. E. B. Du Bois,* 105.

13. Fox, *Guardian of Boston,* 65.

14. Lewis, *W. E. B. Du Bois,* 340.

15. Despite his documentation of the racial prejudice and violence experienced by African Americans, Baker advocated a cautious and gradualist approach. Like many white liberals of the time, he was sympathetic to Booker T. Washington. In the conclusion of *Following the Color Line* he wrote, "There must always be men like Dr. Du Bois who agitate for rights; their service is an important one, but at the present time it would seem that the thing most needed was the teaching of such men as Dr. Washington, emphasizing duties and responsibilities, urging the Negro to prepare himself for his rights." Ray Stannard Baker, *Following the Color Line* (1908; New York: Harper and Row, 1964), 304.

16. Baker, *Following the Color Line*, 123.

17. "The Color Line in the North," *Cambridge Tribune*, February 1, 1908.

18. Patricia Sullivan, *Lift Every Voice: The NAACP and the Making of the Civil Rights Movement* (New York: New Press, 2009), 6.

19. Mary White Ovington, *Black and White Sat Down Together: The Reminiscences of an NAACP Founder*, ed. Ralph E. Luker (New York: Feminist Press, 1995), 59.

20. Initially Ida B. Wells's name also was absent, but after objections from some delegates, it was added to the list of members. This episode reveals the underlying tensions around both politics and gender among the early members of the NAACP. See Paula Giddings, "Missing in Action: Ida B. Wells, the NAACP, and the Historical Record," *Meridians* 1, no. 2 (Spring 2001): 1–17.

21. Lewis, *W. E. B. Du Bois*, 387.

22. Circular letter from William English Walling to NAACP executive committee members, ca. 1910, http://credo.library.umass.edu/view/full/mums312-b004-i002.

23. Giddings," Missing in Action," 10.

24. Patricia Schechter, *Ida B. Wells-Barnett and American Reform, 1880–1930* (Chapel Hill: University of North Carolina Press, 2001), 135.

25. Charles Kellogg, *NAACP: A History of the National Association for the Advancement of Colored People* (Baltimore: Johns Hopkins University Press, 1967), 121.

26. Trotter had been in conflict with Clement Morgan for several years. Stephen Fox argues that the real source of Trotter's suspicion of the NAACP was "the presence of white money and white leadership. . . . In contrast, Trotter's group, the Negro-American Political League, was virtually all black." Fox, *Guardian of Boston*, 140.

27. Fox, *Guardian of Boston*, 136.

28. The minutes for the Boston Literary and Historical Association for this period show the predominance of Monroe and Geraldine Trotter in the activities of the association. Minutes of the Boston Literary and Historical Association, 1913, 1918, box 11, The Guardian Collection, Howard Gotlieb Archival Research Center, Boston University.

29. Mark Schneider, "The Boston NAACP and the Decline of the Abolitionist Impulse," *Massachusetts Historical Review* 1 (1999): 95–113.

30. Cited by Paul Polgar, "Fighting Fire with Fire," *Massachusetts Historical Review* 10 (2008): 94.

31. Robert Hayden, *Boston's NAACP History, 1910–1982* (Boston: Boston Branch, NAACP, 1982), 1.

32. Charlotte Hawkins Brown, "Some Incidents in the Life and Career of Charlotte Hawkins Brown Growing Out of Racial Situations, at the Request of Dr. Ralph Bunche," A-146, folder 2, Charlotte Hawkins Brown Papers, Schlesinger Library, Radcliffe Institute, Harvard University.

33. Ceci Jenkins, "The Twig Bender of Sedalia," incomplete draft, 1946, 19, A-146, folder 7, Charlotte Hawkins Brown Papers, Schlesinger Library, Radcliffe Institute, Harvard University.

34. Glenda Gilmore, *Gender and Jim Crow: Women and the Politics of White Supremacy in North Carolina, 1896–1920* (Chapel Hill: University of North Carolina Press, 1996), 179.

35. Brown described her meeting with Palmer and her decision to attend normal

school in the unpublished manuscript "Charlotte Hawkins Brown: A Biography," Charlotte Hawkins Brown Papers, Personal and Biographical, A-146, folder 1, Schlesinger Library, Radcliffe Institute, Harvard University. The reference to Baldwin's exchange with Palmer is in Charles Wadelington and Richard Knapp, *Charlotte Hawkins Brown and Palmer Memorial Institute* (Chapel Hill: University of North Carolina Press, 1999), 34. I have been unable to locate the correspondence between Hawkins and Palmer.

36. Gilmore, *Gender and Jim Crow*, 183.

37. Sandra Smith, "Charlotte Hawkins Brown," *Journal of Negro Education* 51, no. 3 (Summer 1982): 93. See also Audrey McClusky, "We Specialize in the Wholly Impossible," *Signs* 22, no. 2 (Winter 1997): 404–26.

38. Maria Baldwin to Charlotte Hawkins Brown, February 6, 1911, Charlotte Hawkins Brown Papers, Correspondence to and from Charlotte Hawkins Brown, 1910–1911, A-146, folder 33, Schlesinger Library, Radcliffe Institute, Harvard University.

39. The association also provided speakers to the community from among its members. In 1905 Maria Baldwin's name was added to the list of possible speakers for the association's speaker service, although it is not clear whether she actually participated. Minutes of the Lecture Service Committee, Twentieth Century Club, March 4, 1905, 29, carton 1, Twentieth Century Association Records. Massachusetts Historical Society.

40. "What Can Hub Do for Negro?," *Boston Globe*, February 12, 1911.

41. "In Memory of Colonel Higginson," *Cambridge Tribune*, June 10, 1911.

42. "Negro Problem," *Cambridge Tribune*, January 20, 1912.

43. "Miss Baldwin's Address and Her Well Known Ability," *Cambridge Tribune,* January 20, 1912.

44. "Commemoration of Paul Laurence Dunbar," *Cambridge Chronicle*, April 7, 1906.

45. "Cantabrigia Club," *Cambridge Chronicle*, March 1, 1913.

46. Stephanie Shaw argues for this long tradition of black women's sense of responsibility and community service. Stephanie Shaw, *What a Woman Ought to Be and to Do: Black Professional Women Workers during the Jim Crow Era* (Chicago: University of Chicago Press, 1996).

47. Sarah Deutsch, *Women and the City: Gender, Space, and Power in Boston, 1870–1900* (New York: Oxford University Press, 2000), 19.

48. Isabel Eaton, "Robert Gould Shaw House and Its Work," *The Crisis* 6, no. 3 (July 1, 1913): 141.

49. "The Robert Gould Shaw House, *"Alexander's Magazine* 7, no. 3 (January 1909): 133.

50. *Robert Gould Shaw House: Fifty Years of Service* (n.d.), 7, Robert Gould Shaw House Collection, Digital Repository Service, Northeastern University, http://hdl.handle.net/2047/D20233549.

51. Isabel Lindsay, "Adult Education Programs for Negroes in Settlement Houses," *Journal of Negro Education* 14, no. 3 (Summer 1945): 347–52.

52. "The Robert Gould Shaw House," 133.

53. Dorothy Salem, "To Better Our World: Black Women in Organized Reform, 1890–1920" (PhD diss., Kent State University, 1986), 185.

54. Eaton, "Robert Gould Shaw House and Its Work," 142.

55. Sarah Boyer, *Crossroads: Stories of Central Square* (Cambridge: Cambridge Historical Commission, 2003), 17

56. "Neighborhood House," *Cambridge Chronicle*, June 6, 1914.

57. "Built on a Foundation of Service, It Has Accomplished Much," *Cambridge Tribune*, May 15, 1915.

58. Although some male leaders—most notably Booker T. Washington and Howard University professor Kelly Miller—opposed women's suffrage, most African American leaders, both men and women, supported women's right to vote. In the nineteenth century, Frederick Douglass was renowned for his support of the vote for women; in the twentieth, W. E. B. Du Bois was committed to women's suffrage, despite what he acknowledged was widespread racism among white women. Beverly Guy-Sheftall, *Daughters of Sorrow: Attitudes toward Black Women, 1880–1920* (Brooklyn: Carlson Publishers, 1990), 116–17.

59. "Cambridge Political Equality Association," *Cambridge Chronicle*, January 9, 1915.

60. Mrs. Paul Laurence Dunbar, "Votes and Literature," *The Crisis* 10, no. 4 (August 1915): 184.

61. Maria Baldwin, "Votes for Teachers," *The Crisis* 10, no. 4 (August 1915): 189.

62. Sullivan, *Lift Every Voice*, 29.

63. "Mr. Trotter and Mr. Wilson," *The Crisis* 9, no. 3 (January 1915): 119–20.

64. Michael Rogin, *Ronald Reagan, the Movie, and Other Episodes in Political Demonology* (Berkeley: University of California Press, 1988), 221.

65. See the summary of the NAACP's actions in this period in "Fighting Race Calumny," *The Crisis* 10, no. 1 (May 1, 1915): 40–42; and "Fighting Race Calumny, Part II," *The Crisis* 10, no. 2 (June 1, 1915): 87–88.

66. Evelyn Brooks Higginbotham, *Righteous Discontent: The Women's Movement in the Black Baptist Church, 1880–1920* (Cambridge: Harvard University Press, 1993), 193.

67. Lewis, *W. E. B. Du Bois*, 508.

68. Stephen Weinberger, "The Birth of a Nation and the Making of the NAACP," *Journal of American Studies* 45, no. 1 (2011): 85.

69. Polgar, "Fighting Fire with Fire," 102.

70. "Mayor Curley Hissed," *Boston Globe*, April 16, 1915.

71. "Colored Women Form a League," *Boston Daily Globe*, April 26, 1915.

72. It is not clear whether this organization was ever established. Olivia Ward Bush-Banks left Boston for Chicago in 1918.

73. "Prominent Men Voice Their Protest," *Cambridge Chronicle*, May 1, 1915.

74. Hallie Q. Brown, *Homespun Heroines and Other Women of Distinction* (1926; Freeport, NY: Books for Libraries Press, 1971), 186–87.

75. Melvyn Stokes, *D. W. Griffith's The Birth of a Nation* (New York: Oxford University Press, 2008), 150.

CHAPTER FIVE: KEEN OF WIT, A BRILLIANT MIND

1. Anthony Neal, "Mary Evans Wilson Was Founding Member of the Women's Service Club, NAACP Boston Branch," *Bay State Banner*, August 18, 2014.

2. Charles Kellogg, *NAACP: A History of the National Association for the Advancement of Colored People* (Baltimore: Johns Hopkins University Press, 1967), 121.

3. *Girls* 2, no. 5 (January 15, 1922): 4, Franklin Square House Papers, 2012-M-132, carton 1, *Girls,* 1921–22, Schlesinger Library, Radcliffe Institute, Harvard University.

4. Alice Baldwin first appears in the 1910 census in Wilmington, Delaware. In 1910 she was boarding with Edwina Kruse and three other women; in 1920 with Kruse, Broadnax, and Etta Roach; in 1930 with Kruse and Broadnax. In 1940, when Alice Baldwin was eighty, she was living with Alice Broadnax.

5. Hallie Q. Brown, *Homespun Heroines and Other Women of Distinction* (1926; Freeport, NY: Books for Libraries Press, 1971), 188–89.

6. "Miss Baldwin Elected," *Cambridge Tribune,* August 26, 1916.

7. Isabel Kimball Whiting, "Character, Accomplishment of Beloved Agassiz School Woman Principal Recalled," *Cambridge Chronicle,* August 20, 1964.

8. "Not Apostle of Any New Theory," *Cambridge Chronicle,* September 16, 1916.

9. "Not Apostle of Any New Theory."

10. W. E. B. Du Bois, "Men of the Month," *The Crisis* 13, no. 6 (April 1917): 281.

11. "A Baldwin Memorial Room," undated newspaper clipping, Maria Baldwin file, Cambridge Historical Commission.

12. Whiting, "Character, Accomplishment of Beloved Agassiz School Woman Principal Recalled."

13. Marion Cannon Schlesinger, *Snatched from Oblivion: A Cambridge Memoir* (Boston: Little Brown and Company, 1979), 74.

14. Schlesinger, *Snatched from Oblivion,* 82.

15. Cornelia James Cameron, "Public Schools," *Radcliffe Quarterly* (May 1917): 73–75. See also Maria Dietrich, *Cornelia James Cannon and the Future American Race* (Amherst: University of Massachusetts Press, 2010), 85.

16. Cited in Dietrich, *Cornelia James Cannon,* 87.

17. Schlesinger, *Snatched from Oblivion,* 25.

18. Deborah Gray White, *Too Heavy a Load: Black Women in Defense of Themselves, 1894–1994* (New York: W. W. Norton, 1999), 113.

19. Francesca Morgan, *Women and Patriotism in Jim Crow America* (Chapel Hill: University of North Carolina Press, 2005), 119.

20. Alice Dunbar Nelson, "Negro Women in War Work," in *The American Negro in the World War,* ed. Emmett J. Scott (New York: Arno Press, 1969), 375–76.

21. Dunbar Nelson, "Negro Women in War Work," 394.

22. Minutes, May 14, 1918, League of Women for Community Service, microfilm, M-48, Schlesinger Library, Radcliffe Institute, Harvard University.

23. Dunbar Nelson, "Negro Women in War Work," 389.

24. Minutes, October 18, 1918, League of Women for Community Service, microfilm, M-48, Schlesinger Library, Radcliffe Institute, Harvard University.

25. "Melnea Cass," Black Women Oral History Interviews, 1976–1981, 32, Schlesinger Library, Radcliffe Institute, Harvard University.

26. Minutes, November 14, 1918, League of Women for Community Service, microfilm, M-48, Schlesinger Library, Radcliffe Institute, Harvard University.

27. Minutes, August 19, 1918, League of Women for Community Service, microfilm, M-48, Schlesinger Library, Radcliffe Institute, Harvard University.

28. Minutes, January 23, 1919, League of Women for Community Service, microfilm, M-48, Schlesinger Library, Radcliffe Institute, Harvard University.

29. Mark Schneider, *Boston Confronts Jim Crow, 1890–1920* (Boston: Northeastern University Press, 1997), 146–47.

30. David Krugler, *1919, the Year of Racial Violence: How African Americans Fought Back* (New York: Cambridge University Press, 2015); Karin Stanford, ed., *If We Must Die: African American Voices on War and Peace* (Lanham, MD: Rowman and Littlefield, 2008), 113.

31. Minutes, March 13, 1919, League of Women for Community Service, microfilm, M-48, Schlesinger Library, Radcliffe Institute, Harvard University.

32. W. E. B. Du Bois, "Returning Soldiers," *The Crisis* 18, no. 1 (May 1919): 14. See also Krugler, *1919, The Year of Racial Violence*.

33. Dunbar Nelson, "Negro Women in War Work," 389.

34. Geoff Ward, *The Black Child-Savers* (Chicago: University of Chicago Press, 2012), 127.

35. Minutes, May 1, 1919, League of Women for Community Service, microfilm, M-48, Schlesinger Library, Radcliffe Institute, Harvard University.

36. Adelaide Cromwell, *The Other Brahmins: Boston's Black Upper Class, 1750–1950* (Fayetteville: University of Arkansas Press, 1994, 147.

37. Over the years, the two clubs became known in the black community simply by their addresses: "464" and "558."

38. Cromwell, *The Other Brahmins*, 147.

39. Minutes, April 8, 1920, League of Women for Community Service, microfilm, M-48, Schlesinger Library, Radcliffe Institute, Harvard University.

40. Lorraine Roses, *Black Bostonians and the Politics of Culture* (Amherst: University of Massachusetts Press, 2017).

41. Ward, *The Black Child-Savers.*

42. Forrester Washington, "Reconstruction and the Colored Woman," *Life and Labor* (January 1919): 3–6.

43. Minutes, April 15, 1920, League of Women for Community Service, microfilm, M-48, Schlesinger Library, Radcliffe Institute, Harvard University.

44. Minutes, April 29, 1920, League of Women for Community Service, microfilm, M-48, Schlesinger Library, Radcliffe Institute, Harvard University.

45. W. E. B. Du Bois, *Darkwater: Voices from Within the Veil* (Mineola, NY: Dover Publications, 1999), 17–18.

46. Du Bois, *Darkwater*, 18–19.

47. Du Bois, *Darkwater*, 47.

48. Schlesinger, *Snatched from Oblivion*, 74.

49. "A Tribute to Miss Maria L. Baldwin," *Cambridge Chronicle*, January 12, 1922.

50. Thomas Leonard, *Illiberal Reformers* (Princeton: Princeton University Press, 2016); Adam Cohen, "Harvard's Eugenics Era," *Harvard Magazine* (March–April 2016): 42–48.

51. Dietrich, *Cornelia James Cannon*, 7.

52. See the discussion of Yerkes in Stephen Jay Gould, *The Mismeasure of Man* (New York: W. W. Norton, 1996).

53. Cornelia James Canon, "American Misgivings," *Atlantic Monthly* 129, no. 2 (February 1922): 155.

54. By the mid-1920s, Cannon was in demand as a lecturer and journalist. She spoke widely and published articles defending Anglo-Saxon purity and

arguing for the need to control "inferior" races in respected journals includ-
ing the *Atlantic Monthly*, the *North American Review, Harper's,* and the *Radcliffe Quarterly*. In "Selecting Citizens" (1923), Cannon argued for greater restrictions on immigration based on a racial hierarchy. Some races were simply barbaric and inferior. "Our civilization," Cannon proclaimed, has a "distinctively Anglo-Saxon foundation." Thus she applauded the Chinese exclusion acts, since "we are confessedly unable to lie happily and without dangerous friction with races so different from ourselves as the natives of Asia." Cannon was more tolerant of "the Jew," or at least the Jews who had "already made so distinct a contribution to the intellectual and business life of this country, and whose ability has been recognized and rewarded." But the new influx of Jews from eastern Europe, "where the Jew is essentially an Oriental," was another matter. These Jews were *too* different, and their presence in this country would encourage "racial preju-dice," which would be unfair to successful Jews who had already amalgamated. In the end, Cannon argued for a "rigid exclusion of any groups whose value to us is problematic," urging, "We must practice a rigid selection of individuals of any race we do admit." Cornelia James Cannon, "Selecting Citizens," *North American Review* 218, no. 814 (September 1923): 332–33.

55. Minutes, December 23, 1920, League of Women for Community Service, micro-film, M-48, Schlesinger Library, Radcliffe Institute, Harvard University.
56. The article quoted a December 27, 1920, letter from Harvard president Charles Eliot supporting the effort: "It is fitting that Cambridge people should support Mrs. Charlotte Hawkins Brown and the admirable work she is doing in the Palmer Memorial Institute; because Mrs. Brown was educated in Cambridge, and her school is named for Alice Freeman Palmer, whose strong educational influence was exerted from Cambridge for many years. Mrs. Brown has acquired the confidence and respect of her white neighbors at Sedalia to a very remarkable degree, and is on that account, among others, rendering the best kind of service to her race." "In Aid of the Palmer Memorial Institute," *Cambridge Tribune,* January 15, 1921.
57. Maria Baldwin to Charlotte Hawkins Brown, February 17, 1921, Charlotte Haw-kins Brown Papers, Correspondence to and from Charlotte Hawkins Brown, January–February 1921, A-146, folder 42, Schlesinger Library, Radcliffe Insti-tute, Harvard University.
58. Minutes, February 10, 1921, League of Women for Community Service, micro-film, M-48, Schlesinger Library, Radcliffe Institute, Harvard University.
59. Minutes, September 8, 1921, League of Women for Community Service, micro-film, M-48, Schlesinger Library, Radcliffe Institute, Harvard University.
60. Minutes, April 28, 1921, League of Women for Community Service, microfilm, M-48, Schlesinger Library, Radcliffe Institute, Harvard University.
61. Patricia Sullivan, *Lift Every Voice: The NAACP and the Making of the Civil Rights Movement* (New York: New Press, 2009), 101.
62. Minutes, September 15, 1921, League of Women for Community Service, micro-film, M-48, Schlesinger Library, Radcliffe Institute, Harvard University.
63. "Miss Maria L. Baldwin Was Popular Teacher," *Cambridge Chronicle,* January 14, 1922.
64. Schlesinger, *Snatched from Oblivion,* 74–75.

65. "Obituary—Maria L. Baldwin," *A.M.E. Church Review,* 38, no. 4 (April 1922): 216–20.

66. "Funeral Services for Miss Maria L. Baldwin," *Cambridge Chronicle,* January 14, 1922.

67. Cornelia James Cannon, letter to the editor, *Cambridge Chronicle,* January 14, 1922.

68. Brown, *Homespun Heroines and Other Women of Distinction,* 189.

69. "The Agassiz" 3, no. 3 (March 1922): 7, Maria Baldwin folder, Cambridge Historical Commission.

70. "Maria Baldwin," *Girls* 2, no. 5 (January 15, 1922): 4, Franklin Square House Papers, 2012-M-132, carton 1, *Girls,* 2, 1921–22, Schlesinger Library, Radcliffe Institute, Cambridge.

71. Schlesinger, *Snatched from Oblivion,* 74.

72. Brown, *Homespun Heroines and Other Women of Distinction,* 185.

73. "Obituary—Maria L. Baldwin," 219.

74. "The Maria L. Baldwin Memorial Number," *The Agassiz* (March 1922): 1, Maria Baldwin folder, Cambridge Historical Commission.

75. Brown, *Homespun Heroines and Other Women of Distinction,* 185–86.

76. W. E. B. Du Bois, "Maria Baldwin," *The Crisis* (April 1922): 248–49.

77. "Pay Tribute to Negro Teacher," *Boston Herald,* March 18, 1922.

78. "A Baldwin Memorial Room," *Boston Transcript,* March 18, 1922.

79. "Dedication of the Maria L. Baldwin Memorial Library, Thursday December 20, 1923," souvenir program, League of Women for Community Service, 1922–1940, B/L 434A, Schlesinger Library, Radcliffe Institute, Harvard University. The Baldwin Memorial Library no longer exists. A few years after Baldwin's death, a gift of her books was made to Atlanta University, which may include the contents of the library, but the details of the gifts cannot be traced at present. "Race Leaders Make Gifts to Atlanta U," *Pittsburgh Courier,* October 15, 1927.

AFTERWORD: MARIA BALDWIN AND HISTORICAL MEMORY

1. David Krugler, *1919, The Year of Racial Violence: How African Americans Fought Back* (New York: Cambridge University Press, 2015).

2. W. E. B. Du Bois, "Maria Baldwin," *The Crisis* 23, no. 6 (April 1922): 248–49.

3. Pauline Hopkins, "Famous Women of the Negro Race VII: Educators," *Colored American Magazine* 5, no. 2 (June 1902): 128.

4. This sense that African Americans have an obligation to contribute to racial uplift and to serve as exemplars of black achievement has a long history. As early as 1860, the Boston African American activist Dr. John Rock argued: "My opinion is, that the only way by which we the free colored people can be elevated is through our own exertions, encouraged by our friends. Every colored man who succeeds is so much added to the cause." "Speech of Dr. John Rock," *The Liberator* 30, no. 11 (March 16, 1860): 42. The pioneering educator Fannie Jackson Coppin, who graduated from Oberlin in 1865, one of the first African American college graduates, later recalled, "I never rose to recite in my classes at Oberlin but I felt that I had the honor of the whole African race upon my shoulders." Fannie Jackson Coppin, *Reminiscences of School Life and Hints on Teaching* (Philadelphia: A.M.E. Book Concern, 1913), 15.

5. "Maria L. Baldwin," *A.M.E. Church Review* 38, no. 4 (April 1922): 218.

6. Dorothy West, *The Living Is Easy* (1948; New York: Feminist Press, 1982), 245.

7. Barbara Ransby, *Ella Baker and the Black Freedom Movement* (Chapel Hill: University of North Carolina Press, 2005); Katherine Charron, *Freedom's Teacher: The Life of Septima Clark* (Chapel Hill: University of North Carolina Press, 2009).

8. A pioneer in the history of African American women's education, Linda Perkins undertook the first scholarly examination of the history of African American women teachers in a series of important articles and in her biography of one of the earliest African American women educators, Fanny Jackson Coppin. Following Perkins, a number of scholars have explored the lives and work of black women educators, while memoirs and oral histories of African American teachers have provided fine-textured accounts of the experience of teaching in segregated schools. Linda Perkins, "The Role of Education in the Development of Black Feminist Thought, 1860–1920," *History of Education* (UK) 22, no. 3 (1993): 265–75; Linda Perkins, *Fannie Jackson Coppin and the Institute for Colored Youth* (New York: Garland, 1987); Valinda Littlefield, "Agency and Constructions of Personal Identity: African American Women Educators in the South," in *Stepping Forward: Black Women in Africa and the Americas*, ed. Catherine Higgs, Barbara A. Moss, and Earline Rae Ferguson (Athens: Ohio University Press, 2002); Valinda Littlefield, "'To Do the Next Needed Thing': Jeanes Teachers, 1908–1934," in *Telling Women's Lives: Narrative Inquiries in the History of Women's Education*, ed. Kathleen Weiler and Sue Middleton (Philadelphia: Open University Press, 1999). Both Mamie Fields and Septima Clark have provided rich accounts of their experiences teaching in South Carolina, while Katherine Charron's biography of Septima Clark, *Freedom's Teacher*, places Clark's work as a teacher in the context of her development as a leader of the civil rights movement. Mamie Garvin Fields, *Lemon Swamp and Other Places* (New York: Free Press, 1985); Septima Clark, *Ready from Within* (New York: Africa World Press, 1990).

9. Audrey McCluskey, "We Specialize in the Wholly Impossible," *Signs* 22, no. 2 (Winter 1997): 403–23; Audrey McCluskey, *A Forgotten Sisterhood* (Lanham, MD: Rowman and Littlefield, 2014). Charles Wadelington and Richard Knapp offer a detailed account of Charlotte Hawkins Brown's life and work in *Charlotte Hawkins Brown and Palmer Memorial Institute* (Chapel Hill: University of North Carolina Press, 1999), and Glenda Gilmore provides an extensive discussion of Brown's activities in North Carolina in *Gender and Jim Crow* (Chapel Hill: University of North Carolina Press, 1996).

10. Charles Lemert and Esme Bhan, *The Voice of Anna Julia Cooper: Including A Voice from the South and Other Important Essays, Papers, and Letters* (Lanham, MD: Rowman and Littlefield, 1998); Vivian May, *Anna Julia Cooper, Visionary Black Feminist: A Critical Introduction* (New York: Routledge, 2007).

11. Karen Johnson, *Uplifting the Women and the Race: The Educational Philosophies and Social Activism of Anna Julia Cooper and Nannie Helen Burroughs* (New York: Garland Publishing, 2000).

12. There were a handful of African American women teachers in integrated urban schools in the late nineteenth century and first half of the twentieth. Linda Williams describes the careers of two black women teachers who taught in integrated Detroit schools, but these two teachers are unusual. In virtually all other examples I have found of African American women teachers in integrated

school systems, they have taught in schools with predominantly black students or other students of color. Linda Williams, Fannie Richards, and Gladys Roscoe, "Repertories of Practice in Two Early African American Teachers in Detroit," in *African American Women Educators*, ed. Karen Johnson, Abul Pitre, and Kenneth Johnson (Lanham, MD: Rowman and Littlefield, 2014).

13. Hallie Q. Brown, *Homespun Heroines and Other Women of Distinction* (1926; Freeport, NY: Books for Libraries Press, 1971); Benjamin Brawley, *Negro Builders and Heroes* (1937; Chapel Hill: University of North Carolina Press, 1965); Dorothy Porter," Maria Baldwin," in *Notable American Women*, ed. Edward James (Cambridge: Harvard University Press, 1971), 86–88; Dorothy Porter, "Maria Louise Baldwin, 1856–1922," *Journal of Negro Education* 21, no. 1 (Winter 1952): 94–96.

14. Porter, "Maria Louise Baldwin," 95.

15. Kevin Gaines, "Rethinking Race and Class in African-American Struggles for Equality, 1885–1941," *American Historical Review* 102, no. 2 (April 1997): 378–87; Kevin Gaines, *Uplifting the Race: Black Leadership, Politics, and Culture in the Twentieth Century* (Chapel Hill: University of North Carolina Press, 1996); E. Frances White, *Dark Continent of Our Bodies: Black Feminism and the Politics of Respectability* (Philadelphia: Temple University Press, 2001)..

16. Robin Kelley's work has been foundational in this area; see *Hammer and Hoe: Alabama Communists during the Great Depression* (Chapel Hill: University of North Carolina Press, 1990); and *Race Rebels: Culture, Politics, and the Black Working Class* (New York: Free Press, 1996). In recent years, feminist historians have offered a number of perceptive studies of resistance in the lives of poor and working-class women. See, for example, Tera Hunter, *To 'Joy My Freedom* (Cambridge: Harvard University Press, 1997); Kali Gross, *Colored Amazons* (Durham: Duke University Press, 2006); Cheryl Hicks, *Talk with You Like a Woman: African American Women, Justice, and Reform in New York, 1890–1930* (Chapel Hill: University of North Carolina Press, 2010).

17. Gaines, *Uplifting the Race*, 2. See also Glenda Gilmore, *Gender and Jim Crow* (Chapel Hill: University of North Carolina Press, 1993). The term "middle class" itself needs to be clarified when applied to black society in the late nineteenth and early twentieth centuries. In his influential study, Gaines argues that "in the light of their tragic plight within a racist social formation," most black people "were not middle class in any truly material or economic sense, but rather, represented themselves as such, in a complex variety of ways." Gaines, *Uplifting the Race*, 19. Gilmore agrees, arguing that black men and women were considered middle class if they "practiced middle-class habits—temperance, frugality, and hard work—as useful tools for living." Gilmore, *Gender and Jim Crow*, xvii–xix.

18. This body of scholarship is now extensive. Key studies include Paula Giddings, *When and Where I Enter: The Impact of Black Women on Race and Sex in America* (New York: Bantam Books, 1985); and Deborah Gray White, *Too Heavy a Load: Black Women in Defense of Themselves, 1894–1994* (New York: W. W. Norton, 1999).

19. Brittney Cooper argues that the concept of respectability does not capture the complexity of black women's resistance, proposing a theory of embodiment that looks more closely at black women's self-image and understanding. She argues that examining the presentation of black women's bodies in their own formal and informal texts reveals an understanding of their lives and politics

beyond the concept of respectability. Brittney Cooper, *Beyond Respectability: The Intellectual Thought of Race Women* (Urbana: University of Illinois Press, 2017).

20. Victoria Wolcott, *Remaking Respectability: African American Women in Interwar Detroit* (Chapel Hill: University of North Carolina Press, 2001).

21. Evelyn Brooks Higginbotham, *Righteous Discontent: The Women's Movement in the Black Baptist Church, 1880–1920* (Cambridge: Harvard University Press, 1993), 45.

22. Michele Mitchell, *Righteous Propagation: African Americans and the Politics of Racial Destiny after Reconstruction* (Chapel Hill: University of North Carolina Press, 2004), 14, 81.

23. Elizabeth McHenry, *Forgotten Readers: Recovering the Lost History of African American Literary Societies* (Chapel Hill: Duke University Press, 2002), 17.

24. Higginbotham, *Righteous Discontent*, 188.

25. Thomas Holt, "Marking: Race-Making and the Writing of History," *American Historical Review* 100, no. 1 (February 1995): 9.

INDEX

immigration and, 141; imperialism compared to, 109; intersection with sexism, 57; lack of personal documentation and, 6–7; Lincoln and, 108; minstrel shows and, 119; Niagara Movement and, 127–29; in the North, 4, 12–13, 17–18, 38, 67, 79, 118–21; quiet activism of middle class and, 187; respectability and, 186–88, 216–17n19; scientific, 1, 93, 171–73, 181; settlement house movement and, 142–43; in song lyrics, 135; teachers and, 145; in US Army, 165–66; violence and, 4, 23, 50–52, 61–62, 77–79, 90–91, 166, 174–75; women's clubs and, 169–70; women's political stances and, 68, 70. *See also* black activism and resistance

rape, 54, 82, 147, 202n121

Reasons Why the Colored American Is Not in the World's Columbian Exposition, The (Wells), 54

Reconstructing Womanhood (Carby), 42

Reconstruction, 3, 18, 25, 147

"Reconstruction and the Colored Woman" (F. Washington), 170

Rector, Estella E. *See* Baldwin, Estella Rector

Red Cross, 162–63

Reed, Tom, 105

religion and spirituality, 95–98. *See also* churches

Representative Women of New England (Howe), 87, 193n32

Republican, The, 100, 204–5n38

Republican Club, 99

Republican Party: Archibald Grimké and, 46; black support for, 14–16, 19, 198n6; Louis Baldwin's association with, 99–100, 102–3, 113; Peter Baldwin's association with, 14–16, 22–23, 35; women's vote and, 173

respectability, 186–88, 216–17n19

Ridley, Florida Ruffin: Baldwin's death and, 175, 179–80; Baldwin's views and, 124; *The Birth of a Nation* and, 150; Boston Literary and Historical

Association and, 108; at Boston Normal School, 29, 33, 44; childhood of, 24–26; church membership, 95–96; *A Columbian Year Contrast*, 54; family life of, 71–72; Georgia Educational League and, 83–84; League of Women for Community Service and, 174; letter to Chant, 61–62; at Louis Baldwin's wedding reception, 112; lynching protested by, 78; marriage of, 44, 156; as member of black elite, 5; national movement formation and, 63–64, 67, 69; photo, 26; political activism of, 44; Robert Gould Shaw House and, 143; Soldiers' Comfort Unit and, 163; St. Pierre family account by, 193n32; teaching profession of, 90; Twentieth Century Association and, 76; *The Woman's Era* and, 58, 70–71; Woman's Era Club and, 51–52, 54–55; woman's suffrage and, 144

Ridley, Ulysses, 44, 176

"Right of the Negro to Be Educated, The" 104

Roach, Etta, 211n4

Robert Gould Shaw House, 141–43, 149–50, 168, 175, 185

Roberts, Sarah, 14

Roberts v. City of Boston, 14

Rock, John, 18–19, 214n4

Rodin, Auguste, 165

Roosevelt, Theodore, 127

Roses, Lorraine, 169

Roslindale Unitarian Church, Woman's Alliance of, 139

Rousseau, Jean-Jacques, 30

Rubaiyat of Omar Khayyam, The, 200–201n96

Rubio, Philip, 20

Ruffin, Flora. *See* Ridley, Florida Ruffin

Ruffin, George, 5, 19, 22–24, 43, 46, 95, 168

Ruffin, George (son), 96

Ruffin, Josephine St. Pierre: Afro-American League and, 50; Baldwin Memorial Library and, 180; *The*

KATHLEEN WEILER is professor emeritus of education at Tufts University. Her research has focused on the democratic possibilities of education, particularly in relation to teachers' lives and work. Committed to recovering and exploring the lives and accomplishments of women educators who have been overlooked and ignored in traditional educational scholarship, she has published widely, contributing theoretical analyses of the ways of gender and race have shaped education broadly as well as ethnographic and historical studies of women teachers. Among her books are *Women Teaching for Change: Gender, Class, and Power*; *Country Schoolwomen: Teaching in Rural California, 1850–1950*; and *Democracy and Schooling in California: The Legacy of Helen Heffernan and Corrine Seeds*.